Chained to the Desk

Second Edition

Chained to the Desk

A Guidebook for Workaholics, Their Partners and Children, and the Clinicians Who Treat Them

Second Edition

Bryan E. Robinson, Ph.D.

New York University Press
New York and London

NEW YORK UNIVERSITY PRESS
New York and London
www.nyupress.org

Library of Congress Cataloging-in-Publication Data
Robinson, Bryan E.
Chained to the desk : a guidebook for workaholics, their partners and children, and the clinicians who treat them / Bryan E. Robinson. — 2nd ed.
p. ; cm.
Includes bibliographical references and index.
ISBN-13: 978-0-8147-7596-7 (cloth : alk. paper)
ISBN-10: 0-8147-7596-9 (cloth : alk. paper)
ISBN-13: 978-0-8147-7597-4 (pbk. : alk. paper)
ISBN-10: 0-8147-7597-7 (pbk. : alk. paper)
1. Workaholism. 2. Workaholics—Family relationships.
I. Title.
[DNLM: 1. Behavior, Addictive. 2. Family Relations. 3. Work.
WM 176 R658c 2007]
RC569.5.W67R629 2007
155.2'32—dc22 2007019116

New York University Press books are printed on acid-free paper, and their binding materials are chosen for strength and durability.

Manufactured in the United States of America
c 10 9 8 7 6 5 4 3 2 1
p 10 9 8 7 6 5 4 3 2 1

To my sisters,
Lynn Hallman and Glenda Loftin

Although we walk all the time, our walking is usually more like running. When we walk like that, we print anxiety and sorrow on the Earth. . . . When we are able to take one step peacefully and happily, we are working for the cause of peace and happiness for the whole of humankind. . . . We can do it only if we do not think of the future or the past, if we know that life can only be found in the present moment.

—THICH NHAT HANH,
from *Peace Is Every Step: The Path of Mindfulness in Everyday Life*

Contents

List of Tables *xi*
Acknowledgments *xiii*

Introduction: The "Blackberrization" of Our Lives 1
Overwork: This Century's Cocaine 3
Workaholism and Work Addiction 6
Why Will This Book Be Helpful? 8

1 Work Addiction: The New American Idol 11
Bryan (My Story) 11
Work Addiction: The New American Idol 14
Who, Me a Workaholic? 16
The Difference between Healthy Workers and Workaholics 17
Are You Chained to the Desk? 20
Workaholism: A Family Disease 22
Suggestions for Clinicians 24

2 Work Addiction: Myths and Realities 30
Margo 30
I Only Work on Days That End with "Y" 32
Historical and Cultural Trends 35
Conditions That Enable Work Addiction 36
Myths about Work Addiction 43
Debunking the Myths 53
Suggestions for Clinicians 54

3 How to Recognize Work Addiction 58
Glenn 58
When Work Steals Your Soul 60
The Tell-Tale Signs of Work Addiction 63
The Many Faces of Work Addiction 68
Suggestions for Clinicians 78

4 Treating Work Addiction as a Family Disease 85
Brenda 85
A Family Systems Addictions Model 88
When Work Addiction Hits Home:
The Smith Family 90
Structural and Dynamic Characteristics of the
Family System 91
Research on the Workaholic Family System 97
Suggestions for Clinicians 99

5 Inside the Workaholic Mind 106
Art 106
I Work, Therefore I Am 110
The Impostor Syndrome 113
The World through Workaholic Eyes 117
The Rigid Thinking That Drives Work Addiction 121
The Mind-Body Link and the
Workaholic's Health 126
How to Think That Black Cloud Away 127
Suggestions for Clinicians 129

6 The Childhoods of Workaholics 137
Ross 137
Childhood Origins of Work Addiction 139
Parentified Kids: Little Adults with Big Burdens 141
Are You A Parentified Careaholic? 143
My Own Parentification: The Workaholic
Poster Child 148
Suggestions for Clinicians 152

7 Spouses and Partners of Workaholics 161
Renee 161
Married to the Job 163
Work, Work Everywhere, Not Any Time to Think 166
Difficulty with Intimacy: When Your PalmPilot Is Your Best Friend 169
Concealment and Deceit in the Couple Relationship 174
Suggestions for Clinicians 176

8 Children of Workaholics 183
Charles 183
Carrying the Legacy of the Pretty Addiction 188
"Daddy Gone": Growing Up with a Workaholic Parent 192
The Making of a Chameleon 196
Suggestions for Clinicians 201

9 Work Addiction in the Company 209
Mary 209
Thank God It's Monday (TGIM)! 213
The Emperor Has No Clothes 214
Work Environments That Promote Work Addiction 216
The Boss from Hell 222
Changes in the Workplace 229
Suggestions for Clinicians 231

10 Workaholics Anonymous and Other Resources 236
Further Readings 236
Audiovisuals 239
Support Organizations 240
Workaholics Anonymous 242
The Psychometric Properties of the Work Addiction Risk Test (WART) 250

Notes *253*
Index *265*
About the Author *274*

Tables

2.1 Portrait of the Realities of Work Addiction 54
3.1 Portrait of the Physical and Behavioral Signs of Work Addiction 68
5.1 Portrait of the Workaholic Mind-Set 122
6.1 Portrait of a Workaholic Child 142
6.2 Portrait of a Careaholic 145
7.1 Portrait of the Partners and Spouses of Workaholics 170
8.1 Portrait of Adult Children of Workaholics 193
9.1 Portrait of Optimal Performers in the Workplace 217
9.2 Corporate Abuse: How Would You Grade Your Job? 223
9.3 Portrait of the Workaholic Boss 225

Acknowledgments

I want to acknowledge the many people whose help and support have allowed me to complete the second edition of *Chained to the Desk.* My colleagues at the University of North Carolina at Charlotte have continued their encouragement and support. I especially want to thank my colleague Dr. Claudia Flowers, who has tenaciously spearheaded most of our research studies on workaholics and families and who tirelessly conducted the statistical analyses for almost all of these studies. I couldn't have completed the studies without her one-hundred-percent participation.

My special thanks to Dr. Julie Maccarin, who was always willing to let me call her at any hour and ask her a question to which she always knew the answer. I also appreciate her unyielding help in reading the second edition of the manuscript and offering excellent advice. And I want to extend my deepest appreciation to my agent, Sally McMillan, who has stood by my side rejection after rejection until something finally clicked and especially for her expert professional advice in regard to questions on the second edition of *Chained to the Desk.*

Then there's always Jamey McCullers, who has put up with me and my work addiction for thirty-six (or as we playfully tease, thirty-sick) years. His devotion and support mean everything to me, especially his support of my healthy working for the next thirty-six ones that we share together.

My special appreciation to the anonymous individuals who

provided case material for this book and to the hundreds who wrote or called to share their personal stories of how work addiction impacted their lives. Thanks especially to Dr. Nancy Chase, Glenn Dulkin, Dr. Phyllis Post, Greg Rosshandler, Daffie Matthews, Dr. Gayle Porter, Jumani Rosshandler, Cynthia Carlson, Art Campbell, Gloria Steinem, Dr. Lyn Rhoden, and Stephanie Wilder for their case contributions.

And finally, to the following people in my life who love me from day to day and help make my life rich and worth living: Sara Thompson, Dr. Stephanie Citron, Faison Covington, Dr. Dan Mermon, Kevin Davis, Karen DuBose, Rick Werner, Glenda and James Loftin, Edward and Lynn Hallman, Jennie Holt, and last but not least my precious nephews, Blake and Scotty Loftin, and their families.

Introduction

The "Blackberrization" of Our Lives

I didn't need to use drugs because my bloodstream was manufacturing my own crystal meth.

—WORKAHOLICS ANONYMOUS MEMBER

Recently I was invited to appear on a major network television show. Three minutes before airtime, the co-host leaned into me, referring to what she called her "crackberry": "I used to sleep with my Blackberry," she said, "so I wouldn't miss anything. But then I realized I really don't need to do that. Do I?"

Before I could answer, we were live in front of an American audience, with her asking me about society's problem with workaholism and what we could do about it. In that same segment a recovering member of Workaholics Anonymous testified that "I didn't need to use drugs because my bloodstream was manufacturing my own crystal meth." Even the producer of the show admitted that the more he read my book, *Chained to the Desk,* the more concerned he became about his own workaholism.

That day I realized a lot more education needed to be done before folks would fully understand the problems of workaholism. Although it had been only nine years since the first edition of *Chained to the Desk* was published, we had entered a new century. And a lot had happened in terms of work and workaholism in that nine-year period. Back then "blackberries" were something *you* consumed, not something that consumed you. If you had a "bluetooth," you went to the dentist instead of to work. The 1990s workday phrase "9 to 5" became obsolete, replaced by the new millennium phrase "24/7." These trends were an indication of how work had slithered its way into every hour of our day—the "Blackberrization" of our lives.[1]

. . .

The same year that the first edition of *Chained to the Desk* was published, the Families and Work Institute reported that the average American worker clocked 44 hours of work per week, an increase of 3.5 hours since 1977, and far more than workers in France (39 hours per week) and Germany (40).[2] That 44-hour work week jumped to 47 in 2000, according to the *US News and World Report*.[3]

Even more disturbing has been the slow evaporation of vacation days. Years ago I never went on vacation without my computer, cell phone, and mountains of work. Although my old habits have changed, they are typical of today's employees, many of whom haul tons of work on vacation. But an increasing number of workers no longer take vacations at all. The Economic Policy Institute of Washington, D.C., revealed that the average American took only two and a half weeks of vacation and holidays in 1990—less than workers in any other developed country, including Germany, where workers take six weeks a year. A 2004 survey by Management Recruiters International reported that nearly one-half of U.S. executives said they wouldn't use all of their earned vacation because they were too busy at work.[4] Another study by the Families and Work Institute found that 36 percent of American workers did not plan to use their full vacation.[5] The average American worker left four vacation days on the table in 2006—mainly, workers said, because too much extra work makes it too stressful: "We have to get ahead of our workload in order to leave, and then we have to catch up to our workload upon our return."[6]

Fear is another reason. Increasingly, patients in my clinical practice say they are afraid to take vacation days for fear they will not be perceived as a team player. Some even said they were afraid to leave the office for lunch because if positions were cut, they would be the first to go. This worry has increased nationwide. In 1977, 45 percent of people felt secure in their jobs, according to the Families and Work Institute. That number dropped to only 36 percent in 2006.[7]

Another decline among workers is the drop in social relationships. A major study in 2006 revealed that Americans are becoming more socially isolated today than two decades ago, presumably because of our love affair with the Internet and our Blackberries. The study also reported a one-third drop in the number of people the average person could call a friend.[8] So not only has the problem of workaholism not gone away, but it has worsened. Hence, this second edition of *Chained to the Desk*.

Overwork: This Century's Cocaine

Our society's dangerous immersion in overwork may help explain why we can't see the water we swim in, why many therapists look blank when the spouses of workaholics complain of loneliness and marital dissatisfaction, and why the concept of workaholism is still relegated to pop psychology. There are hundreds of studies of alcoholism, substance abuse, and eating disorders but only a handful on workaholism. This is a profound omission. Overwork is this century's cocaine, its "problem without a name." Workweeks of sixty, eighty, even one hundred hours are commonplace in major law firms and corporations; tribes of modern-day male and female Willy Lomans, manacled to cell phones, trundle through the nation's airports at all hours with their rolling luggage; cafes are filled with serious young people bent over laptops; young workers at dotcoms are available for work, as the slang phrase has it, "24/7"—twenty-four hours a day, seven days a week. It is high time that all of us stopped relegating compulsive overwork to the pop-psychology bookshelves and took a hard look at our lives.

Chained to the Desk is a metaphor for the agonizing work obsessions that haunt workaholics even when they are away from their desks. The director-actor Penny Marshall, confessing to being a workaholic in a *People* magazine interview, said that when she's working, she's obsessively working and that she loses all concept of what day it is. Her devotion to work means that she puts her personal life second. Throngs of workaholics openly admit their obsession for work while concealing the darker side of their addiction. They testify to their passion for work, their nonstop schedules—all of which present them in a favorable light. They fail, however, to mention their episodes of depression, anxiety, and chronic fatigue, which almost always occur as an aftereffect of working obsessively for days on end. The upside of workaholism brings honor, but the downside carries a stigma.

Workaholism is the best-dressed problem of the twenty-first century. Workaholics often have comfortable incomes, and their families appear to have all the material comforts. Not only does work addiction look good on workaholics, but it also is becoming on their families from the outside. But behind closed doors workaholics are breaking down inwardly, and their families suffer in quiet desperation. Here's how one adult who grew up with a workaholic parent expressed her frustration in a letter to me:

> On the outside workaholics are glorified do-gooders and hard workers. Our society praises workaholics, but what workaholism does to people on the inside is harmful. It cuts them off from the rest of the world, including friends and family. It causes them to work constantly without rest, to be in their own cold, dark, lonely world—all alone with room only for other tasks to be completed. Outwardly, workaholics are good citizens; inwardly, they're dying a slow death.

Workaholism is widespread in its devastation. It infects other family members, causing them to experience a whole set of mental health problems of their own. I use an addiction model, combined with a family systems model, throughout this book to show the downside of work addiction and its impact on the individual workaholic, as well as on the workaholic family as a whole. The chapters that follow expose the dark side that successful people are either too ashamed to admit to or too blind to see—that cycles of prolonged highs are always followed by low periods that can last for days or weeks.

Work addiction or workaholism is an addiction in the same way that cocaine and alcoholism are addictions. Progressive in nature, these addictive behaviors are unconscious attempts to resolve unmet psychological needs that have roots in the family of origin and can lead to an unmanageable everyday life, family disintegration, serious health problems, and even death. Similar to alcoholics, workaholics have rigid thinking or "stinkin' thinkin'" patterns that feed their addiction. Because of their self-absorbed preoccupation with work, workaholics often do not notice signals, such as physical aches and pains or reduced ability to function, that can be warnings of serious health problems. Work addiction damages the mental and physical health of the workaholic. It is physiological and chemical in nature and can lead to anxiety and depression and even to suicidal ideation. Work highs, reminiscent of the alcoholic euphoria, run a cycle of adrenaline-charged binge working, followed by a downward swing. Euphoria eventually gives way to work hangovers characterized by withdrawal, depression, irritability, and anxiety.

Members of Alcoholics Anonymous often speak of the moment they "hit bottom." The glamour peels off like old varnish, alcohol stops working for them, and they can no longer think of themselves as simply "bon vivants" or "men-about-town." Workaholics, too, hit bottom: a spouse may threaten divorce; a long-ignored back problem or stress-related illness like psoriasis may become painfully disabling; or valued employees may quit, tired of trying to meet impossible deadlines. Some hit bottom before they can admit they have a problem and get the help they need. Some workaholics become so depressed that they cannot get out of bed. They find themselves alone, unable to feel, and cut off from everyone they care about. Marriages crumble, and health problems hit crisis proportions. Breaking through the denial shakes workaholics into facing the truth and getting the help they need.

Many of the workaholics I see in private practice are dragged there kicking and screaming by their partners; others finally burn out or get tired of being perceived as the impossible boss at work and the distant parent at home. "It finally reached a point that I hit a wall!" exclaimed Ed, smacking his right fist into his left palm. "And I couldn't escape it anymore. I was either going to deal with it or I was going to die."

Workaholism and Work Addiction

The term *workaholic* was coined by Wayne Oates in the first book on the subject, *Confessions of a Workaholic,* in which he described workaholics as behaving compulsively with work in the same ways alcoholics do with alcohol.[9] More than thirty years later, no consensus exists among clinicians on how to define or categorize workaholism. Neither workaholism nor work addiction is defined in many dictionaries, and the latter term wasn't included in the spell-check on my brand-new Dell computer, on which I wrote the second edition of this book.

Clearly, we still haven't developed a language that would enable us to properly refer to the problem of workaholism or to distinguish among its various nuances. And although it has become a household word, workaholism has not been accepted into the official psychiatric and psychological nomenclature. The American Psychiatric Association considers it a symptom of obsessive-compulsive personality disorder. Jeffrey Kahn, consultant for the American Psychiatric Association committee on psychiatry in the workplace insists that "other professionals who think workaholism is an addiction or a diagnosis in and of itself are 'missing the boat.'"[10] It is shocking that in 2006 the Priory, Great Britain's high-profile clinic for addiction, charged that "workaholism is just something journalists like to write about."[11]

Sadly, in the twenty-first century work addiction has become so pervasive that many of us don't see the condition or realize how serious it really is. Many clinicians—vast numbers of whom are also workaholics—still do not recognize workaholism as a problem. They see nothing wrong with eighteen-hour, pressure-cooker days. They deny that workaholism is a factor in their patients' problems or in troubled relationships among couples who see them for psychotherapy. Although it surrounds us daily, they look on it much as we do caffeine or prescription drugs—as harmless, even beneficial.

Uninformed clinicians often prescribe work as a solution to emotional problems, rather than identify it as a cause. In the course of my research, writing, and national speaking engagements, I have been appalled by the inability of the psychotherapeutic community to recognize, understand, and treat workaholics. I have seen misdiagnosis after misdiagnosis because of this lack of awareness. I have also been shocked and dismayed at the pervasiveness of workaholism among practitioners and the attendant denial about their own out-of-control work habits.

So for purposes of discussion, I often use the terms *workaholism* and *work addiction* interchangeably throughout this book. My definition of *workaholism* is as follows: *an obsessive-compulsive disorder that manifests itself through self-imposed demands, an inability to regulate work habits, and an overindulgence in work to the exclusion of most other life activities.* Workaholism is a form of escape from unresolved emotional issues, and the relief it provides has an addictive quality. In the clinical work that I do, workaholism is considered a "firefighter," which means that overworking puts out emotional fires.[12] The addictive nature of workaholism comes from the fact that workaholics are temporarily delivered from the red-alert condition through the distraction of working. But because the deeper issues are not addressed, constant working is necessary to keep the simmering flames from becoming wild fires.

Why Will This Book Be Helpful?

This book provides an inside look at work addiction. It debunks the myths, refutes false claims, and sets the record straight, using the clinical, empirical, and case studies currently available. Since the first edition of this book, new studies have emerged that provide deeper insights into the disorder and into the effects it has on the workaholic's family. From California to the Carolinas, men and women recount their agonizing bouts with work addiction and the devastation left in its wake. It's no accident that personal stories in San Diego resemble almost detail by detail the accounts of those in Atlanta. It's no coincidence that patient after patient in Asheville, North Carolina, who grew up in workaholic homes describe hauntingly similar feelings that parallel those of children of workaholics in Peoria, St. Louis, and Houston. It's not a fluke that partners of workaholics in New York describe, almost in minute detail, the exact experiences of partners in other parts of the country. These personal accounts, though not scientific in the quantitative sense, carry their own validity because they document the psychological experiences of individuals impacted by work addiction—the details of which provide an uncanny match in such high numbers that the emerging profiles cannot be attributed to chance alone. In this respect we do have a qualitative science of work addiction derived from the parallel themes and feelings that have been observed by clinicians in the field.

Many aspects of this book are groundbreaking. It is the first book on work addiction to show not only its devastating effects on workaholics but also its effect on those who live and work with workaholics—their partners, offspring, and business associates. It contains new and innovative research not reported anywhere else on the outcomes of adults who carry the legacies of their workaholic parents and the problems this presents for their own adult relationships. Each chapter opens with a case study, and some chapters contain portrait tables, assembled from hundreds of case reports and a small body of clinical and empirical research. Each chapter concludes with a section called Suggestions for Clinicians, which provides practitioners the strategies and techniques they need to treat workaholics, their loved ones, and their employers and colleagues in the workplace.

In writing this book, I have drawn on my own personal experiences, the research I've conducted at the University of North Carolina at Charlotte for the past twenty years, my vast clinical practice with workaholics and their families, and correspondence from around the world. This information is presented in a readable way for the average person who is struggling with these issues in his or her personal life. Combining scientific knowledge and clinical implications with personal accounts, this book also is unique because it is the first informative source for clinicians to help them respond to the work-addiction epidemic that is sweeping this country. Written for psychologists, social workers, marriage and family therapists, counselors, health educators, the clergy, medical practitioners, teachers, health-care administrators, corporate heads, and employee-assistance personnel, *Chained to the Desk* apprises professionals of the origin and scope of the problem, its pervasiveness within the family system, and how they can diagnose, intervene, and provide treatment for workaholics and their families.

Chained to the Desk is for all the people who are struggling with this insidious and misunderstood addiction. It aims to provide both counseling and consolation when they cannot find them elsewhere. It is my hope that people will be able to get the help they deserve from the medical establishment, from professionals in the addiction and treatment fields, and from clinicians in various capacities. It is also my hope that work addiction will be more openly accepted, diagnosed, understood, and treated as a serious condition. May it help you, the reader, find that place in your life where career success and personal and intimate fulfillment reside side by side—where you will know more about special times to pamper yourself, to just *be* with others, and to have idle moments with nothing to accomplish. You might not be ready to pack your bags and head for the woods, but you might carve your life more in the mold of Henry David Thoreau, who said, "Time is but the stream I go a-fishing in."

1

Work Addiction

The New American Idol

They intoxicate themselves with work so they
won't see how they really are.

—ALDOUS HUXLEY

Bryan (My Story)

There was a time when I needed my work—and hid it from others—the way my alcoholic father needed and hid his bourbon. And just as I once tried to control my father's drinking by pouring out his booze and refilling the bottle with vinegar, the people who loved me sulked, pleaded, and tore their hair out trying to keep me from working all the time. Every summertime, for instance, just before we left on vacation, my life partner, Jamey, would search my bags and confiscate any work I planned to smuggle into our rented beach house on the South Carolina shore. But however thoroughly he searched, he would always miss the tightly folded papers covered with work notes that I had stuffed into the pockets of my jeans.

Later, when Jamey and our close friends invited me to stroll on the beach, I'd say I was tired and wanted to nap. While they were off swimming and playing in the surf—which I considered a big waste of time—I secretly worked in the empty house, bent over a lap desk fashioned from a board. At the sound of their returning footsteps, I'd stuff my papers back into my jeans, hide the board, and stretch out on the bed, pretending to be asleep.

I saw nothing strange about my behavior; it's only in hindsight that I say that I was a workaholic. By this, I mean something quite different from saying I worked hard. I mean that I used work to defend myself against unwelcome emotional states—to modulate anxiety, sadness, and frustration the way a pothead uses dope and an alcoholic uses booze.

Since childhood, work had been my sanctuary—my source of stability, self-worth, and meaning and my protection against the uncertainties of human relationships. In elementary school, the subject I hated the most was recess. When a teacher forgot to assign homework over Christmas vacation, I was the one who raised his hand to remind her. In high school, I wrote, directed, and produced the church Christmas play, also designing and building the sets and acting the lead role of Joseph. Doing *everything* for the play gave me a sense of control and mastery missing from my chaotic family home, where furniture-breaking fights between my mother and my father were a regular occurrence.

As an adult, the thought of a vacation or weekend without work was terrifying to me, and I structured my life accordingly. Throughout the 1970s and early 1980s, I carried a full college teaching load and volunteered for committee assignments, while also writing books, conducting research, and establishing a full clinical practice. Ignoring Jamey's frequent pleas that we "just do something together," I would work in my windowless office in our basement through evenings, weekends, Thanksgivings, and Christmases. I even worked through most of the day of my father's funeral: while my mother and sisters broke bread with our old neighbors, I was in my university office twenty-five miles away, working on a project so insignificant that I no longer remember what it was.

I hit bottom in 1983, when I stopped thinking of myself as an extraordinarily talented and dedicated professional with so much to offer the world and realized how empty my life had become. Up until then, I'd been proud of my workaholism, and well rewarded for it. Jamey might complain that I was never home—and that when I was, I didn't listen—but my university colleagues called me responsible and conscientious. Jamey might call me controlling, inflexible, and incapable of living in the moment. But the promotions, accolades, and fat paychecks that came my way built an ever-stronger case against his accusations, and I used them to further vilify him: *Why couldn't he pull his own weight? Why couldn't he be more supportive? Why didn't he appreciate my hard work and the creature comforts it provided? Why was he constantly bothering me with problems that distracted me from earning a decent living?*

In 1983, after nearly fourteen years together, Jamey—who had been trying without success to talk to me about my absence from our relationship and his growing problems with alcohol—told me that he had found someone who *would* listen to him, and he moved out. I was thirty-eight. My first book had been published, and I had two more books and several funded research projects in the works. I was also recovering from surgery from stress-related gastrointestinal problems. My life was crumbling under my feet, and there was nothing I could do about it. I lost weight. I couldn't eat. I didn't care if I lived or died.

I was a chain-smoking, caffeine-drinking work junkie, dogged by self-doubt. I had no close friends. I didn't smile. I felt that my colleagues didn't really appreciate my hard work and were breathing down my neck. My memory got so bad that members of my family wondered if I was developing an early case of Alzheimer's. I snapped at colleagues, and they snapped back. I once angrily confronted a college librarian, demanding the name of the irresponsible faculty member who had kept, for three months, a book I wanted. She gave me the name: my own. Work had been the one thing that I had always done well, and now even that was failing me. Yet I couldn't stop working.

In the summer of that year, Jamey and I reconciled, and in the fall, he checked himself into a treatment center for alcoholism. When I eagerly took part in the family treatment component to "help Jamey with his problem," a facilitator confronted me with my own work obsession. I joined Workaholics Anonymous, entered therapy, and began my climb out of the pit into a saner life. And Jamey and I started to understand the crack in the foundation of our relationship. Today, we celebrate thirty-seven years together in sobriety.

Now, instead of spending my Saturdays in my basement office, I look forward to weekends of yard work, garage sales, and Saturday-afternoon matinees. When we go to the South Carolina shore or to our remote cabin on the Suwannee River in northern Florida, I don't pretend to nap anymore. I'm fishing off the dock or on the beach now, building sandcastles and swimming in the surf. I enjoy and savor my life and our time together as much as I had once savored my endless work.

But old habits die hard. In the course of writing the second edition of this book, when Jamey yelled from downstairs, I felt, at first, the workaholic's reactive annoyance—*Don't you know how important my projects are?* But this feeling was immediately replaced with love and gratitude as I realized he was calling me to a big breakfast of French toast, warm maple syrup, and butter.

Work Addiction: The New American Idol

In a society based on overwork, my behavior had plenty of camouflage. Flextime, twenty-four-hour Wal-Marts, and laptops have vaporized the boundaries that once kept work from engulfing the sacred hours of the sabbath and the family dinnertime. Likewise, the modem, cell phone, and pager have blurred the spatial boundaries between workplace and home: anyone can fax a memo at midnight from the kitchen table, bend over a laptop on an island in paradise, or call the office via cell phone from the ski lift. But work performed in exotic environments is still work, however much we tell ourselves it's play. And when any place can be a workplace and any hour is worktime, some people will work themselves to death, just as some people will drink themselves to death in a culture in which any hour is cocktail hour. Little in our present culture teaches workaholics when or how to say no. Nancy Woodhull, a founding editor of *USA Today,* is living proof of this trend:

> I'm not the type of person who can just sit around the pool and not do anything. So I take a Dictaphone to the pool, and when I have ideas, I can record them. Not being able to do that would be very stressful to me. People will say to me, "Nancy, relax, recharge your energy," and I say, "I'm being energized by getting these ideas down." Having access to a Dictaphone allows you to be more productive. So does having a cell phone, and so does having a computer. You take all these tools and there really is no need for downtime. Anyone can find me, anywhere, anytime.[1]

Achieving life balance is perhaps one of the biggest challenges facing us in the twenty-first century. Trying to hit the mark, millions of Americans are overinvesting in their jobs in such epidemic proportions that we have become a nation that enables workaholics—unbalanced and out of control and unable to slow down and nurture ourselves and our loved ones. Increasingly, working Americans are using their jobs as an anesthetic to relieve emotional pain, help them forget their worries, boost their self-esteem, gain comfort and safety, entertain themselves, and provide intimacy and silent companionship. In the same way that alcohol or food provide comfort and escape for some, work is the drug of choice for millions, providing them an emotional sanctuary while distancing them from loved ones and friends. These wearying realities have so pervaded our lives that people speak of needing “downtime” as though they were machines.

Who, Me a Workaholic?

The concept of workaholism is a hard sell. You might be thinking that some of these trends and stats apply to you. You work hard and put in long hours because you have a mortgage, two children approaching college, and payments for two cars. If you don’t work hard, how would you stay afloat financially?

Actually, you might not be a workaholic at all. You may simply be a hard worker. There is a big difference between hard work and workaholism. Hard work put us on the moon. From time to time, all of us put more hours and effort into working than we do into being with loved ones or relaxing. Starting a new business can be an all-consuming affair at first. Finding a cure for a disease can make one single-minded. Or a new employee may be determined to make a good impression at the start of a job. But these examples are exceptions that all of us encounter at some point in our lives. Workaholics operate in this fashion all the time, using their jobs as escape.

So it’s possible for you to work long hours, carry a mortgage, send your kids to college, pay for the two cars, and not be a workaholic. Working long hours alone does not make you a workaholic. If, however, friends or loved ones have accused you of neglect because of your work or if you have used or abused work to escape from intimacy or social relationships, you might want to take a closer look.

Perhaps you’re a single parent or someone who has to work overtime to make ends meet, and you’re thinking, “From morning to night, it’s go, go, go. I’m barely scraping by as it is, and now you’re saying I have another problem?”

This is not necessarily the case. A workaholic is not the single mom who works two jobs to pay mounting bills. Neither is it the tax accountant who works extra-long hours on weekdays and weekends until April 15 rolls around. True workaholics are driven by deeper, internal needs, rather than by external ones—not that it's tax season or that baby needs a new pair of shoes but that the process of working satisfies an inner psychological hunger.

The Difference between Healthy Workers and Workaholics

In a society where many people work long hours, it's important to make a distinction between healthy workers and workaholics. Workaholics tend to be separatists, preferring to work alone and focusing on the details of their work, to which their egos are attached.

In contrast, healthy workers can see the bigger picture and work cooperatively with others toward common goals. Whereas workaholics often create or look for work to do, healthy workers enjoy their work, often work long hours, and focus on getting the job done efficiently. Healthy workers think about and enjoy whatever they're engaged in at the present moment; workaholics think about working a disproportionate amount of time, even during social activities or leisure times, when their minds wander and obsess about work.

Healthy workers experience work as a necessary and sometimes fulfilling obligation; workaholics see it as a haven in a dangerous, emotionally unpredictable world. Healthy workers know when to close the briefcase, mentally switch gears, and be fully present at a son's Little League game or the celebration of their own wedding anniversary. Workaholics allow work to engulf all other quarters of life: sales reports litter their dining tables; their desks are covered with dinner plates; commitments to self-care, spiritual life, household chores, friends, partners, and children are frequently broken to meet work deadlines.

Workaholics seek an emotional and neurophysiological payoff from overwork and get an adrenaline rush from meeting impossible deadlines; healthy workers do not. The accountant who works night and day during tax season and the single mother who holds two jobs are hard workers, not workaholics. Healthy workers can turn off their work appetites; workaholics are insatiable. Workaholics are preoccupied with work no matter where they are—walking hand-in-hand at the seashore, playing catch with a child, or fishing with a friend. The healthy worker is in the office looking forward to being on the ski slopes; the workaholic is on the ski slopes thinking about the office. The relationship with work is the central connection of the workaholic's life, as compelling as the connection addicts experience with booze or cocaine.

Workaholics include the lawyer who always brings his briefcase on family picnics, while his wife carries the picnic basket; the therapist who schedules appointments six days a week between 8 A.M. and 8 P.M.; and the real estate saleswoman who cannot have a heart-to-heart talk with her husband without also watching television, eating dinner, and going over property-assessment reports. In each case, work has become a defense against human relationships and balance has been lost.

Workaholism is not a black-and-white matter. Just as *alcoholism* refers not only to the bum in the gutter but to the relatively well-functioning professor who gets quietly soused every night, the term *workaholism* describes a wide spectrum of behaviors. For some people, workaholism takes outwardly bizarre forms, such as working around the clock for three or four days straight and periodically catching a few hours' sleep in sweat clothes. For others, workaholism is subtler: work is the place where "life" really takes place, the secret repository of drama and emotion. Family and friends are little more than a vague, if pleasant, backdrop.

By now, you might be saying, "Fine, I'm a workaholic. It makes me miserable, but I prefer it to having to confront intimacy issues, living without my second home, taking my kids out of private school, and giving up all the other advantages my work brings me." So you've settled on being miserable at work rather than being miserable at home. The belief that you can have happiness only at home *or* only at work but not both is black-and-white thinking. Whether you are a workaholic or simply caught up in the workaholic pace of juggling work and family, this book can help you see that you don't have to give up your lifestyle to change your work habits. The key is balance, not sacrifice. You don't have to choose misery in one arena or another to put balance into your life. It is possible to work hard, to have all the material advantages that result from your hard work, *and* to have a full and satisfying personal life outside the office. Healthy work, in contrast to workaholism, helps you lead a more balanced life, one with time for social and leisure activities and personal and family pursuits. The payoff is a fresher, more clear-minded approach to your job that makes you more efficient at what you do. This book helps you find the proper integration of work and personal time that supports you in all areas of your life.

Millions of Americans, although not workaholics in the literal sense, find themselves caught in a workaholic lifestyle that creates for them some of the same physical and psychological symptoms that workaholics have. They are exhausted, emotionally burdened, and suffering from stress and relationship problems because of the disproportionate amount of time and emotional energy they put into their jobs. Bound by never-ending, obsessive thoughts about work and work-related functions, they find it difficult to be emotionally present with their loved ones or to engage in meaningful intimate, spiritual, and social relationships. They are the ones who are always thinking about their jobs, whether they are at work or play. Their partners feel lonely, isolated, and guilty in these vacant relationships and frequently question their own sanity even as friends and employers applaud the workaholics for their accomplishments.

There are different degrees of workaholism. Some people fall in the low to mild ranges, and others fall in the higher ranges. The more severe the workaholism, the more serious the physical and emotional side effects.

Are You Chained to the Desk?

Could it be that you are chained to the desk? Or are you just a plain hard worker? To find out, rate yourself on the Work Addiction Risk Test (WART) using the rating scale of 1 (never true), 2 (sometimes true), 3 (often true) or 4 (always true).[2] Put the number that best describes your work habits in the blank beside each statement. After you have responded to all twenty-five statements, add the numbers in the blanks for your total score. The higher your score (highest possible is 100), the more likely you are to be a workaholic; the lower your score (lowest possible is 25), the less likely you are to be a workaholic.

___ 1. I prefer to do most things rather than ask for help.
___ 2. I get impatient when I have to wait for someone else or when something takes too long.
___ 3. I seem to be in a hurry and racing against the clock.
___ 4. I get irritated when I am interrupted while I am in the middle of something.
___ 5. I stay busy and keep many irons in the fire.
___ 6. I find myself doing two or three things at one time, such as eating lunch and writing a memo while talking on the telephone.
___ 7. I overcommit myself by biting off more than I can chew.
___ 8. I feel guilty when I am not working on something.
___ 9. It's important that I see the concrete results of what I do.
___ 10. I am more interested in the final result of my work than in the process.
___ 11. Things just never seem to move fast enough or get done fast enough for me.
___ 12. I lose my temper when things don't go my way or work out to suit me.
___ 13. I ask the same question over again without realizing it, after I've already been given the answer once.

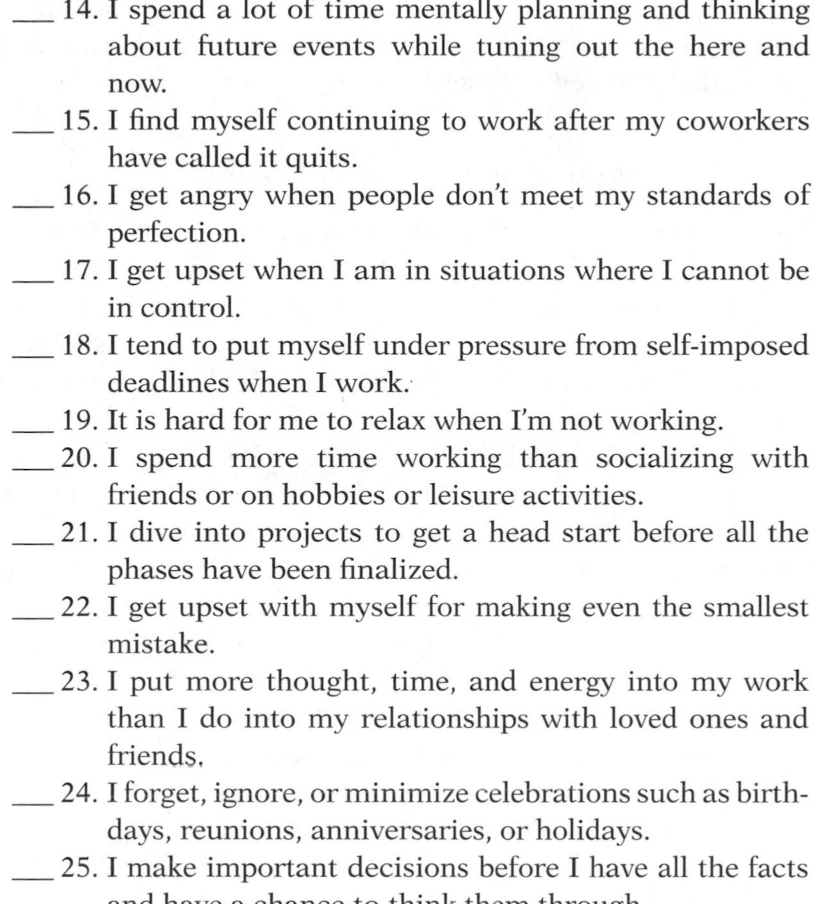

___ 14. I spend a lot of time mentally planning and thinking about future events while tuning out the here and now.

___ 15. I find myself continuing to work after my coworkers have called it quits.

___ 16. I get angry when people don't meet my standards of perfection.

___ 17. I get upset when I am in situations where I cannot be in control.

___ 18. I tend to put myself under pressure from self-imposed deadlines when I work.

___ 19. It is hard for me to relax when I'm not working.

___ 20. I spend more time working than socializing with friends or on hobbies or leisure activities.

___ 21. I dive into projects to get a head start before all the phases have been finalized.

___ 22. I get upset with myself for making even the smallest mistake.

___ 23. I put more thought, time, and energy into my work than I do into my relationships with loved ones and friends.

___ 24. I forget, ignore, or minimize celebrations such as birthdays, reunions, anniversaries, or holidays.

___ 25. I make important decisions before I have all the facts and have a chance to think them through.

For clinical use, scores on the WART are divided into three ranges: those scoring in the upper third (67–100) are considered highly workaholic. If you scored in this range, it could mean that you are on your way to burnout, and new research suggests that family members may be experiencing emotional repercussions as well. Those scoring in the middle range (57–66) are considered mildly workaholic. If you scored in this range, there is hope. With acceptance and modifications, you and your loved ones can prevent negative lasting effects. Those scoring in the lowest range (25–56) are considered not workaholic. If you scored in this range, you probably are a hard worker instead of a workaholic. You needn't worry that your work style will negatively affect yourself or others.

Workaholism: A Family Disease

For the past twenty years my colleagues and I have studied workaholics and their families at the University of North Carolina at Charlotte. Although no formal records are kept on the numbers of workaholics, we estimate from our extensive studies that one-quarter of the population can be classified as workaholic.

Many workaholics, I find, grew up in homes dominated by parental alcoholism, mood disorders, or other problems that forced the children to take on adult emotional and practical responsibilities. They became gravely serious "little adults" and were young when they first forgot how to play. One star saleswoman I treated—who was afraid she'd be considered lazy if she took a lunch break—had gone to work picking tobacco and raking yards at the age of twelve in order to eat.

My research suggests that workaholism has devastating systemic effects on other family members—as severe, or even more severe, than the familial effects of alcoholism. Like the partners of alcoholics, the partners of workaholics often play the role of resentful "enablers" who try to limit their partners' overwork while unwittingly supporting it. Just as the wives and husbands of alcoholics will cover bounced checks or serve a hot dinner whenever the drinker returns from the bar, the partners of workaholics do the workaholic's home chores, give alibis to children and party hosts, build the family schedule around the workaholic's impossible work schedule, and put dinner on the table at midnight for the umpteenth time after the workaholic promised to be home by 7:00. Other partners put their workaholic spouses in a double bind, complaining about their absenteeism while spending thousands of dollars of the monetary rewards for that absenteeism on clothes or tens of thousands on remodeling the kitchen.

The partners of workaholics also may plead, threaten to leave, insist on weekends together, and otherwise try to control the work addict's behavior, much as the partner of an alcoholic searches for hidden gin bottles—the way Jamey had once searched my luggage. Like the partners of alcoholics, these unhappy spouses live with loneliness, try to control the uncontrollable, and build up enormous resentments. They often experience the workaholic's emotional unavailability and unreliability as a personal rejection and failure.

There is one major difference, however, between the spouses and children of alcoholics and those who live with workaholics. In our present culture, the partners and children of alcoholics usually are given understanding, professional help, and referrals to self-help programs like Al-Anon. But when the partners and children of workaholics complain, they get blank looks. Therapists—some of whom are workaholics themselves—may suggest that the partner simply swallow and adapt to the workaholic's schedule or tell the spouse not to be a "pop psychologist."

This can lead spouses to blame themselves for their gut sense that something is wrong. "I know how pathological it sounds, but my feelings of rage, confusion, and abandonment are such that I often wish that my husband would bruise my face or break my arm," one woman, married to a famous New York lawyer, told me. "That would enable me to say to myself and everyone else, 'See, he really is hurting me. He's doing something terrible to this marriage, and it's not my fault.'" The woman's relatives looked at her expensive townhouse and European vacations and couldn't understand what she was complaining about; she had tried couples counseling, only to be told by the therapist at the first session that she'd been reading too many pop-psychology books.

Likewise, the children of workaholics often grow up in a vacuum of parental attention, feeling valued only for what they achieve and not for themselves alone. They look at their externally picture-perfect lives and draw the conclusion that "something must be wrong with me," silently reprimanding themselves for being the unappreciative bad guy. The children of workaholics also report that they sometimes find themselves colluding with a parent's workaholism, the way that some children of alcoholics let themselves be propped up on the counter at the corner bar in order to have time with Daddy. One woman told me that when she was thirty-five and her workaholic father was dying, she smuggled memos and contracts into his hospital room for him. "It was the only way I could be with him," she said. "The only time he'd pay attention to me was around the subject of his work. He died working, a pen in his hand."

Given that our culture so often admires this sort of "dedicated" devotion to work, it is not surprising that it is the wives and husbands who often bring their workaholic partners into my office to force them to invest in their marriages. They say they feel like widowed partners and solo parents. With little support from the workplace, the mental health system, or their families, many are self-doubting and depressed.

"There are times that I would actually be relieved if my husband were dead," said the woman married to the attorney who carried his briefcase on family picnics when the kids were small. "He doesn't hit me, he doesn't drink, he doesn't use drugs. There are a lot of things he doesn't do—the most important being that he doesn't do anything with me or our three kids." When she asked him to spend more time with the family, he called her an ingrate and said he was only working day and night for her and the kids and their future. Without support from her family or friends, she tucked her feelings neatly away inside and tried to fix some faulty aspect of herself that she couldn't put her finger on.

Suggestions for Clinicians

The problem is doubly difficult when clinics and clinicians don't tune their radars to pick up workaholism. Often, I find, therapists either suggest that the workaholic just cut back on working hours, subtly pressure the spouse to adapt to the partner's work obsession, or miss the issue altogether.

Establishing Abstinence

An alcoholic who decides to get sober and joins Alcoholics Anonymous is expected to follow simple, black-and-white rules. He or she may be told, "Just don't drink, no matter what" and "Go to ninety meetings in ninety days." But workaholics can't quit working any more than compulsive eaters can quit eating. Transformation involves becoming attuned to shades of gray and making gradual, gentle changes. The goal is not to eliminate work and its joys but to make it part of a balanced life rather than the eight-hundred-pound gorilla that sits wherever it wants. First, of course, workaholics have to recognize that there's a problem and be reassured that the therapist does not plan to force them to quit work or even necessarily to reduce their working hours.

In my own recovery, and in the clinical work I now do with workaholic clients, therapy usually involves an ordinary, commonsense blend of emotional and interpersonal work, cognitive techniques, family-of-origin work, self-nurturing exercises, pencil-and-paper exercises, and behavioral tactics to help people reorganize time and space so that they're not working or thinking about work 24/7. The only thing unique about therapy with workaholics is focusing the microscope so that overwork comes into view as a problem to begin with.

I often tell workaholic clients that the goal is not to cut back on work hours, which they find immensely relieving. The goal, rather, is to create water-tight compartments between work and other areas of their lives and to prepare for easy transitions between them. Some solutions are simple, modest, and practical. Mildred, an overweight, forty-three-year-old psychotherapist, for instance, had no sense of containment for either her work or her diet. She scheduled clients six days a week anytime between

8 A.M. and 8 P.M. She literally didn't know when her plate was full because she would open the refrigerator and drink or eat directly from a milk container or take-out carton. At my suggestion, she discarded a day planner that listed hours from 7 A.M. to 11 P.M. and replaced it with one that stopped at 5 P.M. I also suggested that when she ate, she pour out a glass of milk and spoon a serving of potato salad onto a plate.

Before she made these changes, my client had felt as though she had to be available to all people all the time. But keeping a more limited Day-Timer and serving herself food on a plate reminded her, physically, and practically, that she had choices, could set limits, and could decide for herself when she would see a client or have a glass of milk. This empowerment and self-care helped her slowly reinstate boundaries that had been blurred in childhood, when she had acted as her depressed mother's emotional caretaker. Over time, she was increasingly able to question old beliefs that had confused legitimate self-care with selfishness.

Putting "Time Cushions" into Work Schedules

Other workaholics need help in making transitions between work and other activities and need to learn not to schedule themselves so tightly that they leave no time for bathroom breaks or travel between appointments. By scheduling "time cushions" around appointments, they can drastically reduce tension. One man, for example, invariably fought with his fiancée when he returned home because she would be eager to talk intimately while he was still tense and preoccupied with work. An earlier therapist had seen the problem strictly in terms of the "pursuer-distancer" dynamic. But once he started to schedule "time cushions," his days became less harried. He also started using his drive home not to chew over the events of the day but to decompress, play enjoyable music, and do relaxation exercises as he mentally thought ahead to seeing his fiancée. By the time she met him at the door, he was actually glad to see her and capable of making the transition.

Many clients find, when they examine the balance in their current lives, that there is no room for any form of play. So I often assign them "homework" that involves doing something fun that produces no end product and requires spontaneity and flexibility. These activities are usually process oriented, like free-form painting, digging in the garden, soaking in a hot bath, or walking barefoot in a rain shower. I also suggest hobbies, sports, and pastimes that can be done "imperfectly" and that immerse the client in process rather than outcome. Richard, a sixty-two-year-old bank president, for instance, took up golf but committed himself not to keep score, not to hurry from hole to hole, and to stay focused on having a good time instead of on winning—the opposite of his behavior at the office. He told me that business associates marveled when, for the first time, they saw his fun, lighthearted, and playful side. Golf, originally a therapy task, became a joy.

Setting Boundaries around Work Hours

Clinicians need to address problems in boundary setting and help clients to say no when choices are available to them or when they are already overcommitted. The boundaries that workaholics set are individual to their unique lifestyles. Some clients can limit their work to eight hours a day, with no weekend or holiday work, and can recognize that additional hours are not honorable but a "fix."

Clinicians need to challenge clients to set weekly boundaries creatively and to evaluate from week to week their success at maintaining healthy boundaries. Clinicians must be prepared to challenge clients' many rationalizations for why they were unable to keep the boundaries they set. The next week then becomes another opportunity for clients to practice this skill.

Many of the techniques I now use with clients are ones that I personally used in the mid-1980s. I ditched a day planner that went from 7 A.M. to 12 A.M. and got one that limited my work from 8 A.M. to 5 P.M. I also set specific hours for working at home, worked only in my study, and gave myself fifteen-minute time cushions between appointments to give myself time to stretch or get where I needed to go. I renewed old friendships and developed new ones. And I confronted the fact that I had been hiding from the world since third grade, using work to keep me from close relationships even though I hungered for them. Closeness had felt scary and unpredictable to me, and I'd work to keep Jamey at arm's length. I felt out of control with someone who in a heartbeat could snap my heart like a brittle twig.

Change was not easy for me, and there was no specific moment when the light switch came on. Like the subtle changing of the seasons, I started to see Jamey with fresh eyes, watching him care for his orchids and realizing the wisdom contained in the pleasure he got from simply working in the yard. One weekend I finally accepted his invitation and tried working with him, just to "do something together." Much to my surprise, I discovered how much I, too, relished the smell of cut grass, the feel of warm earth, and our chats with our neighbors.

I know I'm not alone. Many other clinicians face similar challenges in their own lives. It's one of the hazards of work that is not merely a job but a calling. It's easy for "callings" to overwhelm other areas of our lives, to become not only our livelihoods but our sole source of spiritual meaning and an oddly safe arena for intense emotional connection without too much personal risk.

Clinicians may, in fact, be particularly vulnerable to the blurred boundaries that can promote workaholism. We have the dangerous freedom to set our own hours; to juggle training, supervision, workshops, and clinical work; to labor on research projects in our home offices until midnight; to leave on our beepers; and to have trouble saying no to clients who insist on evening or weekend appointments.

When we live like this ourselves, and swim in the soup of a work-obsessed culture, it's hardly surprising that we miss the cues our clients and their partners drop about the misshaping power of overwork on their families' lives. By way of analogy, many alcohol-naive therapists, before the 1980s, worked earnestly with couples without directly addressing substance-abuse issues and wondered why they seemed to be treading water.

Likewise, many of us may have failed to notice that workaholism is the unacknowledged common element in many of our treatment failures. We hear that the man isn't devoting time to the relationship, perhaps, and we focus on the pursuer-distancer dynamic, unaware that the man's compelling and unacknowledged relationship to work may be at the bottom of the couple's distress.

This is a larger issue than it may at first seem. In the case of alcoholism, therapists eventually got more sophisticated and began to name it for what it was, to refer clients to Alcoholics Anonymous as a condition for continuing therapy and to understand that until the centrality of the relationship to the substance was addressed, little else was likely to change. It's time we got more sophisticated about overwork as well and see it as yet another way that vulnerable human beings seek, for understandable reasons, a sanctuary from the uncertainties and vulnerabilities of really living their present lives, with all their textures and disappointments.

When clinicians restore balance to their own lives, they will be far more likely to recognize, and effectively treat, this century's "problem without a name" when it bedevils the clients and families who come into their therapy offices.

2

Work Addiction
Myths and Realities

More men are killed by overwork than the importance of the work justifies.

—RUDYARD KIPLING

Margo

I got my first job at fourteen, not out of necessity but out of want. I went to school to finish my senior year in the morning and at noon to work in a grocery store for forty hours a week. I bragged about what a great work ethic I had, but little did I know that that was just the beginning. I went to college and found myself studying and usually working some kind of job—always busy, working too many hours. After a year and a half, I quit college to start a family. But the real workaholic came out in my mid-twenties and well into my thirties, when the pace I set and kept landed me in my first strong depression.

Around the age of twenty-four, I was driven to succeed in the company that I worked for and determined to go back to college and finish the degree I had started. I enrolled in a university to study business management at night. During the day, I had the stressful job as general manager for a wholesale manufacturing firm, a $3.5 million company that produced twenty-four hours a day, six days a week. I had a wonderful husband who supported my efforts and a beautiful baby boy.

I continued this regimen until I was thirty years old. After I graduated with a bachelor of science in business management, I continued school during the summers. The last year or so I really pushed myself. I took two courses while still running the company, which had grown to a $5 million business. The last semester I took three courses while working over forty hours a week. I made almost all A's and won the President's Award for the best-managed plant—twice. As you may have noticed, my family hasn't been mentioned. My husband still supported me, and my son was ten years old. But my relationship with both suffered because of my not being there. I was constantly working at my job or doing school assignments at the university. I was obviously gone on weekends and many nights during the week.

I thought I was superwoman. I succeeded at everything, or so I thought. Although I had a lot of guilt where my son was concerned, I tried to be the best mother I could. In reality, I was on a collision course and didn't have any idea how to relax. I hit a wall at age thirty. Even though I had graduated, I missed college. I was still in the same position, making a lot of money but no longer fulfilled by the job. I felt like I was eighty years old. I hardly listened to radio for pleasure, read only educational books, and felt miserable if nothing was planned for every second on a weekend. I was used to being busy every second of my life and hated slowing down.

My marriage was suffering, I was having horrible mood swings, and I was angry at everyone and everything. Through therapy I came to realize that I was going through a major depression brought on by years of workaholism. So what did I do? You guessed it. I went back to work. I enrolled in an MBA program and took two graduate classes each semester. I poured myself back into school and immediately felt better, or so I thought. I was doing what my father had done: when things get tough, work harder. I was withdrawing from my husband more and more and, regrettably, expected perfection from my son, just as I did myself.

In addition to classes during my last year of graduate school, I taught a night class at the local community college and ran the manufacturing plant. I knew I needed to slow down but didn't know how. After I received my master's degree, I found the perfect job. My plan was to slow down, relax, and enjoy. It was hard to leave the company because my employees were my family. I had given my heart and soul to that job for almost twelve years. But I managed to walk out the door for the last time as the "boss."

I knew my life was unmanageable when one Friday afternoon I called a local mental health hospital. Feeling desperate, I was ready to commit myself. I would have done anything to stop this all-too-familiar roller coaster ride. I cried for two solid weeks for no apparent reason. My life had slowed to a snail's pace, which would have been great for most people but not for a workaholic like me. In desperation, I emergency-beeped my therapist, whom I had not seen for some time. I was now willing to try anything, and I shamefully took the new antidepressants that I had refused to take before. How could I stoop so low? Why couldn't I just work harder and fix everything? I had finally found one thing I couldn't fix.

I Only Work on Days That End with "Y"

To say that the general public and the media do not take work addiction seriously is an understatement. Because the facts have been unavailable and because work addiction is so misunderstood, our society operates from myth and stereotype. How much do you know about the best-dressed addiction? How much of your knowledge is based on superstition and how much on fact? This chapter provides answers to those questions, clarifies the myths that our culture perpetuates, and describes the societal conditions that make it difficult to overcome work addiction.

When it's not praised, workaholism is dismissed as a joke. The light-hearted portrayal of work addiction is reflected in newspaper cartoons, one of which shows a huge, empty meeting room with a sign posted at the front that reads, "Workaholics Anonymous" and a caption that says, "Everybody had to work overtime." Advertisers bathe workaholism in the same glamorous light that they poured over cigarettes and liquor in the ads of the 1930s—a 1994 Lexus ad in the *Wall Street Journal* boasted, "Workaholic? Oh, you flatter us. The relentless pursuit of perfection." A radio commercial for a truck praises the versatility of the "Workaholic 4 by 4." If you tell people you're a workaholic, they might chuckle. But if you say you're a work addict, watch out for out-of-control laughter, punctuated with something like, "Boy, that's a good one." The term *workaholic* is tossed around with abandon and is often perceived not as a problem but as a badge of honor. Business associates brag about being workaholics in social gatherings or announce to colleagues that they binged for eighteen hours or three days on a project as something of which to be proud. Rarely, however, do we hear adults boast about a three-day drunk or proclaim that they binged on an entire apple pie. But many corporate climbers wear the workaholic name tag with pride, indirectly proclaiming their loyalty and tireless efforts on behalf of the company.

Well-intended advice from public figures reflects this lack of understanding. Larry King, on one of his nightly talk shows, extolled Lucille Ball for being a workaholic. "That's why she was so good," he said. On another segment, the actress Ally Sheedy told of her recovery from bulimia and drug addiction and how she had become a workaholic, which she considered to be a good thing. The evangelist Billy Graham wrote a newspaper column titled "Try to Change Workaholic Husband" in which he advised a spouse that it was her responsibility to help her husband stop working too much and to take control of his compulsive disorder.

These kinds of comments reflect the general lack of knowledge about a condition that wreaks misery and havoc on millions of people in this country every year. Still, supporters of work addiction reform have been targets of ridicule and butts of jokes, as the following commentary by Daniel Seligman from *Fortune* magazine illustrates:

> Along with heroin, gambling, sex, and sniffing model airplane glue, work is now taken seriously as something people often get addicted to, in which case they need to get cured. . . . The references to work addiction are instantly psychiatric. The phrase is enveloped in psychobabble about inner insecurities, lives destroyed, and—could it be otherwise?—support groups needed.
>
> How did work addiction make it to the social-problem big leagues? Ploughing through our mound of articles, we posit that one source of support has been the universe of corporate human resourcers, always on the lookout for new workplace woes. The ever-emerging "men's movement" also seems to be supportive. Finally, the specter of widespread work addiction—an article in *Vibrant Life* puts the number of addicts at 12 million—appeals to unionists and others looking for excuses to impose legal limits on hours worked. And coming any day now: massive support from Donahue and Oprah.[1]

What's the truth about what's behind this mad rush of workaholism? And where does this desperation get its start? Is it our fast-paced culture, or the way we were brought up? Is it in our genes? What feelings rage? What memories lurk? What motivates people like Margo to push themselves and their loved ones beyond human limits? What drove her to stay on a self-destructive path, and how was she able to finally break the cycle? These questions and many more are answered in the chapters that follow. But a broader historical and cultural context will begin to provide answers as well as to help separate myths from realities.

Historical and Cultural Trends

During the 1980s, the age of the "yuppie"—the young, upwardly mobile professionals—came into vogue, at which time it became fashionable for baby boomers to think of themselves as workaholics. A sixty-hour workweek was standard, with many workers—especially the younger singles and entrepreneurs—working seventy, eighty, even ninety hours per week. Emphasis on heavy socializing and heavy work glamorized the lives of yuppies. Trendy lifestyles required a workaholic pace to support their social and financial requirements. This faddish, here-today-gone-tomorrow trend stressed material gain through hard work. Asked what they wanted on their tombstones, yuppies commonly responded, "Off to another meeting," accompanied by a chuckle.[2]

Alcoholism was associated with skid-row bums, instability, and irresponsibility. Workaholism was associated with status, power, and material gain. Alcoholism was a character defect; workaholism was a character strength. At social gatherings, corporate climbers proudly referred to themselves as workaholics to underscore their tireless efforts and to elevate their status in the eyes of colleagues. Baby boomers said they worked hard because they loved it—it was fun, creative, and stimulating. Many of them were athletes growing up. The workplace was their performance arena, their chance to win the gold, if you will, and relish the applause from their colleagues.

If alcoholism was the "ugly addiction," workaholism was popularized as the "pretty addiction." A book on workaholics by Marilyn Machlowitz that appeared during the eighties applauded the workaholic lifestyle as being as much a virtue as a vice and suggested that workaholics are surprisingly happy because they are doing what they love.[3]

The pendulum of the 1990s swung in the opposite direction for twentysomethings. Members of this generation were not as driven as were those who came of age during the previous decade; although they saved money and built careers, they embraced a philosophy that said there's more to life than work. They were stamped as slackers and ridiculed as underachievers by workaholics, and they seemed almost out of place in the mad-pace of the nineties, where the sixty-hour workweek ruled. During the 2000 decade, the pendulum swung back again. A fascination with new technological advances erased the already-blurred line between work and other life activities. And popular phrases like "24/7" and "downsizing" became household expressions.

Nevertheless, work addiction is distinct from historical trends and cultural whims. My grandmother, who worked in a cotton mill from the time she was seven years old and who gave birth to my mother at the end of a back-breaking day in 1925, was never a workaholic; neither did the upwardly mobile trend of the 1980s breed workaholics. That work ethic was driven by the historical and cultural trends of the time. Historically, for example, the cultural expectation has existed in Japan that people work hard. The Japanese have a term, *Karoshi,* to refer to the ten thousand workers a year who drop dead from putting in sixty- to seventy-hour workweeks. Otherwise healthy, they keel over at their desks after a long stretch of overtime or after consummating a high-pressured deal, usually from stroke or heart attack. Karoshi among corporate workers in their forties and fifties has become so common that the Japanese workplace has been dubbed "a killing field."[4] Still, it is important to bear in mind that although cultural and historical trends may support and encourage work addiction, they do not cause it, any more than they create addictions to drugs and alcohol. There are, however, certain conditions at every level of our society that do make work addiction irresistible.

Conditions That Enable Work Addiction

Although the source of work addiction is within the person, the *enablers*—risk factors that encourage work addiction or make overcoming it so difficult—exist in the context of everyone's life.

Enablers can be other people or circumstances that feed the cycle of work addiction by sending the message that the person needs to do more. Because each person's life conditions are different, so are their enablers. There are four levels of enabling, each level nested within the next.[5]

Daily Surroundings

The first level is the immediate context in which we come face to face with factors that directly affect our daily lives, such as family, school, work, and church or synagogue. The families we grew up in, the families in which we currently live, and the jobs we currently hold—all are potential enablers of work addiction at this level. One example includes adults who overwork to finance the material demands of their spouses and children. Situations where financial demands outweigh income can encourage working overtime, working extra jobs, or competing for job promotions and salary increases. In some instances, family members may send workaholics mixed messages, on the one hand making demands for material comforts and on the other complaining about the wage earner never being at home. A chaotic home situation can be an enabler that makes it preferable for a family member to stay at work to avoid the unpleasantness. Single parents who find themselves trying to wear two hats or work two jobs to make ends meet can be enabled into work addiction by these conditions. The downsized workplace or high-stress job that demands workaholic-like performance as a minimum standard is an enabler, as is the slave-driving boss who has impossible standards and who relentlessly watches over employees' shoulders.

Interconnections between Settings

The second level of enabling comes from the interconnections between two contexts at the first level, such as home and work, home and school, or home and religious institutions. An example is a company that requires employees to sacrifice personal and family time for the financial rewards, praise, and recognition available through the job. One workaholic manager actively looks for workers who have the same hard-driving, frantic edge:

> I try to head problems off at the pass by finding people like me to hire. When I'm interviewing, applicants who are laid back or can't buy into the loyalty and hard work of the company don't get picked. I look for enthusiasm, dedication, and commitment to do the job well, no matter what it takes.

Another example of enabling at the second level is the technologies that have helped erase the line that once separated the contexts of home and school and home and work. Ironically, these telecommuting arrangements and the new trend of home-as-workplace—intended to make the workplace more flexible and family friendly—actually have enabled work addiction. Other enablers are practices such as *flextime,* which allows workers to complete a fixed number of hours per week, scheduled around their personal lives, and *flexiplace,* which allows workers to perform their work duties at home. The home-as-workplace trend, which causes the office and home to become an inseparable blur, enables people to work around the clock.

Neighborhood and Community

The third level of enabling comes from the larger contexts of neighborhood and community resources such as newspapers, television, and government agencies. Examples of enabling at this level are the media stereotypes and jokes that support positive portrayals of workaholics, advertisements that recruit workaholics, and media images that reward workaholics with fame and fortune. Asked what a spouse can do to change a workaholic, the management consultant Marilyn Machlowitz gave some less than salutary advice in a popular magazine interview:

> Family members should make every effort to be exposed to the workaholic's work world. They should meet for lunch if possible. Even a small child can be taken to the office, shop or lab on a weekend. To make time together enjoyable, they must simplify household chores—pay bills and shop by phone, for example, and buy a microwave oven. Most important, they should anticipate spending a lot of time on their own. As one stockbroker told me, "I may be a lousy father, but when Merrill Lynch needs me, I'm here."[6]

The message is basically to center your life around the workaholic and his or her work schedule, join in the addiction whenever possible, and settle for being alone a lot. In other words, bite the bullet and enable the problem to continue.

Also included at this level of enabling are laws that either encourage work addiction or fail to regulate the number of hours adults can work, especially those in high-stress, safety-related professions such as emergency room medicine or airline traffic control. A flextime law, for example, that was proposed in the U.S. Senate in 1997 would allow employers to require hourly employees to work up to sixty hours a week without receiving overtime. In theory, this Family-Friendly Work Place Act would let parents choose cash or compensatory time off for their extra hours. In reality, it would wipe out overtime and the forty-hour work week.[7]

The glamour of technology has made work and work addiction appealing. Advertisers have jumped on the bandwagon to make work addiction alluring and sexy in the same way the tobacco industry used to promote cigarette smoking as mysterious and evocative in the 1940s and 1950s. It is politically incorrect to portray a sexy movie star with a cigarette dangling from her mouth, scotch in hand, and a come-hither look in her eye. Now try to imagine IBM, after many complaints, being forced to remove a billboard of a workaholic slaving over his computer with one hand and receiving a big bonus in the other, a billboard that had been strategically erected at the entrance to the computer giant's corporate headquarters, where all workers were forced to view it each morning. Far-fetched, you say? Such public pressure forced the R. J. Reynolds Tobacco Company to remove a Camel cigarette billboard near a Winston-Salem school after parents complained that the advertisement encouraged teenagers to smoke. Instead of establishing taboos against work addiction, however, we promote and sanction it as the norm:

> Not until recent times has the notion of being a relentless drone actually been portrayed as attractive. Men and women lug around their laptop computers with the bravado of Arthur brandishing Excalibur, cracking them open whenever there's a spare minute to crank out another business plan.[8]

Embedded Beliefs of Culture and Society

The fourth level of enabling occurs in the overall patterns and ideology of the society, culture, politics, and economy. Work addiction, for example, is aggravated by religious and cultural support via such maxims as "idle hands are the devil's workshop." The Puritan work ethic, alive and well, values hard work and productivity and extols it as an antidote to sin and evil. Our culture values work addiction so highly that it applauds workaholism, even when it is life threatening or families are in collapse. A relentless economy that requires long work hours in order for workers to make enough money to have an acceptable standard of living also can be an enabler.

Disenfranchised groups such as women and gay men and lesbians often unwittingly become workaholics to prove to a society that devalues them that they have worth.[9] These individuals often receive subtle or direct messages (real or imagined) that they are devalued by their immediate contexts (such as families or workplaces) and larger contexts (community and culture). Perhaps as children they led lives as underdogs in which they had to continually fight to prove their self-worth. Over time they have come to believe the insidious message that they are inadequate, sinful, or defective, yet learn that performance is a viable —albeit temporary—compensation for the stereotypes in which they are portrayed.

Some disenfranchised groups start the compensation process early in their lives, outperforming or outproducing their peers in school. Carried from campus to career, these individuals learn that working long and hard provides them with a feeling of satisfaction that to some degree assuages their feelings of self-depreciation. They get hooked on proving their worth to the world through achievements, and it pays off with recognition, approval, and money. The fifty-year-old adult, for example, who grew up with the parental message that her performance always fell short may still be trying to gain her dad's approval through overachievement. Gender messages from the culture, directly or indirectly and for a prolonged period of time, support and perpetuate workaholic gender prisons for both men and women that can enable work addiction on a grand scale.

Our society depicts the ideal woman as the one on the fast track who can do everything. Not only must she be a full-time mom; she must have a full-time career and manage a home, relationships, a social life, and, if there's time left over, leisure for herself. Unless women can match the mythical standard of Martha Stewart, juggling their roles as CEO, mother, accomplished gardener, cook, and expert on every subject in the world, and then have a private physical fitness instructor to stay beautiful, they feel like failures, as Stephanie confessed:

> There are enough of us in my generation now who've come through women's lib from the beginning and who have received that message, "Yes, you can do it all." I make a vow to myself every morning as my feet touch the floor that today is going to be the day that I'm going to balance it all. I'm going to get it right. But I never do, and I always feel bad about myself.

Because they cannot deliver, supermoms feel guilty about everything: for staying home, for not having a career, for having a career, for putting kids in day care, for taking off early, for not making enough money, for not disciplining children more, for not making it to PTA meetings. The feelings of failure reinforce the belief that they are somehow inadequate, and the cycle starts over again with women digging their heels deeper into work and production as atonement for their "unforgivable sins." In contrast, men in our society try to live up to the image of the ideal dad—a fast-track, superachieving father who makes lots of money and provides all the material comforts but cannot express feelings and intimacy—an enabler of work addiction for men in our society. They forfeit paternal leaves of absence when their children are born for fear of ridicule from the company or say they're off to another meeting when, in fact, they surreptitiously pick up their children at day care.[10] Our society has blessed all the choices between family and work but has failed to build in the support systems for them.

Gloria Steinem further describes how the gender masks that society forces us to wear can enable work addiction:

> A "masculine" paradigm often becomes ever more punishing when race, class, or sexuality stand in the way of realizing the impossible ideal of power that is not only male but white, heterosexual, and successful. And a "feminine" paradigm is often redoubled for women of color, poor women, lesbians and others who cannot "find" themselves through subordination to the proper kind of husband or family and so are made to feel lacking.
>
> Only when men are equal *inside* the home can women be equal *outside* the home. Women's overdoing it—and the male-dominant culture that compels it—allows this country to be the only industrialized democracy in the world without a national system of child care, the rudiments of flexible work schedules, parental leave for fathers as well as mothers, shortened workdays or work weeks for *both* parents of young children—and so much more.[11]

Myths about Work Addiction

Influenced by insufficient data, cultural and historical trends, and the media, myths about work addiction masquerade and help to perpetuate misunderstanding and denial of the problem. Although work addiction is the most accepted and encouraged of all the addictions, it is a serious disorder that is camouflaged by societal and cultural approval. As in the case of Margo, it draws praise despite the workaholic's frustration, misery, and despair. It masquerades as a positive addiction, insinuating itself throughout our society. Although scientific study of work addiction has lagged far behind that of the other addictions, increasing clinical and empirical research and greater understanding of the addiction process have clarified what is work addiction and helped to separate the realities from the myths.

The Job Makes Me Do It

Workaholics race against the clock, shake their fists at the heavens, and moan about shortage of time. Because they feel they cannot get on top of things, they live with the agony of never-ending defeat. Hurrying, staying busy, and judging themselves by what they do rather than by who they are—these are the evidence of their work addiction.

A common myth is that work addiction originates in such pressures as high-powered jobs or downsizing, which demand more than the regular nine-to-five workday. Evidence suggests that although modern technology and the workplace might enable work addiction, they don't cause it. Work addiction is primarily a psychological problem and secondarily a sociological problem. Workaholics feel inadequate, regardless of their accomplishments, and are constantly setting higher, impossible goals. They will not try new challenges unless they can excel immediately. Yet despite all their activity, they feel an inner emptiness, a feeling that something important is missing inside. They are often lonely people who arrive at the office before anyone else and are the last to leave. They prefer not to take time off, or, if they do, they take their work along with them. Fun and laughter are frivolous wastes of time, and workaholics often have contempt for people who are humorous and carefree and underproductive or who keep an even pace in their work regimens.

Work addiction is not a sudden eruptive reaction to an event in an adult's life. It has its roots in childhood and is a developmental phenomenon, often camouflaged in the child's overdoing, overachieving, and overcompensating, which become accommodating behaviors that children unwittingly develop in order to stabilize their roller-coaster existence.

Clinical evidence suggests that work addiction is a consequence of family dysfunction in childhood and that it contributes to continued family dysfunction in adulthood.[12] Workaholics carry their perceptions and compulsive habits into their families of procreation and into the workplace. Margo is a case in point. She started working at fourteen, partly because she was the child of a workaholic who wanted to please her father. A deep yearning to please, fix, and be perfect became her downfall in adulthood and a legacy she realized she was passing to her young son.

Barbara Garson has delineated three stages that work addiction follows from family of origin to adulthood.[13] In stage 1, the workaholic is reared in a family in which either a parent is alcoholic or workaholic. Or the family dysfunctionality sets oppressive rules that prevent open expression of feelings or direct discussion of personal and interpersonal problems. This sets up unrealistic standards of perfection and conditional approval between parent and child that is usually based on good grades and acts of accomplishment.

The second stage covers young adulthood (twenties and thirties), when work addiction can become acute in the presence of institutional deprivation of approval and appreciation. At this stage, career advancement and rewards for accomplishment fuel the flame of work addiction.

In stage 3, work addiction becomes aggravated in middle adulthood (forties and fifties) by the mid-life crisis. Health and interpersonal crises become issues at this stage, and if work addiction is not reversed or arrested, it can become chronic and may lead to relationship deterioration or death.

Adult workaholics are drawn to high-stress jobs where they act on their perceptions and their compulsive habits. Richard Weinberg and Larry Mauksch suggest that patterns of interaction to which people become accustomed in their families of origin often play unacknowledged roles in their lives and work and can contribute to unwanted pressures and stresses on the job.[14]

Reality 1: The source of work addiction is inside us. The workaholic who blames the high-pressured workplace for his or her work addiction is as much a stereotype as an alcoholic who blames a "nagging" spouse for his or her alcoholism.

The Virtue Myth

It is not uncommon to open a newspaper and find advertisements that read, "Wanted: Workaholics." Although the belief that workaholics make better workers is pervasive, nothing could be further from the truth. Corporate America traditionally has valued and perpetuated workaholism, and the types of destructive environments that it creates are rapidly coming under fire from critics. Anne Wilson Schaef and Diane Fassel argue in their book, *The Addictive Organization,* that business and industry encourage the denial of work addiction and promote it as acceptable and preferable because it appears to be productive.[15] They suggest that American work organizations support work addiction by denying, covering up, and rewarding dysfunctional behaviors among their employees. They assert that workaholic managers and those in key corporate positions negatively impact the organizational system and the employees of that system. Other experts argue that adults from dysfunctional families of origin unconsciously seek out stressful occupations so that they can practice their work addiction by reenacting unresolved family issues.[16]

. . .

Generally speaking, workaholics are not team players in the workplace. Their need to control makes it difficult for them to solve problems cooperatively and to participate in give-and-take situations. They believe their approach and style are best, and they cannot entertain less-perfect solutions. Spontaneity is diminished and creativity stifled when the narrow view of one person prevails. Unable to delegate, many workaholics overload themselves, becoming resentful, irritable, and impatient. Flared tempers and angry outbursts are not uncommon. Their standards are impossible for them or their colleagues to meet. Disharmony prevails, and group morale nosedives. As they try to squeeze more work into less time, burnout occurs for them and those under their supervision. They are less efficient than their coworkers who put in fewer hours planning and working toward a job goal. As they continue to overinvest in their jobs, stress and burnout grow and efficiency declines.

Reality 2: Workaholics create stress and burnout for themselves and for their fellow workers, creating negative fallout in the form of low morale, disharmony, interpersonal conflict, lower productivity, absenteeism and tardiness due to stress-related illnesses, loss of creativity, and lack of team cooperation. Work addiction, therefore, is not a positive quality.

The Superhero Myth

Workaholics are the envy of their peers: accomplished, responsible, and able to take charge of any situation. At least that's how they look to the outside world. The harder people work, the more they are put on a pedestal. Colman McCarthy, a nationally syndicated columnist, said it best:

> The workaholic's way of life is considered in America to be at one and the same time a religious virtue, a form of patriotism,

> the way to win friends and influence people and the way to be healthy, wealthy, and wise. Therefore, the workaholic, plagued though he be, is unlikely to change. Why? Because he is a sort of paragon of virtue. He is chosen as the one most likely to succeed.[17]

The American work ethic prevents us from faulting workaholics for their hard work, which is a sign of being fine, upstanding, and righteous citizens. During childhood, workaholics were often family heroes who learned that compulsive overachieving provided a sense of being in control. The need to control helps workaholics dissociate from unresolved feelings and allays fears and anxieties. Research confirms earlier anecdotal reports that work addiction has severely negative consequences, including depression, anxiety, anger, perfectionism, job stress, inability to delegate, and health complaints.[18] Moreover, other studies report that workaholic-headed families are dysfunctional and that paternal work addiction is associated with anxiety, depression, and external locus of control in the offspring of workaholics.[19]

Reality 3: Workaholics suffer from a compulsive disorder that masks a range of feelings, from anger to depression, and maladjustment in the form of feelings of poor self-worth, difficulty with intimacy, and fear of loss of control.

The Messiah Myth

Workaholics swear they're just working hard for their families. They often give the excuse that they overindulge in work to provide a good life for their families, because of company loyalties, or to contribute to society. However, their motives are much more narcissistic and ego driven than their denial allows them to admit.

Underneath a stack of accomplishments and successes swirls an obsessive need to excel, a compulsive need for approval, a deep-seated unhappiness, and a sense of low self-worth. Feeling incomplete and unfinished, workaholics become dependent on their work to define who they are and to gain a positive sense of themselves. They often measure their own worth by the concrete results they achieve. They need to quantify their successes through observable outcomes.

Reality 4: Workaholics overextend themselves to fill an inner void, to medicate emotional pain, and to repress a range of emotions.

The Wedded-to-Work Myth

There is a common misbelief that workaholics must enjoy their jobs to be work addicted because they spend so much time with their nose to the grindstone. In reality, workaholics tend to work for the sake of working. Regardless of work conditions or salary scales, they are willing to do whatever it takes and go the extra mile to get the job done, even when the company doesn't reciprocate with material rewards.

The reason they are accused of "romancing the grindstone" is not necessarily that they love their work. What they love is the escape from intimacy that the work provides them, and its accompanying boosts of self-esteem. Immersion in work feels safe and secure for workaholics, whether or not the work itself is satisfying.

Reality 5: Although most workaholics say that they enjoy their jobs, work satisfaction is not necessarily a prerequisite to work addiction.

The Impostor Myth

The impostor myth holds that work addiction is not a legitimate addiction because it doesn't have a physiological basis as do the chemical and food addictions. The truth, however, is that work addiction is both a process (overdoing) and a substance (adrenaline) addiction. Long-standing research has linked work addiction to the release of adrenaline in the body. Adrenaline is a hormone, produced by the body in times of stress, that has an effect similar to that of amphetamines or "speed." Workaholics often describe the rush or surge of energy pumping through their veins and the accompanying euphoria as "an adrenaline high." Addicted to adrenaline, workaholics require larger doses to maintain the high that they create by putting themselves and those around them under stress. Some researchers believe workaholics unconsciously put themselves under stressful situations to get the body to pump its fix.[20]

After a long week, a university professor left his office, butterflies in his stomach at the thought of facing an unplanned weekend. On his way out, he was handed a memo announcing grant-proposal deadlines. Suddenly, calm descended over him, and the adrenaline began to flow as he folded the three-inch-thick computer printout under his arm. Like an alcoholic, bottle under arm, who was assured of plenty to drink, he was calmed by the assurance of more to do; this knowledge filled the hours and gave him purpose. It was an anesthetic, a tranquilizer. But after the proposal was written, the emptiness, unrest, and depression returned.

Adrenaline addiction, in effect, creates addictions to crises that lead the body to produce the hormone and provide workaholics their drug. On the job, workaholics routinely create and douse crises that require the body's adrenaline flow. Pushing subordinates or themselves to finish designated assignments within unrealistic deadlines is one way crises are achieved. Another is biting off too much at one time or attempting to accomplish many tasks at once. While the workaholic gets high, however, coworkers and subordinates experience stress and burnout and many of the same emotions as children in alcoholic homes, notably unpredictability, confusion, and frustration. The adrenaline flow also boomerangs for the workaholic in the form of physical problems. Too much adrenaline blocks the cell's ability to clear dangerous cholesterol from the bloodstream. Elevated cholesterol levels clog arteries, damage their inner lining, and can cause heart attacks.

Reality 6: The release of adrenaline, like other drugs, creates physiological changes that lead to "work highs" that become addictive and potentially fatal.

The Stepchild Addiction Myth

There is a general belief that work addiction is not a true member of the addiction family and that it is secondary to the more serious, primary addictions. Even some clinicians view it as a positive habit that carries nowhere near the social stigma of alcoholism, eating disorders, or any of the other compulsive behaviors that are considered character defects. Work addiction has even been hailed as a positive addiction by some management consultants.[21] This myth also hurts the workaholic family, as Brenda relates in chapter 4, because people buy into the myth that says living with a workaholic is not as bad as living with an alcoholic. One factor that has delayed the consideration of workaholism as a serious addiction is that society considers it, if not healthy, at least harmless. That outlook makes work addiction more insidious and in some ways more dangerous than the other addictions, because it is culturally rewarded. In some ways overworking is harder to kick than the other addictions because it is an addiction that draws applause and wins approval at every level.

Many alcoholics find that once their substance abuse is peeled away, an addiction to work lies underneath. Work addiction has a high correlation with the disease of chemical addiction. Many of the doctors and nurses admitted to one treatment facility for impaired professionals had profound disturbances in their lives because of their habit of working seventy to eighty hours a week in addition to the chemical dependency for which they were admitted.[22] But for others, work is a primary addiction. It is estimated that between 25 and 30 percent of the population is addicted to work. A survey by Patrick Carnes revealed that 27 percent of the respondents gave work addiction as their primary addiction, and 28 percent of another research sample was identified as workaholic.[23] Workaholics often have more resistant denial systems than those who suffer from other addictions because of the societal approval workaholism earns. Amid praise and cheers, marriages break, friendships dissolve, work effectiveness ebbs, and physical side effects and health problems appear. No one, least of all the workaholic, understands what is going wrong. Amidst their crumbling world, workaholics drown their sorrows by rolling up their sleeves and digging their heels ever deeper into their jobs. The case of Margo is a testament to this addictive cycle.

Reality 7: Work addiction can be a primary addiction, or it can be secondary, blending with other addictions.

The Gainfully Employed Myth

This myth holds that if you are not gainfully employed, you cannot be work addicted. Most workaholics express their compulsive behaviors through their careers. But others express measured success through housework, volunteering, hobbies, fitness, raising kids, or such activity addictions as planting a tree, making a dress, or painting the bathroom. Melda had a successful law practice until she had a complete breakdown from work exhaustion. She retired from her practice and, along with her husband, bought an old house to restore. She realized early that the workplace is not a prerequisite for work addiction to occur. Working day and night, she almost sabotaged her recovery by transferring her compulsive work habits from her law practice to her work on restoring the house.

Reality 8: Work addiction is not limited to paid gainful employment. It can manifest itself in many forms by consuming the workaholic's identity, time, energy, and thoughts.

The Slacker Myth

Webster's Dictionary defines "slacker" as a person who shirks work or obligation. Workaholics fear that if they moderate their work habits, they will be perceived as slack or remiss in meeting their obligations. At the bottom of this attitude is a fear of failure. They often have a deep-seated fear that if they slow down, they will lose their momentum and never regain it. They drive themselves because they worry that if they slack off, their lazy side will surface. Part of this fear is generational and comes from deprivation in childhood. The Japanese, for example, carry the legacy of postwar economic ruin, and older Americans, that of the Great Depression of the 1930s. For these folks, no matter how rich they are, there's a pervasive fear that if they slack off, they'll end up in the poorhouse.

Compounding this fear is a pervasive belief in the workplace that recovery from work addiction will impair work quality and productivity, although overworking does not guarantee a high-quality product. The quality of work does not improve just because workaholics spend more time at it. Workaholics are interested in "quantity control," whereas healthy workers are interested in "quality control." Workaholics can place themselves and others in danger when employed in certain hazardous jobs. Rushing a job that requires manual dexterity with tools, machinery, or heavy equipment can cause physical injury as well as damaged goods. Other occupations that require mental alertness, such as piloting airplanes or brain surgery, where patience, precision, and clear thinking are critical, do not lend themselves to the workaholic's constant mental preoccupation with the next item on the agenda. Thus, reformed workaholics actually can improve the quality and productivity of their work.

Reality 9: Workers who live balanced lives are more efficient and productive and bring greater quality to the job because they are less stressed and more clear-minded.

The I'll-Quit-Tomorrow Myth

There is a mistaken belief that recovery from work addiction requires simply cutting back on work hours. Although work moderation is important, cutting back on the number of working hours alone is not the solution. The fact is that workaholics are not always physically active when they are working. Much of their work takes the form of obsessive mental preoccupation, even while they appear to be relaxing or socializing.

Workaholics cannot be diagnosed by how much they work, alcoholics by the number of drinks they have, or compulsive overeaters by how many helpings of mashed potatoes they eat. Recovery that is limited to mere reduction of work hours with an increase of recreation and leisure is like putting Band-Aids on a festering sore. The crux of the addiction runs deeper. Workaholics cannot control their compulsive work habits. They use different words to reflect their true feelings about "the great divide": work responsibilities and family obligations.

All addiction programs require abstinence from the drug of choice. For those who are chemically dependent, that means total sobriety, because alcohol and drugs are not necessary for the body to sustain itself. But because even workaholics have to work and compulsive overeaters have to eat, abstinence for them requires avoidance from *compulsive overworking* or *excessive overeating* Abstinence for workaholics essentially means work moderation along with balance in the other areas of their lives—the family, the social, and the personal/spiritual areas.

Reality 10: Like that for other addictions, recovery from work addiction goes deeper than simply measuring the number of work hours. It requires insights into unresolved emotional needs, difficulty with intimacy, and need to control.

Debunking the Myths

Typically, individuals who call themselves workaholics are not workaholics at all. True workaholics go to the office when there is no external reason or demand that they be there. Workaholics often don't take time off for vacations and holidays; if they do, they take work along. They are rarely out sick, unless they have started the downward spiral of burnout. They suffer from health complaints, anger, anxiety, depression, and stress-related illnesses. They are perfectionists who have difficulty delegating,

TABLE 2.1
Portrait of the Realities of Work Addiction

- Work addiction is a compulsive disorder that workaholics carry into the workplace. It is not created by the workplace.
- Work addiction is a mental health problem, not a virtue, and it can create more problems than it can solve for the workplace.
- The superhero facade masks deeper emotional and adjustment problems that workaholics shield with their accomplishments.
- Workaholics do not sacrifice free time and families for their work; they do it for ego gratification.
- Although most workaholics say they enjoy their jobs, work satisfaction is not a prerequisite to work addiction.
- Workaholics become chemically addicted to their own adrenaline because of the stress they put themselves under, and they crave additional crises to maintain the work highs.
- Work addiction can be a primary addiction or a secondary one that blends with other addictions.
- Workaholics do not have to be gainfully employed to become addicted; it can happen with any compulsive activity.
- Recovering one's balance after work addiction improves work quality and productivity and helps workaholics be happier and more effective at what they do.
- Achieving balance from reduced work addiction requires more than cutting back on work hours; it involves deep personal introspection and insights as well as attention to the parts of life that have been neglected.

have more problems with feeling than thinking, and have impaired social functioning. In the workplace they often create disharmony and do not work well with business associates. Their families are often in complete disarray, and their relationships with family members and friends eventually become dysfunctional.[24]

Healthy, nonworkaholic employees are turned off or stressed out by workaholic jobs and are less likely to stay in them as long as workaholics. Nonworkaholics are less willing to sacrifice their boundaries, families, and personal selves for work that does not give them anything back.

Suggestions for Clinicians

Because of the myths surrounding work addiction, clinicians have paid little attention to the needs of workaholics and to the impact of workaholism on the individual and the family. Work addiction is often attributed to other factors that detract from the significant issues that need to be addressed in treatment. Lack of awareness and misunderstandings of work addiction can be obstacles to treatment. One of the best ways clinicians can effectively help clients is by being able to distinguish myth from reality, by understanding the seriousness of work addiction and its associated underlying feelings. Clinicians must look at a deeper level than simply overt work patterns. They must be alert for signs of depression, anxiety, and anger that drive the work addiction and find constructive outlets for the expression of these feelings. In addition, to ensure full recovery they must address other underlying issues, such as low self-esteem, difficulty with intimacy, and need for perfectionism and control. Once clinicians educate themselves and break through their own denial, they can offer the help that is needed.

Helping Clients with Resistance

Work addiction is a disorder that tells you that you don't have it. Many workaholics disassociate themselves from the traits of work addiction. Comments such as "I don't work that much" or "I spend lots of time with my family" or "I have lots of friends and hobbies" are part of the process of denial. Upon closer look, however, their family lives, vacations, friendships, and hobbies often resemble the overly scheduled, rapid-fire pace, and money-making aspects of their jobs.

Clinicians can have clients describe these aspects of their lives and probe workaholics about comments that family members or colleagues make in regard to their work style. This feedback is often in direct contradiction to the workaholic's assertion. Clinicians can use these contradictory reports and comments as challenging evidence with which to confront the denial. Also, spouses, partners, or other loved ones can be invited for sessions to give firsthand accounts that might contradict and break through the workaholic's denial. For most workaholics the denial already has been penetrated before they present themselves for psychotherapy.

One of the first comments workaholics make when they come to therapy is "Don't tell me I have to quit my job," punctuated by rationalizations such as "I have two kids to support. Are you going to pay my mortgage while I quit work?" or "I love my job." The workaholic's biggest fear is that the only way to recover is to slash work hours or change jobs. The implied belief is "Either I work or I don't. There is no in between." These statements reflect workaholics' rigid black-and-white thinking (see chapter 5) and are typical of their inability to envision a flexible balance between work and leisure or work and family. It also reflects the driving fear that if they give up their compulsive working, there will be nothing left of their lives and their world will fall apart. This comes from having their identity wrapped up solely in work. These beliefs cause workaholics to avoid therapy and in many cases to cling more tenaciously to their work for security.

It is important to be prepared to deal with clients' resistance and to reassure them that the number of working hours has little to do with the kinds of changes necessary and that they will be the architect of any and all changes in their lives. This can relieve clients, give them a sense of control, and help them focus on the pertinent issues in therapy. Typical clients blame their jobs or their families for their work addiction. Here's where clinicians can explain the enabling process and help clients identify their enablers from the four levels described earlier in the chapter. They can also help them to separate the enablers in their lives from their work addiction—for which they must assume responsibility.

Clients often need help in understanding that the source of their pain is inside, not outside. It is not unusual for workaholics to blame their problems on today's lifestyles and pressures. But blaming the company, the recession, or the need for two paychecks only rewards self-destructive behaviors and distracts clinicians and patients from the real source of the problem. Blaming fast-paced society and modern technology takes workaholics off the hook. Although they have choices about the way they live, they may be unwittingly choosing an addiction while claiming they have no choices. Having workaholics become aware of their responsibilities, instead of blaming the enablers, helps them become more accountable and empowers them instead of victimizing them. Clinicians can ask workaholics to do a cost-benefit analysis of the advantages and disadvantages of work addiction to help them see concretely what their losses are and to weigh the advantages against the disadvantages.

Managing Time

Clinicians can help clients evaluate how effective they are at managing their time. They can discuss the art of prioritizing and delegating responsibilities and have clients bring in specific examples of ways they practiced these skills. They can also help clients focus on the things that require immediate attention and refrain from imposing unrealistic deadlines; evaluate their ability to ask for help when they need it; explore reasons why asking for help is difficult; and propose how they might be better served by delegating work in the office or at home.

Clinicians can suggest that clients set aside daily personal time. Eating right and getting ample rest and exercise are important for stress-free lives and clear-minded thinking. Clinicians can recommend three balanced nutritional meals a day rather one or two and advise clients to avoid eating on the run, while working, between meals, or while watching television. It is important to evaluate whether clients build personal time into their schedules each week and to investigate the underlying reasons why they inevitably fail at following a regimen that many other people find simple and easy. Thus, the underlying reasons for the difficulty and failure become the focus for the therapeutic session, and even the smallest gains are acknowledged and rewarded.

3

How to Recognize Work Addiction

Without work all life goes rotten. But when work
is soulless, life stifles and dies.

—ALBERT CAMUS

Glenn

It was only when I grew up, went to work, married, and had children of my own that I could begin to see my own emerging patterns of work addiction. And even then, insight didn't come easily. It took the awareness and constant loving petition of a dedicated wife to help me see I was giving all of my energy to my work and leaving none for my children or her.

Someone once asked me what is it like to grow up with a workaholic father. That's like asking a fish to be aware of what it's like to live in the pond. It was the water I swam in, the air I breathed. My father traveled, that's all. He was in sales, responsible for opening the market in this country for a brand of high-quality Swiss textile machinery. For a man in his generation, he was doing everything he was supposed to do. He was a hard-working and successful provider. What more could one ask for? What better role model could one have in a father?

As a child, I could no more have identified what was

wrong with our family than the fish could identify what was wrong with the pond. As a husband and father, I simply and blindly followed for a decade the modeling I had received as a child. I worked long and hard. As the founding pastor of a successful young congregation, I had found a place where I could "swim in my familiar waters." All of my focus was on making the church a success. I attended to every need of the congregation. Working sixty, seventy, and more hours a week, I poured my life's energy into what was widely seen as a great success. And those hours that I was not working, I was "on call." I can remember tumultuous evenings with my family that would be constantly interrupted by the phone ringing. Everything would stop while I politely conversed as if I lived in a sea of tranquillity. I can remember extremely important husband-and-wife dialogues that would end at a moment's notice for lengthy phone conversations on matters of grave importance such as "The songs we sang last Sunday weren't my favorite ones" or "I don't think the choir director likes me" and, most important of all, "What was Cheryl's phone number?" Sadly, to my unconscious ears, every ring of the phone was more important than the cries of my own children for attention. Where was I when my children needed me? I was doing what every father is supposed to do—working hard, being a provider, and being successful.

Driven by internal forces that seemed greater than me and strongly supported by a culture that prizes its men for being self-sufficient, hard workers, I became more and more a success at my work and felt more and more like a failure at home. Needless to say, this only served to perpetuate my own growing work addiction. Where did I want to spend my time, anyway? At home, where I felt like a failure? Or at work, where I felt like a success?

Finally, at the urging of my life partner, we got into counseling. It was only there that I could really begin to see clearly what I was re-creating in my life. There I began to understand this feeling that had always seemed like a hole in my heart; the loneliness of my childhood; the desperate need to fill that hole and that loneliness with something—anything in my difficult adolescence. I did try everything, it seems: alcohol, drugs, travel food, gambling, sex, motorcycles, sky diving, scuba diving, even high-speed dangerous driving in combinations with many of the above. But nothing, nothing filled that hole as well as work. Nothing was so addictive, so well accepted, and so rewarded by society.

In counseling I started to truly understand that powerful, near-suicidal force that had been propelling me—that deep, unfulfilled need that had driven me, that could have and should have been filled, among other things, by a present and loving father.

I can still feel the hole, but it is smaller and fainter now. When I do hear it, I don't run to my work addiction or lash out at loved ones with anger. I know I simply need to take even better care of myself. After years of work on myself, I now have real choices about my involvement as a husband and father and what I do with my most precious commodity—my time. I was fortunate to catch this before my children were grown. Hell, I was fortunate to catch it in my lifetime. Now I spend more time with my family. I make plenty of mistakes, but out of the quantity time comes some real quality time.

When Work Steals Your Soul

Now that we have looked at some of the myths and realities behind work addiction, we can proceed to examining the signs of workaholism more closely and analyzing how they can be recognized. There is a time when you wear your workaholic label like a prize. You don't party or stay out late. You don't waste your time or throw money down the drain. You're level-headed and rational. You've been called dedicated, responsible, and conscientious. You work long and hard, and you're always at your desk. At first the accolades and applause, slaps on the back, fat paychecks, and gold plaques feel worth the effort. But, after a while, the addiction starts to feel like an unwelcome burden. You have a lot on your plate. You've got to do it perfectly. Can you measure up? Will you be able to perform? Or will you let others down? You've got to prove that you can do it. If you fall short, you've got to dig your heels in deeper. You can never let up. Everyone is depending on you.

Burrowing itself deeper into your soul, work addiction is like a prison chain that moves with you wherever you go. When you're not at your desk, your compulsive thoughts are there. They beat you to the office before you begin the day. They stalk you in your sleep, at a party, or while you're fishing with a friend. They lurk over your shoulder when you're trying to have intimate conversations with your partner.

Despite longer hours and more determination, your life is falling apart. Your company doesn't appreciate your hard work. Your boss is breathing down your neck. No matter how hard you try, nothing seems to satisfy him. You're impatient and restless at work. You snap at coworkers, and they snap back at you. You resent that you get to work earlier and stay longer than anyone in the office. You feel contempt for colleagues who don't work on weekends and who goof off on holidays.

Your family doesn't appreciate your hard work and the creature comforts it provides. You can't depend on them to handle things at home in your absence, and they're constantly bothering you with problems that distract you from earning a decent living. They complain that you're never around and that when you are, you never listen. They drag you into their disputes, and your kids are out of control. Sometimes it feels like they gang up on you. You're starting to feel like an outsider in your own home. Your old friends don't call anymore, and you never seem to have fun. Work is the one thing you do well, and now even it has soured. If you don't have your work, there's nothing left of you. Still, you keep plugging away, hoping it will get better. Your life has become cold, dark, and lonely—without meaning. You are dogged by self-doubt and failure. You wish you could talk to someone who would understand and help you remove the invisible chains.

For people who reach this point, there is often no place to turn. Even the clinicians they seek out may be oblivious to their problem or ignorant of how to treat it. Ironically, when this happens, it makes the workaholic feel even more disconnected from others, more lonely, and more hopeless. They have lost their soul to work. In 2006, my research team at the University of North Carolina at Charlotte compared a sample of 109 workaholics with nonworkaholics. Across the board, workaholics had statistically higher burnout rates, were more disconnected from their inner selves, and had less self-insight than nonworkaholics. Whereas workaholics were more controlling and more impaired in their communication, nonworkaholics showed more soul-like qualities of clarity, compassion, calmness, and confidence.[1] And it's no wonder, because workaholics focus—for the most part—outside themselves on the tsunami of work that they take on.

At the beginning of some of my lectures, I conduct an exercise with the audience that gives them a taste of how workaholics feel. I ask them to sit with another person, who then bombards them with a litany of questions such as: What is your social security number? street address? home phone number, including area code? work number, including area code? business address? E-mail address? fax number? driver's license number? birthdate? The receiver must answer each question immediately while writing the Pledge of Allegiance and counting the number of items in the room that are blue—all within a one-minute time limit. Although this activity is next to impossible to accomplish, those who put forth the effort feel the body's adrenaline rush and the frustration, irritability, and sometimes the sense of failure that come with impossible standards. Try this exercise with a friend and see if you, too, feel the adrenaline kick. This is the way workaholics operate in the world with their jobs, vacations, and families. Let's look at the signs.

The Tell-Tale Signs of Work Addiction

Work addiction can consist of a number of symptoms. Over the years I have collected hundreds of case studies from self-professed workaholics in my clinical practice. The following ten warning sings were synthesized from my own case studies.[2] It is important to remember that all of these signs are not always present and that they may appear in various configurations in different individuals. Still, these are important guidelines by which work addicts, their family members, and clinicians can learn to recognize workaholics.

1. *They are always in a rush and hyperbusy.* "As I'm walking out the door, I glance at my watch and realize I have ten more minutes before my next appointment. I just have to cram in one more thing. So, I rush back to my desk, put in a call . . . and before I know it, fifteen minutes have passed. Of course, I'm late to the appointment."

Nothing moves fast enough for Jim. The more items he can cross off his list, the better he feels. When a job is left hanging, he feels anxious and afraid. To curb his anxiety, he has to have two or three activities going at once. So, with the phone in one hand, he's writing with the other and mentally planning a third project.

The need to have many things happening at once and to conduct two or three activities simultaneously gives them the sense that they are getting more accomplished. To perform only one activity at a time feels underproductive. Typically they schedule back-to-back appointments and do not give themselves enough time to complete tasks, the pressures of which provide their adrenaline rush. Or they create minicrises, as when a balky computer system or paper-clip shortage flips them out.

2. *They play the Control Game.* "I have to write, produce, and star in my life. I really do not have time to develop this new account, but I know if I hand it over to someone else, it won't be handled right. I'll have to work nights to write and design this

new ad campaign, but it's worth it. In the long run, we'll keep the client. I'd rather do it myself than waste time with a bunch of bad ideas from everyone else."

Sally's successful advertising agency is built on her own strength. As a work-addicted employer, she has trouble delegating authority.

Sally's need to control her life is prompted by insecurity; she feels uncomfortable in unpredictable situations. Working alone gives her security. Projects come with a beginning, middle, and end. When she's in control of all three stages, she feels like her entire life is in control.

Workaholics fear that delegating tasks or asking for help will be perceived as signs of weakness or incompetence. And once something is out of their hands, they feel a loss of control. So they cannot and will not ask for help. There is a tendency to overplan and overorganize through work so that conditions feel predictable, consistent, and controllable, which inhibits spontaneity and flexibility.

3. *Nothing is ever perfect enough for them.* "I think I'm superhuman. I cannot be content to accomplish something without laying the groundwork for something else. Fearing that I'll somehow fall behind or get out of control, I constantly have to be striving to accomplish some kind of goal or some block of work."

Lynne judges herself and others by inhuman standards. In her view, there's no room for mistakes. Anyone falling short of her idea of perfection is lazy.

Even at home, Lynne is a critical judge. "This house isn't clean enough! Who left crumbs in the den? You forgot to wipe your feet. If I've told you once, I've told you a million times, 'Close that basement door when you come upstairs!'"

Perfectionist workaholics are difficult to work for, and even more difficult to live with. Lives are narrowed to only those things at which the workaholic can excel. Both the self and others are judged unmercifully. Common sayings include "If you want it done right, do it yourself" and "If I do it, I know it's been done the way I want it done." Because of these superhuman standards, failure and anger at others for not meeting high standards are constant companions.

4. *Their relationships crumble in the name of work.* "At rehearsals, I would imagine my smiling dad in the front row. He looked so proud of me. His imagined presence really motivated me to learn my part. But when it came time for the actual performance, he had an out-of-town business meeting. He promised to dash back from the airport to catch my second act. All through the first act, I was distracted by opening doors and shuffling feet. I'd look into the audience, searching for his face. But his meeting ran over, and he missed my school play."

This was not the first play that Sandy's father had missed. He often forgot, ignored, or minimized many family rituals and celebrations. His wife had to remind him about birthdays, reunions, anniversaries, and holidays. Even when he made it to a family event, he had trouble concentrating. His mind was at the office. Wedded to work, he had little time left over for others.

5. *They produce work in binges.* "I self-impose deadlines all the time. The price I have to pay for procrastinating just isn't worth it. I go nuts! I panic. I can't sleep. I have such anxiety until a project is completed. So finally I just buckle down and do it. I get in this altered state where I chain-smoke, don't eat, screen all of my phone calls, and avoid sleep. When I'm done, it's like crawling out of a work cave. I look and feel pretty disgusting. But, with that finished project in my hand, nothing else seems to matter."

Everyone occasionally works overtime to meet a deadline. But workaholics create personal deadlines that mandate binging on every project. Some workaholics would rather work nonstop for days than spread out tasks over a reasonable period of time.

In extreme cases, the workaholic mimics the alcoholic who stashes booze wherever he goes. Instead of liquor, notebooks are shoved into suitcases, under car seats, or in glove compartments. Even at leisure events, where the addict has promised not to work, papers are shuffled inside pant or skirt pockets. It's as if the addict needs a work "fix" everywhere he or she goes.

6. *They are restless, no-fun grumps.* "I always have this annoying voice in my head. It tells me I don't have the right to relax or unwind. This voice says, 'Look, fun is a waste of time. What do you have to show for it? Go do something productive, you jerk.'"

Workaholics feel guilty and useless when they do something that does not produce results. If they are exercising, cleaning, or doing a job-related activity, they feel okay. But if they're just out with friends, they tend to feel restless and irritable. Free time is viewed as a frivolous waste of time, and they become so restless that hobbies and recreation get turned into productivity or money-making ventures.

7. *They experience work trances and "DWWs."* Work trances or brownouts are comparable to the alcoholic's blackouts. Workaholics experience memory losses of long conversations because they are so preoccupied with work. They literally tune out the here and now. DWW, or driving-while-working mentally, can cause them to drive past stop signs or designated points. Busily focusing on tomorrow's presentation, they can't pay attention to the road. While some workaholics claim they can get their best ideas while driving, operating an automobile requires full attention. Not surprisingly, work addicts usually have faulty driving records.

> It was my boyfriend's birthday, and I had spent most of the day with him. We were supposed to have dinner together. He was even going to cook. But just before dinnertime, I became so anxious I had to get out of his apartment. I hadn't done one work-related thing all day. I told him I needed to run home to change clothes. But once in my car, I found myself driving toward my office. I told myself I would merely type a few paragraphs and go over tomorrow's appointments. I don't remember the three hours that passed. It was 9 P.M. when I rushed to my car and floored it back toward his apartment. I was stopped by a police officer for speeding. I tried to explain my situation to

him, but to no avail. When I finally made it back, my boyfriend had already eaten his birthday dinner alone. I felt so terrible. Yet even worse, I didn't know why I did it.

8. *They are impatient and irritable.* Since time is their most precious commodity, workaholics hate to wait. They'll try almost anything to get to the front of the line at the grocery store, restaurant, or movie. You've probably noticed them at the doctor's or dentist's office. They're the ones with open briefcases and fast-scribbling pens.

In the long run, their impatience can result in impulsivity. Decisions may be made prematurely, and projects may be started before all the facts are gathered. Avoidable mistakes are made because workaholics bypass research and exploration.

9. *They think they're only as good as their last achievement.* "Work was my security, promising to fill the hours and give me purpose, meaning, and self-esteem. But as soon as a project was done, the emptiness, unrest, and depression returned. The only time I felt good about myself was when I was producing 'things' so that I could constantly prove that I was okay."

Natalie gets a temporary high when she completes a project. In between achievements, she feels empty and lost. This feeling of inadequacy bothers her until she is immersed in her next project. Work is her security blanket. It's the one thing that used to bring her love and attention from her parents when she was younger. She still believes she has to prove herself through work in order to be accepted by others.

Self-worth is sought through performance and achievement. A sense of inadequacy and poor self-esteem lead to a strong emphasis on production, with concrete results giving a temporary high and feeling of self-worth.

10. *They have no time for self-care.* Work addicts spend all their time taking care of their jobs, rather than themselves. Little attention is paid to physical needs like nutrition, rest, and exercise.

When coping mechanisms such as chain-smoking, caffeine

TABLE 3.1
Portrait of the Physical and Behavioral Signs of Work Addiction

Physical Signs	Behavioral Signs
Headaches	Temper outbursts
Fatigue	Restlessness
Allergies	Insomnia
Indigestion	Difficulty relaxing
Stomachaches	Hyperactivity
Ulcers	Irritability and impatience
Chest pain	Forgetfulness
Shortness of breath	Difficulty concentrating
Nervous tics	Boredom
Dizziness	Mood swings (from euphoria to depression)

abuse, and compulsive eating are added to the picture, health deteriorates further. Even when real symptoms such as headaches, ulcers, or high blood pressure crop up, work addicts tell themselves they don't have time to go to the doctor. Part of them knows there's a problem. Another part instructs them to ignore it. Table 3.1 presents the physical and behavioral warning signs that accompany work addiction.

The Many Faces of Work Addiction

All workaholics work too much, but not all workaholics act alike. Some are too careless; some are too ploddingly scrupulous; some can't get started; others plunge in on a dozen projects and finish little. The end result of these differing work styles may look the same from the point of view of a therapist or an unhappy spouse—an unbalanced life dominated by long hours at the office—but each style expresses a different set of emotional and cognitive vulnerabilities, and each needs different therapeutic treatment. The broad umbrella term *workaholism* is only a starting point. There are four major styles of workaholism: the *relentless* style, the *bulimic* style, the *attention-deficit* style, and the *savoring* style. Some workaholics employ only one style; others mix and match, blending styles or alternating among them. For example, a perfectionist may sometimes procrastinate on a major project in a bulimic workaholic style and at other times be unwilling to let go of finished work in the savoring style. And an attention-deficit workaholic may sometimes procrastinate and at other times impulsively start projects, only to lose interest and abandon them. Whatever the style of overwork, a careful assessment can help unravel the assumptions and fears that lie beneath it and point the way to an effective therapeutic approach.

As you consider the signs and traits, however, keep in mind that not all workaholics fit the general pattern. Work addiction has many faces:

- The CEO who sneaks a beeper, cellular phone, fax machine, computer, and modem into the hospital where she has just undergone major surgery
- The minister zipping down the highway at seventy miles an hour while writing the text for his sermon and promising himself to carry a Dictaphone next time so he won't have to slow down
- The psychotherapist who cannot say no to all the patients who need her and ends up overscheduling herself, burning out in the process
- The architect who confides that she mentally worked on a client's house during sexual intercourse with her husband
- The supermom who has a career, manages the house, carpools the kids, gets dinner on the table, and perhaps even takes a class at night

Workaholics are not always the Donald Trumps of the corporate world. In fact, the number of women workaholics is climbing as women enter more traditionally male-dominated jobs. Workaholics are not always in corporate or office jobs; neither are they always in high-paying positions. Plumbers, electricians, waitresses, and maintenance workers are included in the ranks of workaholics.

Notice if you see yourself, a loved one, or a colleague in any of the following classifications of workaholics.

The Relentless Workaholic Style

The stereotyped workaholics are what I call *relentless workaholics*—those who work compulsively and constantly day and night, holidays and weekends. There is no letup, no periods of downtime, and leisure and recreation are rare, as Gary describes:

> When I am fatigued and have had only three hours of sleep after staying up all night at the computer, something in my body and my mechanism keeps me moving, even when there's no energy left. It isn't easy for me to give up, no matter what the clock says. I take a break to eat and try to work out once in a while. But I usually don't stop until eleven or twelve o'clock at night, and many times not until two in the morning. Because I want to bear down on myself, I tend to put too much on my list, stay up past the time I should have, and do projects that really could be done the next day. I want to make sure that I put forth some blood, sweat, and tears so that I will remember that I've done the work and I did not come by it in an easy way. I have headaches almost every afternoon to the point that I'm keeping Extra Strength Tylenol in business. I'm tired all the time, but I don't allow the kind of rest I need. I haven't made time for it because there's too much work to be done.

Instead of dragging their feet, they are relentless in meeting deadlines, often completing work weeks ahead of schedule. Approaching a six-month deadline as if it were due tomorrow gives the adrenaline charge, and nothing and no one stands in their way in getting the job done. Having the project out of the way early leaves time to focus on other work items. Work is more important than relationships; work addicts appear to have disregard for people's feeling where getting the job done is concerned. Marge, for example, was so affirmed for her tireless dedication by the hospital where she worked that it stimulated her to do more, despite her husband's objections. Her addiction got so bad that she actually stepped over dog excrement on the floor at home for days because she didn't have time to pick it up. Needless to say, this marriage ended in divorce. Marge lamented after the breakup:

> Only after I was separated from my husband did I realize that I wasn't supposed to do all of this as part of my job. I'm aware that I've been addicted to my own adrenaline for a long, long time. My mind never stopped at night, because I was running on adrenaline. When I couldn't sleep, I'd put a yellow pad by my bed. Every time I had a thought, I'd turn on the light and write the thought down, thinking maybe it would help me sleep. My husband continually wanted to know why I couldn't turn it off because I was working day and night. The adrenaline made me feel like I didn't need sleep, except for two or three hours a night. But I wasn't tired. I was having a ball and on a roll!

Once a task is completed, relentless workaholics move to the next item on the agenda, and they have many activities going at once. They are hard-driving perfectionists; their work is thorough, and their standards practically unreachable. Relentless workaholics are those Oates referred to as *dyed-in-the-wool workaholics* who take their work seriously, performing to nothing short of the highest standards.[3] Overcommitted, this type of workaholic abhors incompetence in others. Relentless workaholics tend to be highly productive and highly regarded by others.

The Bulimic Workaholic Style

The second category is the *bulimic workaholic,* who has out-of-control work patterns that alternate between binging and purging. Faced with a time crunch, bulimic workaholics create adrenaline as they engage in frantic productivity followed by inertia. They overcommit, wait until the last possible minute, then throw themselves into a panic and work frantically to complete the task. Jenny worked for two or three days straight and slept off her work high for two days. She collapsed, sleeping in her clothes, just like an alcoholic sleeping off a drunk:

> When I used to binge, I would take on a project and stay up until three or four in the morning to get it finished, just compulsively thinking that morning's not going to come and that if something happened to me, I have to have it done today. That binge would go into fourteen and sixteen hours, and then I'd have two or three hours of sleep and then go on a roll and do this for two more days. Then I would be exhausted and sleep it off. It's almost like I've heard alcoholics talk about sleeping off a drunk. I would sleep off that binge of work. Sometimes I would sleep in my clothes, and I hated it! I just hated it!

In contrast to relentless workaholics, whose productivity is clearly visible, bulimic workaholics go through long periods where they do not work. In fact, you'd never know they have a problem if you caught them during their downtime. When it comes to deadlines, they procrastinate and then put themselves under the gun to finish. Procrastination and frantic working are two different sides of the same coin of work bulimia. Underlying the procrastination is the fear that they will not do the task perfectly. Bulimic workaholics may become so preoccupied with perfection that they cannot start a project. Yet, while they engage in behaviors that distract them from the task, they obsess over getting the job accomplished. Outwardly, work bulimics appear to be avoiding work, but in their minds they are working obsessively hard.

Although physically present during family gatherings or even Workaholics Anonymous meetings, work bulimics are perceived as preoccupied because they are working in their heads. During the procrastinating phase, when they feel paralyzed and unable to work steadily and within healthy boundaries, bulimic workaholics are referred to as *work anorexics*—the ones for whom avoidance of work is as much a compulsion of work addiction as is overworking because of their obsession with it.[4]

The Attention-Deficit Workaholic Style

Lee represents the third type of workaholic, *attention-deficit workaholics*—adrenaline-seeking workaholics who are easily bored and constantly seeking stimulation. Lee leaves the house most mornings in a huff because either his wife or his kids did something that upset him. On the way to work he weaves in and out of traffic and shakes his fist and curses at the other commuters. By the time he gets to the office, he feels settled and ready to work. The appetite for excitement, crisis, and intense stimulation is a strategy that attention-deficit workaholics unwittingly use to focus themselves. They are often the revved-up workaholics who click their nails on table tops, twiddle their thumbs, or fidget or pace about erratically. They like risky jobs, recreation, and living on the edge at work and play.

Living on the brink of chaos gives attention-deficit workaholics a constant adrenaline charge. Some, like Lee, seek diversion from boredom through stimulation in a relatively safe fashion, such as creating tight work deadlines, keeping many projects going at one time, taking on big challenges at work, and having a chronic inability to relax without intense stimulation. Others live on the edge and engage in high-risk jobs or activities such as playing the stock market, parachute jumping, or working triage in a hospital emergency room.

All of them have difficulty keeping their focus on the job before them, get bored with what they are working on, and jump ahead to the next item on the agenda to get another charge of adrenaline. Attention-deficit workaholics constantly create crises over the smallest things to get the adrenaline rush. They may throw a fit because there is no paper in the fax machine. It is not uncommon for workaholics to generate the crisis but also to get attention and praise for resolving it.[5]

Some but not all attention-deficit workaholics are struggling with attention-deficit disorder (ADD), which is often undiagnosed. Adrenaline acts as self-medication that functions as an antidote against the ADD and provides the needed focus that allows the workaholic to buckle down to work. Unlike bulimic workaholics who are so preoccupied with perfectionism that they cannot start a project, attention-deficit workaholics start many projects but cannot carry them out. Unlike relentless workaholics who compulsively follow through, attention-deficit workaholics leave projects unfinished and half-baked to move on to the next excitement. Easily bored with the details of follow-through, they get high from creating ideas and start many projects but have difficulty seeing them through to completion. Diane Fassel has observed this workaholic type, which she calls *the innovators,* on the job:

> They cannot keep their attention focused long enough to finish what they have created. Moreover, they report boredom with follow-through. Upon deeper investigation, I discovered that these workers were hooked on the adrenaline rush of the new idea, and felt let down by the painstaking development work. They jumped to the new projects to get their high. Of course, with inadequate product development, these great innovations were just sitting on the shelves and not making profit for the company.[6]

The compulsion to jump impulsively into work projects before plans have been thought through or solidified makes it hard for attention-deficit workaholics to complete projects in a timely manner. Instead of giving serious consideration to alternate behaviors or possible consequences or waiting and planning, their need for immediacy often causes them to become locked into a course of action. They proceed with projects without giving thorough attention to details or receiving valuable input from others. Results can be disastrous when the addiction outruns careful thought and reflection. Nowhere is the adage "haste makes waste" more appropriate than when attention-deficit workaholics make decisions or launch projects before gathering all the facts and examining all options. Lack of forethought often sends them back to clean up the resultant messes.

The Savoring Workaholic Style

The fourth type, *savoring workaholics,* are a contrast to attention-deficit workaholics because they are slow, deliberate, and methodical. Consummate perfectionists, they are terrified deep down that the finished project is never good enough. This type of workaholic has difficulty discerning when something is incomplete or when it's finished. They savor their work just as alcoholics would savor a shot of bourbon. When Norm balances his accounts, he'll take eight hours to do some tabulating that most people could do in one. According to his wife, Norm has the same sort of intoxication with work that people who eat too much do with food. He's always working but never seems to accomplish much. Norm's wife said, "Sometimes I look at what he's done, and it doesn't look like he's produced anything. For all I know, he's adding up the same column of numbers day after day."

Savoring workaholics inadvertently prolong and create additional work when they realize they are nearly finished with a project. They are notorious for creating to-do lists that often take longer to generate than the tasks themselves require. Norm says he takes great pride and pleasure in generating to-do lists and in marking off each item as it is completed: "Creating lists dictated my work life. I always found a way to fill in any extra spaces or lines on my yellow pad with obscure chores so that I would always be busy." He says that each line that is marked off is a great sense of satisfaction for him. It is a visible trophy to his sense of accomplishment.

It is this tunnel vision, this detailed and self-absorbed approach to work that makes it hard for savoring workaholics to work as part of a team. Norm drives colleagues and loved ones crazy with his nit-picking and his inability to let things go because to him nothing ever feels finished. Colleagues complain that savoring workaholics drag their feet because they have to dot every "i" and cross every "t." When others are ready to move on, savoring workaholics hold them back by overanalyzing and taking ideas apart, thinking them through from every angle, getting bogged down in detail, and sending things back to committee fifteen different times. Because projects always feel incomplete, even when others feel they are finalized, savoring workaholics have difficulty with both closure of old tasks and initiation of new tasks in their work.

Careaholic Workaholics

Roberta represents a fifth type of workaholic, the *careaholic workaholic,* who cuts across the typology in figure 3.1 and can be found in combination with any of the other four types. Careaholic workaholics have a compulsive need to be overly responsible for others, to feel the feelings of others, and to overdo for them. Roberta doesn't feel normal unless she's helping or doing something for someone else. She works full time, cares for a husband and two children and volunteers in her church helping the needy and traveling to third-world countries to help the poor. She believes that every person who comes into her life is sent by God, which gives her justification to work compulsively through caring day and night. Despite constant overload caused by caring for everyone but herself, she wonders why she is burning out.

Careaholism is work addiction veiled in noble intentions. Careaholic workaholics are not sitting behind desks or in front of computers. They are tending to the sick, caring for the young, advocating for the needy, or saving the souls of the lost. Found more in the clergy and helping professions, careaholic workaholics feel happy only when helping others, because it makes

FIGURE 3.1
Typology of Workaholics

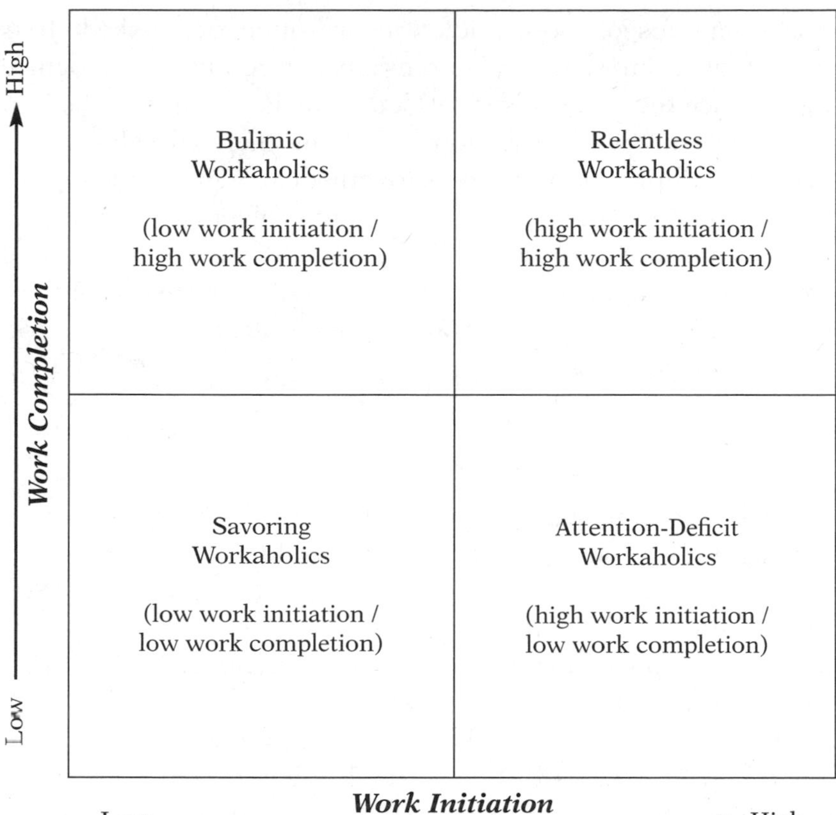

them feel needed, keeps the focus off themselves, and gives them a type of "high." They think, feel, and act as if they are omnipotent and can take care of everybody's feelings and problems, while their own worlds are crumbling under their feet. Careaholic workaholics who overload themselves out of obligation contribute to their own stress and burnout. A nun once said, "I believe that some religious persons often seek salvation through the number of souls they save and sick they attend to; thus, the more they do, the better human beings they are."

Suggestions for Clinicians

The symptoms of work addiction are often overlooked. It is important to know the symptoms and to be able to recognize them. Once the pattern is identified, clinicians can take the first step in treating work addiction by helping clients develop a self-care plan. Clinicians and clients together can identify the type of work addiction and the accompanying problems that are presented and can match counseling goals with the specific type of work addiction. It is important for clinicians to be aware of their own abusive work patterns and to evaluate their own work-addiction tendencies.

Using the WART

I developed the Work Addiction Risk Test (WART), shown in chapter 1, as a tool to screen for the symptoms of work addiction. The WART has been tested for its clinical preciseness. Statistical studies show that it has high reliability and validity: scores on the instrument tend to be consistent over time, and it measures what it is supposed to measure.[7]

Those who are truly workaholics can use the WART to identify problem areas and to set goals. Readers can use the WART to become aware of areas of concern that they would like to modify and then apply some or all of the tips that are presented throughout the book. Reading the test again and identifying those statements assigned a score of 3 or 4 will tell readers a lot about how they are living their lives. Then they can ask themselves what steps they can take to reduce the risk involved in each situation by changing their lives so that they can answer honestly with a 1 or 2 score. Clinicians can help clients make each situation that they would like to change a goal in which they can begin to reverse their compulsive work patterns.

Wayne and Mary Sotile modified the WART for those they call *high-powered couples* and discovered that it provides a vehicle for stimulating helpful conversation among couples.[8] Couples can read the WART together and decide how much each item pertains to each of them. After tallying their two scores—a "mine" and a "yours" score—they can note how they define their own and each other's "work." They can note where they agree and disagree in self- and other-ratings. They can note changes in perceptions of each other and ask such questions as "Have you changed in ways that your partner is not recognizing?" or "What are small changes in your own and in your partner's work style or work orientation that might make a difference in the quality of your day-to-day life together?"

Matching Counseling Goals to Type of Work Addiction

Different workaholic types experience different kinds of job and family problems. Clinicians and clients together can set therapeutic goals that match the client's type of work addiction. Relentless workaholics need help with impulse control, forethought, and attention to detail. They need to slow down the pulse and rhythm of their daily lives—to deliberately eat more slowly, talk more slowly, walk more slowly, and drive more slowly. Developing a work pace commensurate with that of their colleagues and learning to delegate tasks can give them the breathing room they need to stay in the present.

Goals for work bulimics might include devising a more consistent and even work style and setting boundaries around the times they work. If people employing this work style learn to accept imperfection, they can move from a stance of "Either I do it perfectly or not at all" to "It's okay if my rough draft contains misspelled words, bad grammar, and incomplete and imperfect ideas." Then bulimic workaholics can get started earlier and spread their work over more realistic time spans. Some workaholics need more help with procrastination and lethargy, along with concurrent mental obsessions and working. Still others need a self-care plan that helps them reduce the frantic, nonstop approach to work; this plan might include time out.

I have noticed in my private practice that many adrenaline-seeking workaholics also have a dual diagnosis of attention-deficit disorder (ADD). Clinicians need to be aware of that possibility and of the client's need for medication where the dual diagnosis exists. Attention-deficit workaholics perform best in positions in which they can initiate ideas and delegate the implementation to others Instead of multitasking, they benefit from making a list of daily (or weekly) goals and sticking with one task on the list until it is completed before starting another.

The physicians Edward Hallowell and John Ratey, authors of *Driven to Distraction,* describe what they call the high-stim ADD individual who abhors boredom. Similar to attention-deficit workaholics, the high-stim ADD seeks diversion from boredom and is unable to relax without intense stimulation. This appetite for excitement and crisis is a strategy that these clients unwittingly use to self-medicate themselves with adrenaline, which helps focus on their work:

> It may be that the thrill of danger helps focus the individual in a way similar to that of stimulant medication, inducing changes at the neurotransmitter level. Stimulant medications, the standard for ADD, enhance the release of epinephrine (adrenaline) in the brain. High-risk behavior does the same thing. Hence such behavior may constitute a form of self-medication. In addiction, a high-risk situation may supply the extra motivation that we know can help with focusing. When one is highly motivated, once again there is a change at the neurotransmitter level that enhances focusing.[9]

Thus, it is difficult to treat attention-deficit workaholic clients without proper medication, thereby reducing their appetite for crises and high stimulation so that therapy can have maximum benefit. Once it is clear that medication is not necessary, clinicians can employ other traditional therapeutic techniques to stress reduction. They can let clients know that it is acceptable to indulge themselves once in a while by setting aside a block of time to soak in a long, warm bath, relax by a fire or on a cool screened porch, or listen to soft music over candlelight. They must have the cooperation of both their body and mind to get the full benefit from this special time. Encourage them to block all work-related thoughts that try to enter their mind. Teach them thought-stopping techniques to make this easier. Advise them that they may feel bored or restless the first time they try it but that they should not become discouraged. The only way to get over adrenaline withdrawal is to go through it. When restlessness occurs, encourage clients to exercise vigorously, use deep-breathing techniques, or meditate but to keep a low-key mood at all costs until the anxiety abates.

Those who practice savoring workaholism need to learn to widen their work lenses, function as team members, and trust their work group's assessment of the time to move forward. They need to learn to let go, to distinguish between perfectionism and high standards, and to work more efficiently without getting bogged down with minutiae and losing sight of their goals.

Work Moderation

Abstinence for those who are chemically dependent means total sobriety. But workaholic clients, most of whom need to work, must learn work moderation—abstaining from compulsive overworking and freedom from negative thinking. For some workaholics, an effective work-moderation plan includes specific activities and time commitments. For others, it is a broad framework that provides maximum flexibility, along with balance in the other areas of life—the family, social, and personal/spiritual areas. Giving time and thought to their work in proportion to other activities in their lives becomes a primary goal. There is a general consensus in the literature that the best predictor of a positive approach to work is a full life outside work. A full home life that acts as a psychological absorber can dissipate work's negative effects and augment the positive effects.[10]

Clinicians can help clients develop a self-care plan of abstinence that is tailored to their personal needs, lifestyles, and preferences. The plan includes ways to instill their lives with social and leisure activities, hobbies, and family, as well as personal and spiritual time. A work-moderation component includes setting regular work hours rather than binging and purging, planning ahead for deadlines, and spreading projects over a realistic span of time. Putting the plan on paper for one week helps clients see how they are spending time and which parts of their lives get overlooked. Clinicians can help clients with lowering perfectionistic standards to more reachable goals and with delegating and hiring out work in the office and at home.

Steps to Developing the Self-Care Plan

As a beginning to the self-care plan, clinicians can have clients imagine their lives as a circle made up of four parts, as described here, and then have them consider the four points that follow.

Self: attending to such personal needs as rest and physical exercise, relaxation, self-esteem, spirituality, nutrition, and free time to meditate or think.

Family: spending time and nurturing the relationships with significant loved ones whom you consider your family. Your family can be a spouse; it can include both a spouse and children; it can include unmarried same-sex or opposite-sex partners; or it can comprise adults who reside with older parents or siblings. Your family, whether related or unrelated, is your major support system.

Play: having fun, hobbies, recreation, leisure, social relationships, and friendships.

Work: being effective and productive on the job, enjoying what you do for a living, working moderately, and giving equal time to other areas of your life.

Now consider these points:

1. Your NOW percentage. How are you living your life? Indicate the percentage of time you NOW devote to each of the four areas. (The total should add up to 100%.)

SELF	_____
FAMILY	_____
PLAY	_____
WORK	_____
TOTAL	100%

2. Your DESIRED percentage. How would you like to be living your life? Indicate the DESIRED percentage you would be devoting to each of the four areas if your life had more balance?

SELF	_____
FAMILY	_____
PLAY	_____
WORK	_____
TOTAL	100%

3. Enter the four NOW and DESIRED percentages in the spaces below. Subtract the NOW from the DESIRED percentages to get the REMAINDER, which is the amount of change you need to make in each area to achieve balance in your life. A plus score means the area needs more attention. A minus score means the area needs less attention.

	SELF	FAMILY	PLAY	WORK
DESIRED	_____	_____	_____	_____
NOW	_____	_____	_____	_____
REMAINDER	_____	_____	_____	_____

4. After reviewing the four REMAINDERS, name three or four goals for each area that you could set to make the necessary changes to bring greater balance into your life. List these goals in the space below. Putting them into practice becomes the basis of your self-care plan. After you try your

plan for a week, revise it by deciding what you want to keep, add, or delete.

SELF:

FAMILY:

PLAY:

WORK:

4

Treating Work Addiction as a Family Disease

Work is the refuge of people who have
nothing better to do.

—OSCAR WILDE

Brenda

I often have called myself the widow of a workaholic because of the overwhelming loneliness, trials, and tribulations of living with my workaholic husband. One day it hit me that I had been enabling my husband's work addiction by (a) trying to keep up with his pace and work schedule, (b) believing his need to overwork was somehow connected with my being defective, and (c) buying into society's myth that says living with a workaholic isn't as bad as living with an alcoholic.

I thought if I were prettier or sexier, he would spend more time with me. His mistress was his work, so I didn't receive a whole lot of support from my friends. They would say, "You should be grateful that he doesn't drink, screw around, or beat you" or "You should be grateful that he stuck by you through your alcoholism." With statements like that, I felt more shame and asked, "What's wrong with me?"

On the outside, Michael looks like the all-time high

achiever; he is paid very well for all that he does professionally. At one time he consulted at three hospitals, along with seeing an overwhelming number of patients. In addition to this, he spent hours involved in court custody cases. Both of us are psychotherapists in private practice together. While I see approximately five patients a day, my husband loads himself down with ten to twelve people a day. He cannot understand why I refuse to increase my caseload and tells me I am not pulling my weight in the office. As he sat at his desk, making phone call after phone call, wolfing down his lunch of Dr. Pepper and peanuts, he would tell me I had problems. At one point in our marriage, he would race home from the office at lunch time to work on home chores. With sweat running down his face, he would return to his desk, which was always piled high with more projects, for his afternoon patients.

The problem with his work addiction was that there was no time left for me and our relationship. Everybody else got a piece of Michael except me. At night he would come home from the office, usually late for dinner, only to collapse on the couch and fall asleep. With this, I would either rage with anger or grieve with loneliness. Neither disturbed him from his exhaustion. In my grief, I would sob by myself and wonder what I was doing wrong to cause him to ignore me.

One Saturday I watched from the sofa as Michael ran around going from one task to another at his usual one-hundred-mile-an-hour pace. It suddenly struck me that during my own bout with alcoholism, Michael's enabling behaviors almost destroyed me, and I realized that, in the same way, my enabling could kill him and destroy our marriage. My enabling behavior was to run around with Michael, trying to keep up with him so that he would not accuse me of being lazy. He was moving so quickly that it took him a while to notice I wasn't involved in the usual load of Saturday chores. When he finally did notice, he asked me what I was doing. When I told him it was Saturday and that I was resting, he looked at me as if I had lost my mind.

For the next week I didn't make the bed, do the dishes, or cook meals. I took a day off and went fishing and started having lunch more often with my friends. I spent more time writing, as I had grown to love writing, and I saw even fewer patients in the office. One day I left town while he was at work and went to visit a girlfriend of mine for a week. While away, I called to tell him that I loved him but that his workaholism is as destructive as my alcoholism was and that if I am to continue living with him, he must agree to seek help.

Michael did agree to get some help, and today he is recovering. He recognized that he was addicted to the adrenaline rush of working and made a decision to do whatever it took to recover. Because I finally gave up control and admitted I was powerless, I was able to get out of his way and let him suffer the consequences of his destructive behaviors. Once I started taking care of myself and not enabling Michael, he was able to see how his work addiction was destroying his life and hurting those around him.

Periodically, Michael slips back into his old compulsive busy habits, and I find myself enabling him. But thanks to our recovery, the barrier to work addiction that kept both of us from experiencing true intimacy for so long has lost its power.

We have learned to set aside more time for our relationship. Not only do we have a once-a-week date night, but we also go on vacations several times a year. It used to be that when we took vacations together, Michael could only be away from the office for three days. We would be on the coast, and as I lay on the beach enjoying the water and sun, Michael would be up at the hotel helping the housekeeping staff move furniture. Today when we go to the beach on vacation, Michael is beside me, holding my hand.

A Family Systems Addictions Model

Now that you know the signs of work addiction and how to recognize it in yourself and others, let's look more closely at how widespread it is in its devastation. This chapter shows how work addiction infects other family members, causing them a whole set of mental health problems of their own.

In exposing the diseased nature of work addiction, I employ a family systems addictions model that conceptualizes work addiction as a symptom of a diseased family system. The principal view from this perspective is that addictions are transmitted through the breakdown of the family system, rendering it dysfunctional. This breakdown is shown in the families of origin of workaholics and in workaholics' intimate relationships as adults with their partners and with their children. Addictive behaviors are intergenerational and are passed on to future generations through family dynamics, often changing from generation to generation. Thus, through the family operation—its rules, beliefs, and behavior patterns—addictive behaviors such as alcoholism, work addiction, and codependent relationships can become an intergenerational cycle. This model views work addiction as a learned addictive response to a dysfunctional family-of-origin system. It employs a nonmedical model of treatment such as family-of-origin work and marriage and family therapy from a structural and systems perspective.

Work addiction is a family disease—one that affects every member in a devastating way. Thinking of the family unit as a system helps us to better understand the disease concept. Suppose I wanted to know how the cardiovascular system works. I might go to a medical lab, locate a heart and the attached blood vessels, then carefully dissect and study them. In this way I would learn something about the basic structure of the cardiovascular system, that the heart has four chambers and a number of valves. But I would still not know how these chambers and valves work, because the heart would not be functioning. Only by studying the cardiovascular system while it is functioning in a living person would I see how the chambers and valves pump blood through the body. I cannot know what happens to the heart when a person is running, for example, without seeing the cardiovascular system in relationship to the whole body system. This holistic approach informs me that, while the person is running, the muscles of the body require more oxygen than they do at rest and the heart beats faster to supply oxygen. In other words, the total body system is affected by the running and must change to adjust to it.

The same is true of the workaholic family. We cannot understand fully what happens to individual family members without understanding the interworkings of that total family system. We must look at the family as a whole composite, because each member, as part of a functioning system, is interdependent on the other. As the family works together to run smoothly, any change in one part of the family will result in changes in the other parts. A family system will always try to keep itself balanced and will organize around its problems, often causing them to continue. Workaholic families alter how they function to accommodate the workaholic's extreme work patterns. The workaholic's out-of-control working throws the whole family off kilter, which causes them to shift the way they function in order to keep themselves in stasis and to maintain a closed system.

Family members are often negatively affected by work addiction and may even develop mental health problems of their own. The workaholic's career dictates family rules that get enforced, often despite their negative effect on the emotional well-being of family members. There is often a tacit family contract that allows workaholics to work, while their partners align with the children against them and the workaholic forfeits a hierarchical family position in order to pursue a career.[1] To better understand the structural characteristics of workaholic families, let's look at the Smith family.

When Work Addiction Hits Home: The Smith Family

Jack Smith, age forty-three, went to his physician because of failing health and was told that the best antidote to his work addiction was long weekends and vacations.

On these vacations Jack lugged his legal files across Europe and around half the world. His wife, Dorothy, said that both Jack and she knew that those files would never be opened, because she would not allow it. She then complained that he worked constantly and of how lonely it was on trips when she would frequent the museums alone while Jack holed up in the hotel working. Even when they took those long weekends to their mountain retreat in the Adirondacks, Jack felt compelled to carry a portable phone with him in the fishing boat. Dorothy complained that Jack maintained direct and constant contact with the other attorneys in his law firm in New York City. A constant source of conflict in their marriage, Jack's workaholism had driven a wedge between him and Dorothy and between him and his now grown children.

When the children were small and came along on picnics, Dorothy carried the blanket and picnic basket while Jack carried his briefcase. Dorothy was angry that Jack was always preoccupied with work. She felt like a single mother rearing the children. In turn, the children are angry at their father because he wouldn't let them get close to him. Although the three children have become successful adults, they admitted to Dorothy that they never believed they could do anything good enough to please their father.

Dorothy regretted that in her marriage Jack was a "no-show" and she was "left holding the bag" when it came to child rearing, managing the house, and attending social gatherings, where Jack would fail to keep his promise to meet her. The family's tone and activities revolved around Jack's moods and whims. Everybody postponed his or her plans, hoping by chance to be able to grab some time with him. The children learned they could have these special times with their dad by photocopying legal papers for him or going to his law office on Saturdays and playing in an adjacent room while Jack worked on important cases. Even when they went fishing, the children resented that their father usually had out-of-body experiences because his mind was back at the office. Dorothy even went to school to become a paralegal and took a job in Jack's office, working alongside her husband "just to nab some time with him." On those rare occasions when Jack tried to take an active role in his family, he said he felt rebuffed by his wife, who felt that he was intruding on her turf.

During the course of therapy, the concept of workaholism was introduced to Dorothy, which helped her see her husband in a different light. "Workaholic, huh? That sounds as if my husband's a sick man. That gives me a whole new way of looking at him—with more compassion and understanding."

Structural and Dynamic Characteristics of the Family System

The structural characteristics of the Smith family are such that Dorothy and the children become extensions of Jack's ego, inevitably leading to family conflict.[2] Tending toward self-centeredness and self-absorption, workaholics typically need an overabundance of attention and want family members to cater to their wishes.[3] With the timing and synchronization of a Ginger Rogers–Fred Astaire dance routine, each family member gets drawn into the act by waltzing around the workaholic's schedule, moods, and actions, which determine family schedules, moods, and actions.

Circularity

Over the course of time, family members develop certain behavior patterns in response to their loved one's work addiction. As workaholics work longer and harder, their spouses, not unlike alcoholic spouses, often react by trying to get them to curb their compulsive behaviors and spend more time in the relationship. Workaholics often hear these reactions as demands, criticisms, or nagging and react by digging their heels in deeper, thus distancing themselves further from the family. Feeling lonely, unloved, isolated, and emotionally and physically abandoned, family members align against the workaholic and retaliate with verbal resentments and emotional distance. Workaholics eventually are left outside the family unit because of their self-distancing and the family's retaliations and coalitions. Family members may habitually complain or become cynical about the work addict's abusive work habits. A common refrain is that even when workaholics are physically present, they are emotionally unavailable and disconnected from the family. Their partners may have single-handedly raised the children and may complain about having had the major portion of parenting responsibilities dumped on them. Filled with resentment at this one-sided arrangement, they tend to react with anger and complaining. Some workaholics then use the verbal complaints as justification for their physical and emotional aloofness. Thus, circularity often results: the workaholic asserts, "I wouldn't work so much if you wouldn't nag me all the time," whereupon the partner retorts, "I wouldn't bug you so much if you didn't work all the time."

Dorothy's presenting problem in therapy was Jack's remoteness and his relationship exits through work; Jack's presenting problem was Dorothy's constant criticism and his feeling that he could not please her. Even his successful career was not enough to satisfy her. He rationalized his intentional exits from the marriage by declaring, "Why would I want to spend time with someone who's on my back about something all the time?" Dorothy had started to withdraw because she felt she was getting nothing from Jack emotionally. Jack's defense was the Messiah Myth (see chapter 2). He claimed his hard work was for Dorothy and the kids, and he couldn't understand how she could criticize him on one hand and reap the benefits of his efforts on the other. As two business-management experts observed, "For the suffering family, the final blow usually comes when the workaholic passes the blame by saying, 'I'm doing all this for you!'"[4]

Power Struggle and Enabling

Paradoxically, family behavior patterns or roles in response to work addiction have the effect of enabling it. By assuming child-rearing and household responsibilities, spouses and older children provide workaholics with the necessary freedom to work endlessly. Shielding workaholics from domestic worries and working alongside them, as the Smith family did, have the effect of enabling the compulsive working.

Additional examples of enabling include building the family schedule around the impossible, workaholic schedule, putting dinner on the table at midnight for the umpteenth time after the workaholic promised to be home by seven o'clock, making alibis for the workaholic's absenteeism or lateness at parties or family gatherings, assuming the workaholic's household chores, covering for the workaholic in business meetings or social gatherings, and returning phone calls meant for the workaholic.

Family demands for moderation of the workaholic's busy pursuits also unwittingly enable the work addiction. Family members become just as obsessed with trying to get workaholics to cut back their working hours as workaholics are obsessed with working. The more family members put pressure on them to take a break, a day off, a vacation, or to slow down or come home early, the more threatened the workaholic family member feels and the more tenaciously he or she resists. Typically, workaholics interpret these pressures as an effort to undermine their control. Cheryl said, "The more my husband complained about my working too much, the harder I worked." When spouses try to dictate to workaholics how to set boundaries or reprimand them when they relapse, the more shamed and out of control the work addict feels. The only solution, from the addict's point of view, is to immerse himself or herself further into work addiction in an attempt to gain control. Challenges to the compulsive working often result in defensive reactions in which the work is rationalized in terms of providing a better life and future for the family, as Jack claimed.

The Societal System

Family members are inhibited in their attempts to deal with work addiction and the workaholic is enabled because of this looking-good camouflage, which is echoed and supported by the larger societal system. Spouses are often branded ingrates and blamed for wanting more, despite the fact that their workaholic partners have given them abundant material comforts. Madge ended up in Duke Medical University to be treated for allergies, headaches, stomachaches, and all the other stress-related symptoms that workaholics have. The paradox was that Madge was the spouse of a workaholic:

> I had to remove myself from him, or I was going to die. I had taken on my husband's work addiction, and it was killing me. I tried to keep up with him for as long as I could, but then his workaholism got the best of me. I couldn't keep up, and I burned out trying. He heads a multimillion-dollar business. Work is everything to him; it's his life. He's always working, always on a "high." I feel totally alone with my two kids. People don't really understand how bad the situation is. They ask me why I'm always complaining. We have two beautiful kids, he has a great job, he makes lots of money, and I don't have to work. I have the dream life, but why am I never smiling?

Dorothy said she felt vilified:

> To everyone else, my husband is perfect. I feel like I'm one of his employees, even at home. He denies there's anything wrong and gets hostile if I confront him about his workaholism. Our friends always want to know why I'm always complaining. I

have become the bitchy wife in the eyes of our friends, but they don't understand what it's like being alone.

Fear of being unappreciative can have the effect of censoring the family, keeping it from speaking out or seeking help and maintaining the denial of the family's problem. This denial can also cause partners of workaholics to wonder if perhaps it is they who have the problem. As they see friends and colleagues heaping praise and financial rewards on the workaholic, spouses may think that something is wrong with them. They may feel undesirable and that they don't measure up compared to their workaholic spouses. If they relax, they might feel unproductive and inferior.

Parentification

When the generation lines that insulate children from the parental adult world get violated or blurred, children can become what family therapists call parentified.[5] *Parentified children* by definition are parents to their own parents and sacrifice their own needs for attention, comfort, and guidance in order to accommodate and care for the emotional needs and pursuits of parents or another family member. Workaholics, who were parentified as kids, often pass their own parentification on to their offspring, who are sometimes chosen to be emotional surrogates for the missing workaholic parent. A typical example is the child who is elevated into an adult position within the family system to accommodate a parent's emotional need for intimacy by becoming the adult of the house during the workaholic parent's physical or emotional absence. Or the nonworkaholic spouse may be consumed by the single-parent role during the workaholic's absence, with the children (usually the oldest) becoming parentified—required to become overly responsible at a young age before they are fully emotionally constructed themselves. They may, for example, assume household chores or caretaking responsibilities for young siblings to bring homeostasis to the family system. The void left when children have to forfeit their childhood—bereft of feelings of approval, reassurance, love, and comfort and protection from adult pressures—shows up years later as an oft-described "empty hole inside."

Triangulation

Triangles across generations can occur when spouses become competitive or the parental bond becomes more valued than the marital bond, as when a mother aligns with a child by secretly sharing her despair over the workaholic father's emotional absence. The father is excluded, and the mother-child bond is strengthened at the expense of the marital bond. This boundary violation can exacerbate the child's resentment of the absent workaholic father and escalate the tension between them. As emotions surface between father and offspring, the mother may intercede on the child's behalf, further eroding the marital and paternal bonds while solidifying the maternal bond.

As alliances are formed, workaholics feel like bystanders in their own homes. They complain about feeling insecure and not fitting in with their families. Milton said he believed his wife and three daughters were in a conspiracy against him. He blamed them for his unhappiness outside the office. The truth was that he participated in the creation of the barriers by extricating himself from their conversations and activities, because his mind was on work. Although he felt like an outsider, he could not see how his own actions had contributed to the condition.

In Japan Milton would be called a "seven-eleven husband," the term for marginal fathers who work from dawn to dusk and live on the fringes of their families:

> For overworked and exhausted husbands, the home becomes just a place where familiar sleeping facilities are provided without much emotional nourishment. Such husbands tend to feel like fringe dwellers whose main responsibility is to bring money

> home, but not to be directly and significantly involved in family activities and raising their children. The seven-eleven husband is often so tired even on the weekends that family outings and chores around the house sometimes become additional sources of stress and fatigue. He tends to have a rather marginal family membership, and receives only limited substantive validation for his familial self from the family. When the family forms an internal alliance excluding the marginal father, he is likely to feel displaced and unwanted at home, which in turn reinforces his wish to be back in a familiar working environment.[6]

After alliances are solidified, spouses often resent having their turfs violated when workaholics do try to become more actively involved in their families. Older children often rebuff the workaholic's attempts to reestablish close contact, because they feel the reentry is too little, too late.

Research on the Workaholic Family System

My colleagues at the University of North Carolina at Charlotte and I tested anecdotal reports by conducting two empirical studies that verified that family members can be harmed by work addiction too.

The first study ever conducted on workaholism in the family developed from our desire to know if there was a relationship between work addiction and family-of-origin or current-family functioning.[7] After all, family systems and psychodynamic theories suggest that adult behaviors have their roots in the family of origin. A body of research had already linked a healthy family of origin to healthy functioning in adulthood, positive marital experiences, and overall family relationships.

We administered a battery of tests to 107 participants from Workaholics Anonymous representing five regions of the United States and Canada. Of our sample, 14.2 percent came from the Northeast, 23.6 percent from the Southeast, 38.7 percent from the Northwest, 18.9 percent from the Southwest, and 0.09 percent from Canada. The average age of participants was forty-four years, and 65 percent were women.

Respondents were classified into two groups on the basis of their responses to a question that asked, "Have you ever joined a group or talked with a professional counselor about your work habits?" A total of seventy answered yes and were defined as the clinical group of workaholics; thirty-six said no and were defined as the nonclinical workaholic group.

Despite the clinical observation that workaholic adults come from dysfunctional families, no relationship was found between work addiction (based on WART scores) and family-of-origin dysfunction in the overall sample. On the other hand, when the sample was divided into clinical and nonclinical groups, the findings changed. Clinical workaholics who had sought help for their condition, compared to those who had not sought help, were more likely to rate their families of origin as dysfunctional and lower in intimacy.

Findings also revealed that work addiction was positively linked to current-family functioning in workaholic-headed families. The work addiction wreaked havoc on the family functioning, and the more serious the work addiction, the worse the family was at communicating, solving problems, expressing feelings, valuing others' concerns, and functioning as a unit.

On the basis of scores on the WART, three groups were established from the sample: low-risk, medium-risk, and high-risk for work addiction. Individuals in the high-risk group were more likely to rate their families as having problems in communication or in the exchange of information than were those in the low- or medium-risk categories. They were more likely to rate their families as having unclearly defined family roles and believed their families were less likely to have established behavior patterns for handling repetitive family functions than were those in the other groups. They also said their families were less likely to express feelings appropriately in response to various events that occurred in the family. High-risk adults said their families were less likely to be interested in and to value each other's activities and concerns. High-risk individuals also perceived their families as unhealthy and as more likely to have problems in their general functioning than individuals at low or medium risk for work addiction.

Maintaining social and intimate relationships was also a problem for workaholics in the sample because of their work. The social relationships of men were affected to a significantly greater extent by their work than were those of women. Intimacy was a problem for the clinical workaholics, both in their families of upbringing and in the families that they established once grown. Perhaps workaholics in the clinical group, with more intimacy problems from their families of origin, had more problems with intimate relationships in adulthood, which may explain their motivation to seek help, compared to the nonclinical group.

The second investigation conducted by my research team examined the influence of work addiction on adults who grew up in workaholic homes—the first study to be done on adult children of workaholics. That study, as well as the earlier one, strongly supports clinical evidence suggesting that work addiction is associated with ineffective communication and that it can contribute to brittle family relationships, marital conflict, and overall dysfunction within the family system.

Suggestions for Clinicians

Several clinical approaches can be taken to help workaholics and their loved ones who, not unlike alcoholic families, are entrenched in denial. Outwardly, workaholic families appear immune to the effects of the hard-driving, compulsive behaviors. Workaholics in particular mask their anxiety, depression, or fear of not being in control by resiliency, perfectionism, overresponsibility, or self-reliance to the point of having difficulty asking for help. Family members often are reluctant to come forward for fear of being branded "ingrates" for the material rewards generated by the workaholic lifestyle. Typical workaholic families dance around this huge "elephant in the living room" without acknowledging its presence, which builds tension and resentment. By helping couples identify and express their feelings about the problem, it is possible to reduce tension and reactivity and set the stage for further work.

Initial Screening and Family Contracts

As part of the initial screening, it is important to identify the struture of the workaholic family. Is there a tacit family contract, for example, that permits compulsive overworking? Are there unspoken expectations of children that place them in parentified roles that could cause them long-term emotional problems? Bringing these unconscious factors into the light can help families restructure their behaviors.

Clinicians, together with family members, can diagram the structure of the family system to help them see clearly where alliances, triangles, enabling, or exclusions exist. In cases where the marital bond has weakened and has been replaced by parent-child alliances or elevation of children above the generational boundary into adult surrogate roles, clinicians can work with couples to strengthen their relationships, consciously work at reinforcing the generational boundary, and perhaps even reverse further parentification of the children. Having revealed the tacit family contract, clinicians can help families rewrite a more deliberate and functional family contract that clearly defines family roles for each member and provides methods for encouraging open communication, valuing each other's concerns, and openly expressing feelings.

Introducing the Concept of Work Addiction as a Family Disease

Presenting the disease concept of work addiction to families can bring them great relief, as it did for Dorothy, and can help families reframe the problem, to go from seeing it as personal rejection to seeing it as a more complex condition that workaholics bring to the marriage. The disease concept also helps family members understand how they are affected in subtle ways of which they are not aware. The disease concept allows clinicians to use a twelve-step approach and many of the principles of Alcoholics Anonymous and Al-Anon that have been extrapolated to work addiction (see chapter 10 for more information). Some families, for example, benefit from help in learning to detach from the addictive process and to focus on themselves and their children when offspring are involved, as Brenda described earlier.

As I have noted, work addiction is a "pretty addiction" that also looks good on the workaholic's offspring. It is important that clinicians apprise themselves of the insidious damage that work addiction inflicts on the offspring and that treatment examine the unrealistic expectations placed on children by the family. Once the family structure is ascertained, screening beyond the surface of this pretty addiction can be undertaken to discern potential anxiety and depression among children. Breaking the cycle of work addiction also is important. Protecting children from out-of-reach aspirations, unreasonable expectations, and parental perfectionism can prevent the development of Type A behaviors and the intergenerational transmission of work addiction.

Confronting the Enabling

Clinicians can help spouses and children identify the ways they are repeatedly pulled into the addictive work cycle and learn how to avoid enabling the addiction when they feel desperate to spend time with the workaholic family member. They can refrain from such activities as bringing their loved one work to do when the person goes to bed sick, making alibis for his or her absenteeism or lateness at social functions or family gatherings, and letting their loved one be responsible for explanations. They can refrain from assuming the workaholic's household duties, returning phone calls for him or her, or "covering" by lying to business associates on the telephone—all because the workaholic is too busy working.

Clinicians can help families explore whether they have postponed their lives for their workaholic family member. Family members can be led to understand that, as with any addiction, building their lives around the addict's behaviors only sets them up for further hurt and disappointment. If, for example, a parent has planned a trip to the zoo with the kids and the workaholic cancels (for the umpteenth time) because of last-minute demands at the office, the parent can go without the addicted spouse. When workaholics promise to be home in time for dinner and never show, families can eat on time and, instead of putting dinner on the table at midnight, let the work addict fix his or her own meal. It is important for families to include workaholics in their plans and to let them know they were missed and how disappointed the family was by their absence, without putting their own lives on hold. Here is a real-life example:

> My husband used to be late for everything—parties, dinners, movies—because he always worked overtime. Then one night, our friends came to pick us up, and as usual, he wasn't home yet. So I left without him, but I wrote him a note that read, "You're always late, and it's embarrassing. We're at the restaurant. I hope you get home in time to join us." He's been much more considerate ever since. He even gets home early enough on Fridays to take me to the movies![8]

Twelve Steps and Referral to Support Groups

In conjunction with individual therapy, workaholics benefit from support groups composed of other members struggling with various addictive behaviors. In group therapy, members help one another to see past denials and distractions that prevented them from taking responsibility for their actions and putting more balance in their lives. Most large cities have support groups such as Workaholics Anonymous (WA) that can provide literature and weekly meetings for workaholics. Clinicians can apprise themselves and inform clients of twelve-step programs such as Workaholics Anonymous or Al-Anon to complement their individual therapy plans.

The Twelve Steps have worked for millions of people with a variety of addictions, including alcohol and other drugs, food, gambling, and shopping. Continuing in the Twelve-Step tradition, Workaholics Anonymous provides a setting that is accepting, anonymous, and safe and where workaholics share their strength, courage, and hope. They follow the Twelve Steps and work with other recovering workaholics and sponsors with solid programs of personal growth who mentor newcomers. Under the guidance of their sponsors, members are encouraged to develop their own self-care plan of work moderation. Abstinence from compulsive working on a physical level is encouraged, as is developing a positive attitude that comes from surrender to a Higher Power greater than humans. The work plan is a guide to daily work that provides healthy limits and moves Workaholics Anonymous members toward a more balanced way of life. Chapter 10 provides more information on Workaholics Anonymous and describes how to find locations and contact persons across the United States and Canada. Elizabeth described how she benefited from Workaholics Anonymous:

> Workaholics Anonymous gives me the opportunity to go and sit down with other people like me, with anonymity. I don't have to worry if I don't want the world to know about me, that what I say will go out of that room. It gives me an opportunity to share with others and to hear myself for an hour. It gives me a chance to calm down. It's very soothing to be with other people just like you who understand and know what you feel. At the same time, listening to them and what they've done to change their behavior helps you realize what you can do, because they share their experience, strength, and hope. They don't give advice.

Support for Family Members

Family members often need help expressing their feelings of emotional abandonment, guilt, inadequacy, anger, resentment, and hurt to their overworked loved ones. Partners especially need help in developing constructive outlets for their feelings, such as journaling, support groups, or individual therapy. They often benefit from understanding that they didn't cause, cannot cure, and cannot control their partner's work addiction and that their partner's problem is a cover for low self-esteem, past hurt and fears, and intimacy problems that remain unresolved.

An organization called WorkAnon was founded in suburban New York at the same time Workaholics Anonymous started. WorkAnon serves spouses, family, and friends of workaholics in the same way Al-Anon serves as a family adjunct to Alcoholics Anonymous. Barbara, founder of WorkAnon and wife of one of the WA founders, got a call one night from a distraught woman who had planned a special dinner for her twenty-fifth wedding anniversary, for which her husband never showed. The woman put his gift on the dining room table, went to Barbara's house, and the two of them started WorkAnon. Some people come to WorkAnon with the idea that it will help them cure their spouse of work addiction. But, like Al-Anon, WorkAnon is there to help spouses deal with their personal feelings about work addiction, not to cure their work-addicted partners. Workaholics have to decide for themselves that they need help and take the responsibility for getting it.

Spouses and children who cannot find a WorkAnon or Workaholics Anonymous group in their area can attend Al-Anon. Although meant for families of alcoholics, Al-Anon addresses issues similar to those that emerge for those living with work addiction. The principles and group interaction can provide partners the needed support to face and deal with the work addiction.

Clinicians can establish structured support groups for partners of workaholics similar to Al-Anon or WorkAnon. These special groups can help spouses cope with their own bruised self-esteem, guilt, stress, and isolation. It can be an island for many families who feel alone and hopeless and who fear that their coming forth will meet with accusations and insults aimed at their lack of gratitude. These groups can provide the support to help spouses feel connected to others who understand and to achieve greater clarity on constructive actions they can take to change their lives.

5

Inside the Workaholic Mind

There is a great fret and worry always running after work; it is not good intellectually or spiritually.

—ANNIE KEARY

Art

From the time I was eighteen, I stuffed into my hip pocket each day a worn week-at-a-glance. It became my Bible and scorecard, dictating every hour of devotion to my disease, ensuring I wouldn't forget an appointment in my daily frenzied pace. Its margins were crammed with lists of tasks to accomplish between meetings and before going to bed. As long as I was working, thinking about work, or lining up work in my notebook, I felt in control, important, powerful. When I recall it, the fearful, shameful, guilty self of my childhood seems like someone from another planet.

Now forty-eight, I'm in my ninth year of recovery from work addiction. My childhood was the meat of a dysfunctional family sandwich. I was pressed on one side by a tyrannical, workaholic father whom I rarely could please. Around him I was always fearful I would be (and often was) scolded or punished for some awkward, selfish, or mean-spirited thing I hadn't intended to do. On the other side was an apprehensive and distant mother always within arms reach of potent prescription drugs. Around her I experienced constant anxiety and rejection, feeling I wasn't worthy enough for kisses, hugs, or other expressions of love. Confusion and conflict dominated my family communication. Exuberance was criticized. Sadness was ridiculed. Tenderness was wrapped in mock gestures, delivered with sarcasm.

Around spontaneous, self-assured kids, I felt puny, ugly, and unpopular. I felt safest and most in control when playing alone. I could then pretend I was one of my favorite radio heroes: a powerful, cherished champion of justice, battling alone (or with some animal companion) against incredible odds on behalf of the unloved and powerless. Thus, my childhood nurtured the lethal seeds that later blossomed into work addiction: self-denial, self-control, self-image.

When I hit puberty, pitching myself wholeheartedly into school and extracurricular projects enabled me to control my emotions at the same time I was creating a socially acceptable self-image. The only price I had to pay was to spend every waking hour working hard at something. By the time I was eighteen, I had become a professional musician, seeded tennis player, boxing champion, state-champion track athlete, straight-A student, and National Merit Scholar. I was president of a statewide youth fellowship and a high-school selection for Boys State. For two years I went steady with the school's most popular cheerleader, and a month before graduation I received a scholarship to Harvard.

Despite the accolades, my parents' attitude toward me did not change: my accomplishments were still never enough to impress my father or to win my mother's warmth. My response? Already deep in my disease, I dug a little deeper, tried a little harder, won more honors. By now I was learning to get strokes elsewhere: from teachers, coaches, friends. Awards and publicity became replacements for acceptance and affection. Most of all, the constant pace of work numbed my mind to unpleasant, unresolved feelings of shame, powerlessness, and lack of love.

College devastated me. My entire sense of self-worth had been robbed in the grandiosity of high-school self-images. My view of life was of perpetual conflict in which only superior people survived and were worthy. At Harvard, however, it seemed every student was better than me! What's more, they all seemed to know exactly who they were and what they wanted to do with their lives—whereas I hadn't a clue. Teenage work addiction had been so all-consuming for me that I'd been too busy—and afraid—to discover who I really was or what career might actualize my true self. For three undergraduate years, I battled suicidal depression.

At the end of my junior year, I decided to pursue a career in law. As a criminal defense attorney, I could actually wield the power I had fantasized about all my life: fight real battles in courtrooms for the sake of justice, the powerless, and the oppressed.

I finished law school and for the next five years litigated criminal cases. Proud of not taking a vacation during that entire time, my relentless activity pitched me day and night into preparing and conducting trials, which continued to anesthetize feelings of self-doubt, while the stakes involved provided me with the adrenalized, grandiose illusion that my work was a matter of life or death. This was years before I realized the powerless, oppressed person I'd been defending in court was really the quaking little child buried deep within me; the causes I'd been championing stood for all the battles I'd never won as a boy; each law student I'd mentored with such loving parental care was really myself.

Nearing burnout in the courtroom, I jumped at an offer to write a law book and teach in law school. Evenings and weekends allowed me to sweep my infant son into a gerry-carry and trudge off on mountain hikes; paternal bonding could take place—and fatherhood justified through my strenuous activity. Thanks to work addiction's blend of anesthesia and adrenaline, ten years of fatherhood flashed by.

One day my wife nearly killed herself and our second son while driving the car under the influence of marijuana. The next day she checked herself into a drug rehabilitation center where she was diagnosed as an alcoholic-addict. Her courageous action not only rescued her life and our marriage but saved my life as well. While participating in her recovery program, it dawned on me that descriptions of the addict's life, thoughts, and feelings fit me perfectly. All I had to do was substitute "compulsive working" for "compulsive drinking/using" and I was as much an addict as anyone.

On August 20, 1983, I drafted a long letter to the rehabilitation clinic, described my symptoms, and asked if there were any treatment programs for work addicts. But this cutting-edge clinic for recovering addicts knew of none. So I attended meetings of Alcoholics Anonymous. On the gut level of shame, fear, desperation, and self-esteem, the stories I heard at AA were my story.

In 1990 I realized I couldn't recover alone and started a Workaholics Anonymous group in my city. In its first two years over a hundred people attended. I volunteered for WA's first World Service Organization. Getting to know scores of other recovering workaholics apprised me of the immensity of this insidious disease: its deep roots, its subtle forms, its range of rationalizations, and its enormous cultural encouragement.

Nearly every day of recovery I unearth some new facet of my work addiction: how its fear of true feelings goads me toward activity and away from contemplation or uncensored feeling of emotions; how its dread of powerlessness tempts me to control everything inside and outside my life; how its anxiety over the worth of my true self urges me to hide behind self-images. I'm fully resigned to the fact that this cunning and baffling disease will never leave me.

> But at every WA meeting I encounter love, strength, and renewed hope; I hear some new wisdom I can apply to my life; I discover another useful tool of recovery. I am discovering, accepting, and nurturing my true self by myself. For the first time in my life I'm in touch with the awesome range of my genuine feelings—and gradually learning not to hide, channel, change, or flee from them. On good days I experience incredible wonder and joy from just being alive. My sick, fictional life is finally over. Though its arrival was a long time coming, my real story's just begun.

I Work, Therefore I Am

Now that you are familiar with the signs of work addiction and the havoc it wreaks on families, let's look beneath the surface at how the workaholic mind thinks. This chapter explores in more detail the psychological workings of the workaholic mind that are manifested in compulsive behaviors of accomplishing and achieving. In the psychological realm, "I work, therefore I am" is the reasoning of workaholics like Mario, a physician who thinks he is nonexistent as a human being unless he is working. Hospitalized for depression, Mario was wrung out like a sponge. He had been putting in seventy-hour workweeks and was still behind. He turned to work for accolades and constantly tried to prove himself to others. His need for approval was insatiable, and nothing seemed to satisfy his craving. He had lost himself in his work for the feelings of accomplishment, importance, power, and admiration it provided. But even all that was not enough to fight off the depression that eventually won the battle.

Work defines the identity of workaholics, gives their lives meaning, and helps them gain approval and acceptance. It becomes the only way they know to prove their human value and to numb the hurt and pain that stem from unfulfilled needs. They believe they must earn the right to be, something that non-workaholics believe is their birthright. Shame is often at the bottom of work addiction—a kind of self-loathing that has earned workaholics the name human doers instead of human beings, a caricature that reflects their need to justify their being. They feel they must make up for the shame by overcompensating. Many of them, like Lyn, believe they must do more than the average person to be legitimate:

> For some reason I can't just be average. I have to do more or be more than the ordinary person. I've always felt that way—that I have to go over, beyond, and above what other people do. It makes me feel like I'm okay.

Although friends and family think workaholics are present and accounted for, in their minds they are working constantly—while driving a car, during dinner, while spending time with loved ones, even while having sex and, sometimes, during Workaholics Anonymous meetings. Workaholics believe they can earn respect and their place among others if they just work hard enough. The masquerade of hurrying, the need to control, and the perfectionism mask a deep feeling of not being good enough. Work addiction has been dubbed the "addiction of choice of the unworthy."[1] Workaholics use the old Groucho Marx line as a standard against which to judge themselves: "I wouldn't want to belong to a club that would want to have me as a member."

Motivated by low self-worth, they define themselves by their accomplishments. The more they do, the better they feel about themselves. Dan is an example of someone who gauges the value he places on himself by what he can produce:

> My self-esteem is defined by my work, and it provides an identity for me. I associate whether I have worth and value with what I achieve, and if I'm not achieving, I have no worth or value. It's like who I am depends on whether I'm able to achieve, not that I'm a good person, not that I have a lot of good qualities and characteristics. But it ties directly with achievement. If I achieve, I have worth and value. That's real distorted, but that's where I'm at.

Workaholics need tangible success, observable outcomes of "how much" they have achieved. Outward manifestations of their importance include how much money they make, how many sales accounts they land, how many pieces of real estate they sell, how many projects they can complete around the house, and how quickly they can get superb food on the table. This is one reason workaholics are list makers and take great delight in marking off the completion of each task.

This type of rigid thinking is typical of workaholics who hold tightly to their unrealistic expectations of themselves and others.[2] Diane Fassel and Anne Wilson Schaef say that the workaholic's to-do lists become a tight girdle instead of a flexible guide:

> One woman allots a certain amount of time each day to spend with her children. If the children are not willing or available between three o'clock and five o'clock, they get no time with their mother. The list is a link to our stash. It tells us what we have accomplished and what is left to be done. The problem, for the work addict, is that the list is never done. There is always another list.[3]

Lyn quantifies all the things she does as a measurement of her personal worth:

> The A-pluses I get in graduate school are a measure of how good I am. Sometimes I sit and count off to myself all the things that I can do so that I reassure myself that I'm doing okay and am accomplishing enough. I speak three languages, I can cook really well, I've been to this many countries, I work out four or five times a week, I'm getting my Ph.D., I have a 4.00 quality-point average. You're okay, Lyn. That part of me has high self-esteem, but I have to tell myself those things and be aware of them, and then there's another part of me that doesn't feel okay.

Instead of thinking, "What can I realistically accomplish?" workaholics think, "What would be so great an accomplishment that everyone (myself included) would see how valuable I am?"[4] The attorney tells herself that winning one more case will put her on top. The writer believes she will be revered after just one more book. The construction worker will have all the money he needs after building just one more house. The avid plant collector needs only one more rare orchid to make him happy for a lifetime. The stay-at-home mother needs to bake the perfect loaf of bread, get the bathroom painted, and make it to all her children's afternoon activities as her crowning achievement. The business manager needs to purchase one more office building to have it made, and the actor needs one more big role to make him famous. When part of a compulsive pattern, all these acts convey similar messages: "Look at me; I am worthy; I have value."

Workaholics depend on their work to define who they are and to gain a positive sense of themselves. Producing and achieving temporarily fill the inner emptiness and give a fleeting and false sense of self-fulfillment. But deeper identity issues are not resolved, and as the good feelings fade, workaholics must work even harder to redeem their value.

The Impostor Syndrome

It was January, and snow covered the ground. Inside my office, Sandy was having an anxiety attack because he feared he would not be able to succeed in the highly competitive real estate field in which he had worked day and night for several years. He believed that it was only a matter of time until the truth about how incompetent he really was came out and he would lose his job. The paradox was that he had just received an award and a bonus for being the top salesperson in his company the previous year. I was puzzled at the contradiction, because I saw him as bright, friendly, and obviously capable and accomplished. He said to me, "At first I felt good about it, but that only lasted for about twenty minutes. Then I realized it was a fluke, and I'll never be able to pull it off again. I feel like I'm going down the tubes this year."

Workaholics feel like impostors. Case examples like those of both Sandy and Art illustrate the common workaholics' belief that they have been able to fool people into thinking they are competent and the fear that if people really knew them, they'd be discovered for the fakes they truly are. They are afraid of failure and success at the same time, and it is these fears that motivate them. Their rigid beliefs about themselves tell them they have to work even harder to keep up the charade. One financial consultant said, "I want to achieve everything there is to achieve in my profession. I am humble in the spotlight, but I am afraid of not being in the spotlight."[5]

The fear of failure drives workaholics to produce harder and harder to ensure that they are worthy of all their achievements. They take on mountains of work even when their professional and personal lives are already overloaded. They set themselves up for failure because their standards are so high that no one could ever meet them. Stephanie described the workaholic mind-set:

> I feel like people judge me on what I do—on what I accomplish, achieve, and on what products I produce and what effect I have in the world. And if I'm not doing the best job I know how, I feel like a failure. And because I can't possibly be doing the best job at everything, I feel like a failure most of the time. I get depressed. Anytime I set a goal for myself that I can actually achieve, I think, "That wasn't worth it; that was nothing." So I create a higher goal which I can't possibly reach.

Like the rigid thinking of the anorexic who looks in the mirror and sees herself as fat at eighty pounds, workaholics have negative feelings because they rely on rigid beliefs that tell them they have to do more and more to be worthy. Although they exceed others' expectations, they never reach their own because their standards (not unlike the anorexic's) are rigid and distorted. On the inside they feel like the small child who never does anything right, while they judge themselves harshly for the most minute flaws. When they eventually do make mistakes, they condemn themselves, as Dan described the self-defeat in his bout with work addiction:

> I set myself up for failure in trying to accomplish all the things I set out to do, because realistically no one person can do it all. But I set myself up with all these things I want to get done without enough time to do them. I'm doomed to failure, and then I kick myself for failing.

Driven by insecurities, workaholics sometimes go to desperate ends to prove their worth. Often at the expense of others, they use superiority to disguise their inferiority. The organizational management expert Gayle Porter suggests that workaholics struggle with low self-esteem to such an extent that they have distorted patterns of working with others, because they focus on how interactions enhance their self-esteem, not on how they can enhance the quality of the task itself:

> The workaholic does receive ego-enhancement from work involvement to the extent that external rewards can temporarily bolster feelings about self. Work will be pursued that is likely to result in raises, promotions, or other recognition, but choices along the way are influenced by the underlying identity issues. The good of the organization, the department, or the work team is secondary to choosing the task or method that will protect the workaholics' self-concept and possibly highlight their efforts.
>
> When choices are available, workaholics may redirect effort in a way that does not risk damage to self-esteem. The job outcome is secondary to ego protection. The most common response to any problems will be to work more hours. It would also be important that the ego be protected from any possible connection to lack of results to accompany those added hours. This requires finding a way to assign external blame when the work does not go well rather than focusing on genuine efforts of problem resolution.[6]

Louis said his workaholic boss went to great lengths to create defeat in subordinates to give his own esteem a boost. The more inept they looked, the more competent he felt. Louis said his boss seemed to feel discomfort when Louis handled the job competently or figured out a computer problem that had stumped the rest of the office staff. In contrast, the boss seemed more secure and in charge when things were falling apart or when an employee made a mistake. Louis said,

> You can see the look of relief on his face when someone in the office makes a mistake or hits a dead end. He swells up like a frog and throws his weight around. It's as if he jumps you when you're down, because it gives him some kind of good feeling to be on top.

Tanya complained that her workaholic boss refused to see her own father when he showed up at the office because he didn't have an appointment with her, and she wouldn't train her employees because she didn't want them to function without her:

> If you're given a project to do, you automatically go under her microscope. Whatever you can do, she can do it better, and nobody gets complimented for a good job. If there's a problem, she'll find it, and if she can't find it, she'll create one to find, because she gets off on that type of superiority.

Workaholics tell themselves that they are the only ones who can solve a certain problem at work, when the truth is that the work could be delegated. The belief that only they can do it in the specific right way or at the speed necessary gives them a sense of superiority and bolsters their self-esteem. Being able to handle heavier loads more swiftly than coworkers makes them think they measure up to the performance of others. But, of course, when workaholics have to denigrate others to prove their own adequacy, it only calls more attention to their feelings of inferiority.

When workaholics stay past five and everybody else goes home, they often quietly fume or smugly demand that coworkers and sub-ordinates do equal time. The thing people applaud workaholics for most, their work ethic, is also the thing people close to them dislike the most. Despite their superior attitudes, workaholics are often surprised to learn from office surveys that business associates do not admire them for their Heigh-Ho Syndrome.[7] Instead, they often are viewed as narrow-minded, difficult to work with, and lacking in vision.

The World through Workaholic Eyes

What workaholics believe about themselves contributes to their addiction, and it is their thoughts that keep them caught in the addictive cycle. All of us, for example, have expectations of how situations will unfold before they occur, and we unknowingly enter situations with these mind-sets. After a three-week trip to China, I returned to my job at the university unaware of having a new mind-set. I remember walking into a faculty member's office and noticing a book on her sofa, only half of which I could see. I thought the title of the book was *Tea Ching* and thought at the time that she too had an avid interest in the Orient. As I came further into the room and upon closer examination of the entire book cover, I chuckled to myself to see that the actual title was *Teaching in the Elementary Schools.* My Asian frame of reference caused me to view that situation differently than I ordinarily would have. Usually, when we expect a situation to be a certain way, that's the way it will turn out, because we think and behave in ways that make our thoughts come true.

A good illustration of how this principle works is the fable about the old farmer and the stranger. Once there was a farmer working in the field, when down the road came a stranger.

"I've been thinking of moving," said the stranger, "and I wonder what kind of people live around here."

"Well," replied the farmer, "what kind of people live where you come from?"

"Not very good," answered the stranger. "They're selfish and mean and not at all friendly. I'll be glad to leave them behind!"

"Well," said the farmer, "I expect you'll find the same sort of people around here . . . selfish and mean and not at all friendly. You probably won't like it here."

The stranger went on.

Shortly afterward, another stranger came along the same road.

"I've been thinking of moving," said the stranger, "and I wonder what kind of people live around here."

"Well," replied the farmer, "what kind of people live where you come from?"

"Oh, wonderful people!" answered the stranger. "They're generous and kind and very friendly. I'll really be sorry to leave them."

"Well," said the farmer, "I expect you'll find the same sort of people around here . . . generous and kind and very friendly. I'm sure you'll like it here."

The point of this fable is that the mind works in such a way that workaholics believe about themselves what they learned as children, and they collect evidence in their adult lives to support this belief. Perceptual studies conducted with animals have implications for the workaholic mind. In a laboratory experiment at Cambridge University in England, the visual field of baby kittens was restricted to horizontal lines from birth. They were never exposed to vertical lines while growing up. Once grown, the adult cats could recognize horizontal lines (——) but not vertical ones (|). They could jump on table tops, but they consistently bumped into the vertical table legs. Vertical lines were not part of the adult cats' perceptual reality because they had never experienced them as kittens. Another way of putting it is that because of their restricted past, the cats had a restricted view of reality.

The way workaholics think about themselves also is formed early in life and depends to a large degree on the cultural norms and daily experiences with which they grew up. As children, people are like clay; they are still under mental construction. The words they hear and the attitudes, feelings, and actions of parents and significant adults define how they view themselves. Many workaholics were children like Art, who were held to high standards that they could never reach (see chapter 6). These repeated experiences of not measuring up to the standard restricted their beliefs about their capabilities, so what they see about themselves as adults is set in a certain direction, like the kittens. Children who believe they never measure up develop a mind-set that they are inadequate, defective, inferior, undeserving, unworthy, and unlovable. In adulthood they are driven by the belief that they are never good enough, and they collect evidence to fit with this belief. They are looking for the horizontal line, because that is what has been shown to them. They put their thoughts and actions into disproving their inadequacy and proving their worth by overcompensating, overdoing, overcaring, overachieving, and generally going overboard with work. But the consequence is the opposite—they prove to themselves that they are inadequate, because that's what they believe.

Try this exercise. Ask a friend to spend one minute looking around your office or whatever room you're in right now. Ask the friend to list mentally as many items as he or she can that are blue—perhaps the carpet, wallpaper, bindings on books on shelves, curtains, the sofa. After a minute have the person close his or her eyes and name out loud all the items he or she can remember that are yellow. Most people go blank and cannot remember any yellow items. Your friend might look at you strangely, wondering what kind of prank you're pulling, and say something like, "I didn't see any yellow, because you told me to look for blue." However, if you had instructed the friend to see yellow, he or she would have seen yellow items. Even if there were only a few of them, the friend would have blocked out everything else to focus on whatever yellow color exists in the room.

The point of this exercise is to demonstrate that the mind sees what it expects to see. Essentially, workaholics make present experiences coincide with their mind-sets. They verify their unworthiness by unconsciously proving how inadequate they really are. They get a 98 on an exam and condemn themselves for not making 100. They receive the promotion, but it's still not high enough up the corporate ladder. They are named salesperson of the month but still didn't break the all-time sales record. They get the bronze medal, but they *should* have won the gold. If they're second academically, they criticize themselves for not being first. If they make an A, they feel as if they have failed because they didn't make an A+, as Lyn admitted:

> The last couple of times I had to get up to speak in class I was so charged up that I had physiological symptoms of shallow breathing and shaking, but I still made it through the presentations. Knowing it was obvious to people watching that I was nervous was hard for me to deal with. I think it started out from the sheer excitement of trying too hard. I felt that I had failed somewhat. Although I gave the presentation well and made an A on it, I had not been perfectly relaxed, and I had not done a perfect job in presenting the material, and that felt like a failure to me.

When incoming feedback from people around them conflicts with their perceptions of themselves, they change it to fit with their belief system. In other words, they turn positive situations into negative ones. If they think they're inadequate (which could be called the blue), they frame each experience through that belief system and collect evidence to fit with it. Any situation that contradicts the belief that they're inadequate is ignored, discounted, or minimized (the yellow) or is not taken in as part of their personal experience. In these ways, they continue to look for blue, despite the fact that they are confronted with a veritable rainbow every-day. Compliments sail over their heads. They tell themselves that their successes are accidents and that their failures are living proof of how inadequate they are.

Workaholics are constantly looking for the blue and constantly find it in their lives, because whatever they expect to see they will see. Their rigid beliefs tell them they must earn the right to be, and because they believe they never achieve enough (the blue), perfect is never enough. So they find themselves always feeling badly about themselves and always working to disprove their negative ideas about themselves. Unable to accept that they cannot measure up to their own impossible standards, they keep pushing themselves to try harder by working harder and longer hours, neglecting everything and everyone else, going deeper into performing, achieving, being out of control, attempting to feel better and hoping to be the best. Elaine said, "If I wasn't accepted, I had to excel, I had to keep pushing to keep working, to prove myself to somebody out there so they would recognize me and think that I had a brain and thought I had something on the ball."

The Rigid Thinking That Drives Work Addiction

The first step in dealing with work addiction is to identify the rigid thinking from which the self-inadequacy originates. Table 5.1 summarizes twelve types of rigid thinking that are characteristic of the workaholic mind-set and that are present in each workaholic to varying degrees.

Perfectionistic thinking tells workaholics to bite off more than they can chew—an action that leads again to feelings of self-defeat and failure, which then lead them back to where they started: self-inadequacy. They engage in *all-or-nothing thinking*—thinking in extremes instead of seeing the shades of gray. They tell themselves that they can either spend time with their families or working to support them, but not both. They think there's something wrong with them if they cannot give 100 percent to every area of their lives, motivated by such cultural maxims as "I must be all things to all people or I'm a failure," "If you cannot do a job right, don't do it at all," or "If I can't do it all, I might as well do none of it."

TABLE 5.1
Portrait of the Workaholic Mind-Set

1. *Perfectionistic thinking.* Things have to be perfect for me to be happy, and nothing I ever do is good enough.
2. *All-or-nothing thinking.* If I cannot be all things to all people, then I'm nothing. I'm either the best or the worst; there is no in-between.
3. *Telescopic thinking.* I always feel like a failure because I focus on and magnify my shortcomings and ignore my successes.
4. *Blurred-boundary thinking.* It's hard for me to know when to stop working, where to draw the line, and when to say no to others.
5. *People-pleasing thinking.* If I can get others to like me, I'll feel better about myself.
6. *Pessimistic thinking.* My life is chaotic, stressful, and out of control; I must stay alert, because if I take time to relax, I might get blindsided.
7. *Helpless thinking.* I am helpless to change my lifestyle. There is nothing I can do to change my schedule and slow down.
8. *Self-victimized thinking.* My family and employer are the reasons I work so much and am stressed and burnt out. I am a victim of a demanding job, a needy family, and a society that says, "You must do it all."
9. *Resistance thinking.* Life is an uphill battle, and I must fight to force my way, resist what I don't want, and cling to keep things as they are.
10. *Wishful thinking.* I wish I could have the things I cannot have because the things I have are of no value. If only my situation would change, I could slow down and take better care of myself.
11. *Serious thinking.* Playing and having fun are a waste of time because there's too much work to be done.
12. *Externalized thinking.* If I work long and hard enough, I can find happiness and feel better about myself. It's what happens to me in the outer conditions of my life that will determine my happiness.

Even when workaholics succeed, their critical inner voice says they have failed. *Telescopic thinking* occurs when the workaholic mind acts like a telescope, blind to anything that raises the person's self worth, and zooms in on and magnifies the negative. This distorted thinking pattern often starts with critical parents in childhood, as Stephanie described: "I had parents who said when I brought home an A– on my report card, 'Well, why couldn't that be an A+?' My dad even said to me when I won a writing contest and I sent him a copy of the story, 'They must not have had too many entries to pick yours.' So I have this real sense of needing to prove something."

Telescopic thinking is carried into adulthood when workaholics set themselves up for failure by comparing themselves to the tops in each category. They must be smart like Einstein, creative like Leonardo da Vinci, compassionate like Mother Teresa, witty like Ellen DeGeneres, rich like Donald Trump, sexy like Brad Pitt, or a brilliant tennis player like Boris Becker. Even if they excel in three out of four areas, they ignore the three areas of achievement and focus on the one in which they fall short. They berate themselves and think of themselves as failures, although they may be perceived as outstanding by others. They continue to overlook their accomplishments and positive actions because they are focused on their shortcomings. Through such superhuman standards, they shower themselves with self-criticism and self-contempt: “That was a stupid thing to do” or “I just can’t seem to do anything right.”

With *blurred-boundary thinking,* workaholics show a lack of clear boundaries. What others consider excessive, workaholics consider standard. Lyn gives a good example in her own life: “I don’t think I overdo it by my standards. Lots of times when I take on projects, other people’s responses are stronger than mine. They see what I do as a bigger deal than I see it.”

It’s hard for workaholics to realize they’re biting off more than they can chew, because they don’t see it at the time. It’s difficult to say no because they don’t know where or when to draw the line. They often sacrifice their own needs by giving in to the demands of others whom they perceive as more needy than themselves. They are so used to doing what others expect them to do that they don’t know what they really want or need to do for themselves. This type of thinking leads to self-neglect, putting their needs at the bottom of the heap until they explode from either burnout or uncontained resentment.

Sometimes what others believe about them becomes more important to workaholics than what they believe about themselves. *People-pleasing thinking* causes them to be indecisive and overly agreeable, because they’re always using the opinions of others to gauge their actions. They figure that if they can get others to applaud them, they’ll feel better inside. It is impossible to please everybody, and when they try, their personalities change with the wind. They lose their self-respect and become unsure of what they believe without someone else to tell them.

When workaholics do get praised by friends or coworkers, their *pessimistic thinking* discounts the praise, and they continue to feel unworthy and unfulfilled. They unconsciously filter the positive aspects of their lives and allow only negative aspects to enter. Their pessimism reminds them that nothing they ever do is good enough, and their flaws usually stand out. This bad habit of selecting the negative over the positive eventually leads workaholics to believe that everything is negative.

They believe that they live in a world where sooner or later the worst will happen. At the core of this fear is shame. No matter how successful they are in the outer world, they attribute their success to luck or accident and believe that it's only a matter of time until their failure is imminent. The fear of failure sometimes becomes a self-fulfilling prophecy, driving them so hard that they unintentionally sabotage their own success. It ruins their physical and emotional health and cripples their relationships with coworkers, families, and friends.

Workaholics feel helpless and unable to change their lives. When they engage in *helpless thinking,* they view their lives as determined by high-pressured lifestyles, how much they accomplish, and how much praise they get. As a result, they externalize their responsibilities and blame other people and situations for their problems—the job, family, or the economy.

Believing that problems and solutions are outside themselves, workaholics engage in *self-victimized thinking.* They characterize themselves as victims by blaming such outside forces as corporate downsizing, a relentless economy, an impossible boss, or a need to support a family. A favorite rationalization is the Messiah Myth: "Honey, I'm doing all this for you and the kids," to which there is little a spouse can say in rebuttal. The more victimized workaholics feel, the more their resentment builds and is expressed through bitterness and cynicism toward a lifestyle in which they feel trapped.

Resistance thinking causes workaholics to perceive life as a struggle. They structure their lives by wearing too many hats and doing too many things. They keep pushing themselves beyond human limits, refusing to take time for themselves and determined to do it all. They straightjacket themselves into a lifestyle that doesn't know spontaneity or flexibility. Rather than relaxing and finding harmony, they fight harder to be more perfect. They try to cram forty-eight hours into twenty-four, to make life's schedule conform to their self-created schedule of trying to force a size nine foot into a size seven shoe. They get frustrated in traffic jams. They become annoyed with people who move too slowly. They get impatient in long, slow-moving lines. They waste a lot of emotional energy getting mad at their daily conditions, instead of accepting them and living their lives within those limits.

Workaholics engage in *wishful thinking*—wishing they had more of something or someone to make them feel more finished, more complete. This type of thinking fans the flames of work addiction to gain more. They want most what they are least likely to get. They want what they cannot have, and they devalue or ignore what they already have, simply because they have it. Wishful thinking defines happiness in terms of lack and discontent. Focusing on what is missing from their lives keeps workaholics in a state of feeling empty and incomplete, which encourages more working to fill up the hole.

Serious thinking tells workaholics that life is all grim determination and that fun and joy are taboo. This rigid belief keeps them from laughing at themselves and seeing the humorous side of life. They tend to take themselves too seriously because they have learned that life is serious business. Perhaps as children they did not get to enjoy the carefree world of childhood and had to grow up as little adults. Laughter and fun are looked on with contempt, because they conflict with the single minded goal of getting the job done. Relaxing is often considered wasteful, and people who fritter time away by playing and having a good time may be considered frivolous and foolish.

As I have mentioned, workaholics are externally focused. *Externalized thinking* is reflected in the need to have a concrete product to show for their efforts. Their value is attached to what they can do, not to how they feel inside. The more they produce, the better they feel, because the more they do, the more worthy they are. Keeping to-do lists is an example of external referencing. Workaholics look outside themselves for their self-worth and put more value on what they accomplish and what people say or do in regard to their accomplishments than on their own inner personal opinions and human qualities.

The Mind-Body Link and the Workaholic's Health

Can you catch a cold because you split up with the love of your dreams? Can your job stress cause you to get the flu? Can long-held anger and resentment give you cancer? Think of how many times you have felt depressed, angry, or stressed out only to have those feelings followed by a cold or other viral infection.

Increasing evidence indicates that both happiness and misery come from our way of thinking. Scientists now know that every time we have a thought or feeling, every cell of our body creates chemicals called neuropeptides that directly affect all of our physical systems and organs. Norman Cousins, in his book *Headfirst,* declares, "Scarcely anything that enters the mind doesn't find its way into the workings of the body."[8] The mind influences every cell because every thought activates hormones or chemicals that carry that information throughout the body.[9] The stress psychologist Hans Selye long ago explained how the body manufactures its own poisons when under siege by negative emotions. The cells of workaholics are constantly eavesdropping on their thoughts and being changed by them. Workaholics become recipients of the effects of their own frustration, anger, or rage. Negative dark moods have harmful physical effects on their bodies, causing their body chemistry to secrete chemicals that can harm them.

On a physical level, recent biochemical research has shown that emotions act as boomerangs. Negative emotions can ricochet on workaholics to cause them biochemical harm, and the people may not realize it until it is too late. Workaholic negative thinking, for example, can create negative emotions, and negative emotions unleash biochemical enzymes in the body that create destructive physical side effects. When workaholics are overly stressed, their brains send that message through cortisol and adrenaline, stress, hormones that destroy the immune system. Anger, hostility, and hurry cause the release of the hormone epinephrine, which makes the heart beat fast and blood pressure rise. High blood pressure leads to damaged arteries and heart attack. Too much adrenaline blocks the cell's ability to clear dangerous cholesterol from the bloodstream, where elevated amounts of cholesterol clog arteries, damage their inner lining, and can cause heart attacks. In addition, high stress and negative feelings have been linked to other body chemistry changes that are believed to produce cancerous cells. Thus, the workaholic's despair, anxiety, and depression can raise the risk of heart attack and cancer, thereby shortening life.

Positive thoughts, on the other hand, create positive emotions, and positive emotions create body chemistry that has beneficial physical side effects that boost the immune system. Body chemistry research indicates that positive feelings such as laughter and optimism enhance the immune system by increasing the number of disease-fighting immune cells. Laughter also activates the secretion of endorphins, the body's own pain killer, which helps reduce physical pain. Humor and mirth generally reduce stress, ease pain, foster physical healing, and generally brighten one's outlook, regardless of how grim the reality. So if workaholics learn to have fun or think positively, their bodies will produce interleukins and interferons, powerful cancer-fighting drugs. As they embrace more optimism and joy, they will become more healthy and live longer. Anger can kill workaholics; laughter can heal and sustain them.

How to Think That Black Cloud Away

Jason spent the majority of his life blaming his work addiction on high-pressured jobs or on the fact that he was brought up in an alcoholic home. The truth of the matter was that he was choosing that lifestyle, and he was the only person on earth who could change it, regardless of cultural norms or society's expectations. Elizabeth, once a dispirited wage earner, was able to stop blaming the workplace and accept responsibility for her job choices: "I have picked high-pressured jobs for my last three jobs. I wasn't aware of it going into them, but now I see that I am doing that. Nobody's doing that to me."

Workaholics believe that they are made miserable by the circumstances of their lives. But where they live and what they do for a living have little to do with whether they can lead a balanced life. Nothing will change until they change on the inside and rethink their priorities and values. They must confront the work addiction and the rigid thinking that have become part of their personalities and commit themselves to changing these habits, instead of blaming family, the media, society, the job, the economy, or the dog. The way to change is to change the negative thinking. As Anthony De Mello said, "Nothing has changed but my attitude; everything has changed."

It is not what life doles out that determines happiness or unhappiness. It is how workaholics consciously think and react to what life deals them that makes the difference. They are given life, but they have the power to create their experience of life. The ways in which they think about what happens to them creates their emotions and reactions, not the incidents themselves. Staying focused on hardships and problems keeps them stuck in rigid thinking. When used to combat feelings of failure, despair, and pessimism, work addiction can become a chronic way of life. But if workaholics view themselves as empowered to use life's disadvantages to learn and improve their lives, then they create a positive experience out of a negative one.

Sometimes critical messages blink in the mind like a neon sign. Some workaholics stew over mistakes, worry about things they cannot control, and expect the worst in each situation. In adulthood, the childhood messages continue to remind them of who they are through mental dialogues they have with themselves. Much of what they think and do is still dictated by their refusal to let go of that inner dialogue. The critical voices of parents and other significant adults from the past continue to drive workaholics and keep them stuck. The negative thoughts are so automatic that they are hardly noticeable unless a concerted effort is made to pay attention to them.

Jason's father often used to tell him that he'd never amount to anything. That critical voice, echoing in his head, reminded him that nothing he ever did was enough, driving him deeper into work addiction. Today, he knows that his father's criticisms, although directed at him, were a reflection of his dad's inner frustration, low self-worth, and deep unhappiness. As workaholics recognize where the critical messages come from, they can give them back to whomever they belong, instead of carrying them around. Jason was able to give his father's critical messages back to him by silently saying, "Dad, I'm letting you have your feelings back. I know you felt like you never amounted to anything. Now I know those feelings are yours, not mine."

Suggestions for Clinicians

Recovery from work addiction is not something clients can dash through like a commuter rushing to catch the 5:00 train. Most workaholics have spent a lifetime developing their habits, and changing them requires a reversal of their mind-set. Clinicians can help them get in touch with the beliefs that drive their behaviors, make appropriate changes, and begin to set realistic expectations for themselves. When they understand that their self-worth is not tied to what they do, they can begin to adopt an internal instead of an external focus.

Written Exercises and Behavioral Techniques

Once clients recognize that compulsive work is a problem, I find that pencil-and-paper exercises can help them assess and visualize how they live now—and how they'd like to live. Using what I call a "healogram," I ask them to make a bar graph assessing five basic life areas: relationships, career, spiritual needs, self-care, and play. How much time, I ask them, do they spend in each area of their lives? Usually, the bar in the category called "career" towers over all the rest. Then I ask them to redraw the bar graph, illustrating how they'd like to live. This simple process gives clients a clear sense that the goal is balance, not elimination of work altogether.

The pencil-and-paper exercise may bring to the surface the catastrophic, all-or-nothing thinking that lies behind some workaholic patterns. One man said to me, "I can spend time with my family or provide for my family financially, but not both." Another client, a successful, thirty-eight-year-old heart surgeon, had not gone on a vacation in ten years because he was convinced that if he took even a week off, his multimillion-dollar business would crumble. I asked him to draw a line across a sheet of paper and write his two extreme beliefs on each end. He put "I must work nonstop to build my business" on one end and wrote "If I take a vacation, my business will crumble" on the opposite end.

This helped him externalize and dispassionately examine the unspoken assumptions that had driven his financially successful but lonely and harried life. I asked him to consider an option and write down a new phrase at the line's midpoint: "It is possible for me to take a week's vacation and for my business to continue to grow." I call this simple process "accessing the graydar," because it helps clients get in touch with an internal radar attuned to shades of gray rather than extremes.

Sometimes I teach simple behavioral techniques to stop work thoughts from elbowing their way into every waking moment: once, for example, I taught a financial planner who worried obsessively about his job to compartmentalize his intrusive thoughts by mentally placing each one in a box, putting a lid on the box, and setting it on a storage shelf in a basement or attic. He was to take the thoughts off the shelf and out of the box only when he planned to give them his full attention. I also suggested he wear a thick rubber band around his wrist and if an intrusive work thought got loose, to snap the band and say, "Stop!" in his mind. You would have thought that this simple rubber band was a miracle cure. He proudly wore it to each session, proclaiming the dramatic changes in his life. Combining these simple strategies with an antidepressant and basic relaxation and breathing techniques, the planner slept better, was more present with his wife and young son, and tackled work problems with more clarity and energy.

Using Cognitive Psychotherapies to Treat Work Addiction

The cognitive psychotherapies of Drs. Aaron Beck and David Burns are excellent approaches to treat work addiction, because they capitalize on the workaholic's reliance on thinking and cognition rather than on feelings and intimacy. They are good strategies for helping clients get to the core of the workaholic cycle and change their incorrect beliefs about themselves. As these beliefs begin to change, the motivation to overwork subsides. Thus, by changing their rigid belief systems, workaholics develop a more flexible, balanced perspective of themselves that automatically translates into a healthier, more balanced, and more flexible lifestyle.

Clinicians can help clients make a mental shift to get them out of the workaholic cycle by following these steps:

Step 1: The first step in modifying incorrect beliefs is for clients to become more aware of them. Start off by helping clients identify their negative thoughts by suggesting that they pay attention to and keep track of their self-referencing, negative thoughts for a one-week period. Tell them to notice each time they have critical dialogues with themselves and write down the negative thoughts, without censorship, in a daily log.

Step 2: Once the list is generated, ask the clients to look over their lists and star the criticisms that occur more than once. They may be surprised at how often they call themselves names such as "stupid" or "unworthy," use shame-based words such as "should" or "must," and downgrade themselves. Next, have clients write beside the thought whether or not the belief is true (these thoughts are almost always untrue). For example, are they really losers? Is it really true that no one loves them or that everything they do is wrong?

Step 3: Have them get a sheet of paper and draw two lines down the page, making three columns. In the left column have them list each negative thought. In the middle column, have clients identify the kind of rigid thinking exemplified in each statement, using the list in table 5.1 or explain why that negative thought is not true.

Step 4: In the right column, have the clients rewrite each negative thought by substituting a positive statement, rational thought, or affirmation about themselves that counteracts the negative thought. For example, if a negative thought said, "I'm a loser," a positive replacement might be "I'm competent and capable" or "I am a worthy person." The positive statements become a more accurate portrayal of who the workaholics really are and the way others probably see them. Here are a few examples:

Negative Thought	*Rigid Thinking*	*Positive Statement*
"I must be thoroughly competent in all tasks that I undertake or else I am worthless.	All-or-nothing and Perfectionism	"Achievements do not determine my worth; I am capable and competent and I do the best I can. When I make mistakes, I can learn from them."
"I should be loved by everyone."	All-or-nothing and People-pleasing	"My worth doesn't depend on everyone liking me; no one is loved universally. Many people in my life love and care for me."

"If only things were perfect, then I could be happy."	Wishful thinking and Perfectionism	"People and myself included are not perfect. I accept myself as I am with all my strengths and shortcomings.
"I cannot help the way things are."	Helpless thinking and Pessimism	"I am in charge of my life; it is not in charge of me, and its up to me to change the things I can."

The positive statements, more than the negative ones, tend to be accurate portrayals of the ways that clients are viewed by others. The positive statements can become affirmations that clients repeat silently to themselves from week to week. The more they use these positive statements, the more they come to believe that these qualities really apply to them. The use of positive affirmations, repeated silently during the day, before the morning mirror, or written in a journal, helps build the nurturing voice to combat the self-critical voice. Written affirmations can be put on mirrors, refrigerators, desks, or even telephone answering machines. Clinicians can suggest that clients keep a bulletin board with all the affirming letters, notes, gifts, and sayings that loved ones, friends, and business associates send them and to look at them often as reminders of their inherent value.

Helping Clients Connect with Themselves

Exploring and learning to validate the existential, authentic self becomes an important therapeutic task for workaholics in recovery.[10] Clinicians can confront them with questions as to how they honestly feel about themselves and their lives, what they value, what their sources of validation are, and whom and what activities they have been neglecting at the expense of their work addiction. There may also be opportunities to explore ego-threatening feelings such as loneliness, ennui, insecurity, and hopelessness.

As clients start to reframe how they think about themselves, their feelings and behaviors automatically start to shift. The shift starts as they redefine themselves, not by what they have or do but by who they are on the inside. This shift takes them from an external, quantifiable focus to an internal, quality-based, process-oriented focus. Helping clients connect with themselves helps them learn to use flexibility and live in the process instead of quantifying their lives through products that they can point to with pride.

Breaking out of the self-destructive cycle of work addiction comes with time for renewal, rest, pampering, contemplation, a time where workaholics intimately connect with that deeper personal part of themselves. Clinicians can share the following tips with clients so that they can develop an internal relationship with themselves:

- *Change how you think about yourself.* Good health and self-esteem are part of a state of mind. Henry Ford once said, "If you think you can or you can't, you're right." The starting point is to realize how negative thinking undermines your health and self-esteem and how an optimistic outlook can change that. See yourself honestly by recognizing your accomplishments along with your defeats, your strengths as well as your faults. The more you look for the positives, the better you will begin to feel about yourself.
- *Learn to identify your feelings and to accept the fact that you're angry or frustrated.* Listen to yourself. Pay attention to your thoughts and feelings. Get in tune with your feelings, and get in the habit of writing them down in a journal. Ask yourself what you're using your activities to escape from. What are you afraid of facing? What resentments or hurts are unresolved? Face your feelings, and feel them completely. Ask yourself where the voice came from that tells you that nothing you do is ever good enough. Is it

your voice, or is it the voice of a critical parent or another adult figure from your past? Learn to stand up to the critical voice and take charge of it, instead of letting it take charge of you.

- *Give yourself pep talks.* Replace the critical voice with one that nurtures and encourages you. Whether you're asking for a raise, making an important presentation, starting a new job, or struggling with parenthood, doubt and lack of confidence can flood your mind. When you have these negative thoughts, ask, "What would I say to my best friend or child if she thought she couldn't do something? You wouldn't say, "Of course you can't do it. You might as well give up." Your confidence in her ability would lead you to encourage her. Value yourself enough to be your own best friend, and give yourself the same encouragement that you give to others. Pep talks bring self-reassurance and ultimate success. Tell yourself, "Yes, I can do this, and I can do it well." Use a mirror as you send yourself positive, encouraging messages. Image the best of outcomes, instead of the worst, before you get into the situation. Encourage yourself just as you would your best friend. Tell yourself, "You can do anything you set your mind to, and you can do it well."
- *Please yourself instead of pleasing others.* When you trim yourself to suit everybody else, you whittle yourself away until there's nothing left of you. Learn to let go of other people's opinions, and form your own. Develop solid values and beliefs, and stand up for them instead of being a chameleon. Keep the company of people you respect and who mirror your positive worth.
- *Learn to accept your human limitations without feeling flawed.* Learn to admit and accept your mistakes and to value yourself in spite of them. Acknowledging and accepting your vulnerabilities and your limits is a character strength, not a character weakness. Begin to think of yourself as a human being who needs nurturance, rather than a machine that can be driven nonstop. Make a mental shift

and begin seeing your limitations as normal instead of as a drawback. Acknowledge those human limitations and value them, instead of trying to push yourself beyond them. Stay away from relationships that drain you, and surround yourself with people who support, love, and affirm you.

- *Recognize that less is more.* Simplifying your life will help you appreciate how rich it already is and recognize that more things will not bring more happiness. Lower your standards, and be more realistic about what's possible for you to do. It is possible to relax your standards and still do a good job. Instead of asking yourself what additional commitment you can make, ask yourself what obligations or chores you can eliminate from your to-do list. Instead of taking on more work responsibilities, decide which ones you can delegate, sell, or give away. Instead of juggling three or four tasks at once, choose only one at a time, and focus on it.
- *Work smarter, not longer.* Make your schedule work for you, instead of your working for it. Instead of overscheduling your life, leave gaps in your calendar for something spontaneous and unexpected to happen. Delegate responsibilities wherever you can at home, at work, or at play. Assign errands and household chores to others with whom you live. Rely on outside help to get the windows washed, the lawn mowed, the house painted, and the rooms cleaned. Tell yourself that you don't have to do it all. Get up earlier or go to bed later to have extra time for yourself and loved ones. Remember, it's your life. You can be in charge of it, instead of letting it be in charge of you.

6

The Childhoods of Workaholics

We're so engaged in doing things to achieve purposes of outer value, but the inner value, the rapture that is associated with being alive is what it's all about.

—JOSEPH CAMPBELL

Ross

For me, work addiction was about abandonment and is a very interesting study as to why people elect to work at the cost of having fulfilling relationships with spouses and children. I was one of two sons, my brother being fifteen months older than I was. From the beginning, I remember nothing but tension, worry, and concern, two parents who did more fighting than loving, and when there was peace we were always waiting for the next blowup. In addition to the worry, the migraines, the vomiting, the loss of vision, and the tablets, there was the aloneness of it all, the shame of it all. Who knew? What did the neighbors think? How would I ever climb out of the sewer?

During these years, my mother and I were very close, perhaps too close. I only realized at a heavy cost much later how unhealthy the relationship had been and what a price I had to pay to exist. She seemed to love me, encourage me, and promote me as her surrogate husband. She came to look to me for guidance, decisions, and support. I paid a heavy price for what seemed flattering to a young boy growing up. She spoke to me about what I now call "adult problems," things I should never have known, from the most intimate details of her private life to relationships with others, and even sex with my father. She spared me nothing. No wonder I grew up feeling burdened and worried. There was no childhood for me. There was no childhood for my brother. The only difference between my brother and myself was that I took it all on board feeling sorry, concerned, and always crying for a solution. No doubt my brother suffered in his quiet way, but because he didn't show it my mother dismissed him, spoke poorly of him, and ridiculed him. "He's weak," she'd say. I was promoted for my allegiance to her; he was demoted for his apparent lack of it.

By the age of eight, I began to figure out that if I did not look after myself, then no one would. I washed cars, saved money, sold old Coke bottles, and did whatever I needed to become strong, independent, and rich. By doing this, I figured that I would be unhurtable, in control, that pain would not touch me. How wrong I was! How much I still had to learn about intelligent balance, that moving from one dysfunctional extreme to another was not the answer. I had to learn how to live properly. It was tough because I hadn't learned the skills of proper living. Sure, I knew about manners, right from wrong, and social skills—but not about unconditional love, leading by example, and tolerance and patience.

I left school at about sixteen and started my own business at twenty. At twenty-three, I married for peace. This was an error, but at that time of my life, I was simply looking for quiet, and I got it. Seventeen years and three children later, I left my wife because I was not prepared to live with this deathly quiet any longer. There was no conflict and no words of anger. My kids never heard a cross word.

They were as surprised as everybody else in our community. I worked like a donkey building my business to deal with my pain. I continued to grow as an individual, I broke off my relationship with my mother, and my business grew tremendously.

During the thirty years that I have been in business, I built a large and profitable company with a team of good people. It became as strong as it did for a few reasons. First, I was and still am very focused. Second, the business was my family, because my personal life was unfulfilled.

Childhood Origins of Work Addiction

Now that we have explored the inner workings of the workaholic mind, we turn to work addicts' childhoods to get a better understanding of the beginnings that shaped their thinking and feelings in their families of origin.

At age seven, Carol stood on a chair in the kitchen to make homemade biscuits. She ironed all her family's clothes and did most of the housework. She already had learned to write money orders so that the electric bill would get paid. Both her parents were alcoholic. Nobody told her to take on the grown-up responsibilities; she did them as an intuitive way of bringing order and security to her young life. Today, at twenty-eight, Carol is a workaholic.

Clinicians generally believe that work addiction is a consequence of family dysfunction in childhood and that it contributes to continued family dysfunction in adulthood.[1] The natural swing and style of all children is to make sense and order out of their worlds as they grow, learn, and develop. When everything around them is falling apart on a prolonged and sustained basis, their natural inclination is to stabilize that world by latching onto something that is stable and consistent—something that will anchor them and keep them afloat amid the chaos, turmoil, and instability. Out of their confusion and desperation, youngsters begin to seek control wherever and whenever they can find it.

Work addiction develops most frequently in kids who get a roller-coaster ride through childhood, rather than in those whose bounces and jostles are buttressed by steady parental hands. Because of their individual family situations, they are propelled into the adult world, where, although unprepared, they are expected to cope even though they lack the emotional and mental resources of an adult.

Lacking the emotional equipment to meet these unrealistic expectations, they instinctively grab onto a life raft to carry them through the storm. For many, it is the security of caretaking, schoolwork, housework, homework, church work, and perfectionism. Examples of family situations that can cause kids to become hooked on work are parental separation or divorce in which children are placed in the middle of a tug of war; the death of a parent, shattering family unity and spirit and perhaps never talked about; devastating unemployment, creating an economic see-saw; a traumatic family move, uprooting the children; parental substance abuse, throwing the family roles and expectations off kilter; parental schizophrenia or other mental illness that sends conflicting Dr. Jekyll/Mr. Hyde messages to children; and emotional incest, in which one parent is physically or psychologically absent (because of workaholism, depression, or other factors) and the other parent elevates a young child to replace the absent parent emotionally, as in the case of Ross.

Families that breed work addiction operate in the extremes and can be placed into one of two categories: the perfect family, on one end of the continuum, and the chaotic, imperfect family, on the other. They either have rigid rules or none at all, boundaries that are too thick or too blurred, lifestyles that are overorganized and perfect or disorganized and confusing. These families are often characterized by open or subtle conflict, poor communication, and lack of nurturance.

In perfect families, looking good and putting up a happy front are unwritten family rules. The message is clear: say and do the right thing, pretend everything is okay even when it isn't, don't talk about your feelings, and don't let people know what you're like on the inside. Being in control, being perfect, and doing what others want are some of the character traits reinforced in some workaholic kids.

In imperfect families, inconsistency and unpredictability are often at the root of childhood work addiction. The common theme in these childhoods is a lack of psychological insulation during the vulnerable childhood years. Although no child's life is completely carefree, children have a basic need to receive psychological protection from their caregivers, who keep them safe and separate from the adult world. When this security is severely breached, as in the case of Ross, children learn that they cannot depend on adults to give them the insulation they need and that they must have absolute control over people and situations in order to survive psychologically and physically. Constant disruptions require children to take charge of a life that feels like it's crumbling around them. Workaholic kids learn to take control of everything around them to keep their worlds from coming unglued. They overcompensate for the confusion and become overconciliatory; eventually, they bring these qualities to their adult jobs. While friends play, the lives of workaholic youngsters are filled with serious, adult issues. Outward success conceals deeper problems of inadequacy and poor self-esteem. Underneath are overly serious children who browbeat themselves into perfectionism and judge themselves unmercifully for making mistakes. Table 6.1 presents a portrait of workaholic children.

Parentified Kids: Little Adults with Big Burdens

One result of parentification is that children become little adults, both emotionally and mentally, and miss the developmental tasks of childhood altogether. Workaholics were often child caretakers of younger siblings or of emotionally dependent, alcoholic, or mentally and physically disabled parents. The role required them to become overly responsible at a young age, before they were fully constructed themselves.

TABLE 6.1
Portrait of a Workaholic Child

- Puts more time into schoolwork than playtime
- Has few friends and prefers the company of adults to that of other children
- Shows signs of health problems related to stress such as chronic exhaustion, headaches, or stomachaches
- Takes on such adult responsibilities as keeping the household running smoothly, cooking, cleaning, or care of a younger sibling
- Strives for perfection in most things he or she does
- Stays serious much of the time and carries the burden of adult worries on his or her shoulders
- Spends little time relaxing, playing, fantasizing, having fun, and enjoying childhood
- Has precocious leadership abilities in the classroom and on the playground
- Seeks constant social approval from adults by striving to be a "good girl" or "good boy"
- Demonstrates compulsive overachievement in church work, schoolwork, or sports or other extracurricular activities
- Gets upset or impatient easily with himself or herself for making even the smallest mistake
- Shows more interest in the final result of his or her work than in the process
- Puts himself or herself under self-imposed pressures
- Does two or three things at once
- Has trouble asking for and receiving help

Adult family members whose own needs were not met in childhood turn to their children to get these needs satisfied, as Ross's mother did. The chosen child may be made into a confidant or an emotional caretaker, or he or she may be required to live out parental dreams, even if it goes against the child's desires and best interests.[2] The child, in order to balance out the family, is used to establish family justice by providing parents whatever they never got from their own families. Children then begin to mold their identities around fulfilling the needs of parents and other adults: "Parentified children take care of their parents in concrete, physical ways by comforting them emotionally, and also by shaping their own personalities to meet the expectations of the parents, thereby increasing the parents' self-esteem."[3]

Parentification can take two routes: the child who is shaped to be "Mom or Dad's Little Helper" or the child who is inducted to live out a "Parent's Dream."[4] The "Little Helper" develops a caretaking, self-defeating character style, the mode of adaption that in childhood offered the best possibility for achieving proximity to the parent.[5] The parent's "Dream Child" is more likely to give up his or her own self to serve the parent and to fall short of self-development, which leaves the child with a narcissistic character style. Either path leads to careaholism and workaholism, a sacrificing of the self in favor of another person or another task. Many parentified children become careaholic grownups who are compelled to take care of others and who seek out and find people to help, either in their professions or in their personal relationships.

Are You a Parentified Careaholic?

A Methodist minister and therapist to his flock believed that every person who came into his life was sent by God. Even when overloaded with congregation members, hospital visits, and pastoral counseling, he had difficulty saying no because his guilt told him it was God's will and that he had to help each and every person, even when his phone, mounted on the headboard of his bed, rang in the middle of the night.

One morning, after a full and hectic week, he got a 2 A.M. call from one of his parishioners who had lost a family member. He told the caller he would come to the hospital immediately, rolled over for what was to be a brief second, and reawakened at 7 A.M. By the time he got to the hospital, the family was furious. Guilt ridden and overburdened, the pastor took ten years to recover from his feelings of failure and inadequacy.

Compulsive caregiving in adulthood is the result of parentified attachment bonds in childhood, where children are expected prematurely to care for their parents emotionally. In such cases, children deactivate and renounce their need for comfort, protection, and reassurance from parents, because their best shot at gaining emotional attachment is giving emotional support to a needy parent:

> The structure of a person's interactions with the parent is carried forward into adulthood and serves as a template for negotiating current relationships. Deference and subjugation of self to others is assured to be the price exacted by attachment. The compulsive caregiver thus develops affectional ties along old relational lines: playing the role of the caregiver is the vehicle through which relational proximity is sought and maintained.[6]

Careaholics have great difficulty in asking for and giving help to themselves. The psychologist John Bowlby explains why:

> The person showing it may engage in many close relationships but always in the role of giving care, never that of receiving it. . . . the person who develops in this way has found that the only affectional bond available is one in which he must always be the caregiver and that the only care he can ever receive is the care he gives himself.[7]

Ram Dass, the psychologist turned spiritual seeker, said, "If you need to be helpful, you'll look for someone to be helpless." Not only does this line of reasoning hurt the caretaker; it damages the people he or she is trying to help. The relationship between the helper and the helped is potentially destructive when carried too far. There are many people who are more than willing to entrust their lives to another person; when they give their power to another, they keep themselves helpless. Careaholism can keep people dependent on the caretaker and unable to move forward with their own lives.

Are you a careaholic who was parentified as a child? Take the test in table 6.2 to find out.

The helping and health professions are bulging at the seams with grownup parentified children who bring their needs to caretake, fix, make peace, and carry others' burdens into the workplace. But, then, so is the entertainment business. The actress Drew Barrymore was her mother's Dream Child. She says she and her mother were more friends than mother and daugh-

TABLE 6.2
Portrait of a Carea holic

Read the following twenty-five statements and grade how much each one pertains to you, using the following scale: 1 = never true; 2 = sometimes true; 3 = often true; and 4 = always true. When you're finished, add the numbers in the blanks for your total score.

___ 1. I get overly involved by taking on other people's problems.
___ 2. I feel overly responsible when bad things happen and feel that it is my role to make them better.
___ 3. I overidentify with others by feeling their emotions as if they were my own.
___ 4. I have an ongoing urge to take care of other people.
___ 5. I neglect my own needs in favor of caring for the needs of others.
___ 6. I take life too seriously and find it hard to play and have fun.
___ 7. I have a need to solve people's problems for them.
___ 8. I have not dealt with a lot of painful feelings from my past.
___ 9. I feel unworthy of love.
___ 10. I never seem to have enough time for myself.
___ 11. I criticize myself too much.
___ 12. I am afraid of being abandoned by those I love.
___ 13. My life always seems to be in crisis.
___ 14. I don't feel good about myself if I'm not doing something for someone else.
___ 15. I don't know what to do if I'm not caring for someone.
___ 16. Whatever I do never seems to be enough.
___ 17. I have dedicated my life to helping others.
___ 18. I get high from helping people with their problems.
___ 19. I have a need to take charge of most situations.
___ 20. I spend more time caretaking than I do socializing with friends, on hobbies, or on leisure activities.
___ 21. It is hard for me to relax when I'm not caring for others.
___ 22. I experience emotional fatigue and compassion burnout.
___ 23. It is hard for me to keep emotional boundaries by saying no when someone wants to tell me about a problem.
___ 24. I have developed health or physical problems from stress, worry, or burnout.
___ 25. I seek approval and affirmation from others through people pleasing and by overcommitting myself.

SCORING:
The higher your score, the more you are a careaholic. Use the following key to interpret your score:
25–49 = you are not a careaholic
50–69 = you are mildly careaholic
70–100 = you are highly careaholic. Chances are you were parentified as a child.

ter. "If we ever were [mother and daughter], it was me being the mother. Our role reversal was pathetic." Drew's mother agreed. "We both had to grow up. I made a tremendous amount of mistakes raising her. I was living through Drew's accomplishments. Now I have my own accomplishments.[8] The actress Brooke Shields exemplifies the Little Helper, fiercely loyal to her mother.

"There were no other kids, no husband. It was just us, and we formed a little team."[9] Her mother was the closest person in her life, and it was difficult for her to let others in: "I preferred crushes and unrequited love, because a real romance threatened my relationship with my mother. To me she was the single closest friend in my life. I was terrified of being vulnerable with anyone else.[10]

Gloria Steinem, a self-professed workaholic, chronicles in her bestselling book *Revolution from Within,* what it was like as a child caring for an invalid mother who alternated between wandering the streets and sitting quietly:

> I remember so well the dread of not knowing who I would find when I came home: a mother whose speech was slurred by tranquilizers, a woman wandering in the neighborhood not sure where she was, or a loving and sane woman who asked me about my school day. I, too, created a cheerful front and took refuge in constant reading and afterschool jobs—anything to divert myself (and others) from the realities of life.[11]

The case of Ross is an example of emotional enmeshment that continued to haunt him into his manhood. When his parents went through a messy divorce, twenty-six-year-old Ross faced his mother's emotional blackmail as he tried to free himself from her grip. Feeling emotionally abandoned when Ross refused her ultimatum to never see or speak to his father again, his mother set out to destroy her son in any way she could. She called him a liar and spread false rumors about him. He sent her flowers for her birthday with a loving note, and they were returned, untouched. She did not see her son for twenty years. Although Ross continues to come to terms with the emotional hurt he incurred from his mother, he is learning not to use his work as a refuge from the pain.

Another example of a parentified child was twelve-year-old Katie, who became a Little Helper when her father died. Her mother had to take two jobs to support Katie and her younger brother, and she was gone from early morning until late at night. Katie was only twelve; yet her little brother became what she called "her baby":

> I got him up every morning, made sure that he got his breakfast, had his lunch, and learned to read when he came home from the first grade every afternoon. I helped him with his ABCs, made the beds, and cooked meals. Mother would come in at supper time, tell me I had made a good meal, and go to her second job. My world was falling apart around me, and by grasping onto those duties, I was able to gain control over my life. I could take care of my brother, clean the house, make cakes, and do a multitude of chores that would make my world stable. And I have been doing this all my life.

The tacit family contract here was that Mom would fill the father's role as breadwinner, while Katie moved into the mother role as partner to her mother and mother to her brother. Katie's hectic childhood contributed to a stressful bout with work addiction and a broken marriage by the time she was fifty, at which time she worked day and night as a nurse administrator:

> My husband complained about me working in the evening. So I bundled up all this work, took it home, and closed myself in my bedroom to work on it into the wee hours of morning. I'd fall asleep with work piled on top of me. My husband would come to bed and find his side covered with ledgers. Finally, he quit coming to bed and slept on the sofa.
>
> It was two years before I realized anything was wrong. When we separated, I wondered why I was crying about the bed being empty on the other side. I'd tell myself how dumb it was because he had been on the sofa for the last year anyway. I'd find myself almost falling off the bed, rolling over trying to find him there. I purposely started leaving books and stuff on his side of the bed so there would be something there for me to cuddle with.

My Own Parentification: The Workaholic Poster Child

The first time I talked with Gloria Steinem, we both said, "I feel like I know you." Although our lives were very different on the outside, the way we experienced them was much the same on the inside. Children who become parentified often have an emotional bond that supersedes their gender, ethnicity, or socioeconomic backgrounds. They share an understanding of the isolation, pain, loss, fear, and, sometimes, embarrassment of a little adult who is carrying emotional burdens bigger than they are. They are comrades of the soul—bound together by common childhood wounds. The following accounts of the childhood of Gloria Steinem and of my own illustrate the connections that can lead two adults of different genders, ethnic backgrounds, and geographic regions who have never met before to exclaim, "I feel like I know you."

Bryan Robinson

I could have been the workaholic poster child. My upbringing in an alcoholic home where I was caretaker of a younger sister and overly responsible for the emotional tone of an out-of-control family led me to use housework, homework, schoolwork, and church work as groundwork to my adult work addiction.

My stomach turned as the jolt of my father's drunken outbursts hit me like a jackhammer. I quaked in my bed late at night as I heard him stagger up the porch steps and fumble around for his house keys. Lights came on all over the house, and everyone was in an uproar. I'd jump out of bed to control the scenario, closing doors, windows, and drapes so that neighbors wouldn't see and hear, hiding lamps and breakables so that the house would not be destroyed and no one would be killed or sent to the hospital. It was not a role I chose; it was one that I took by default, out of necessity and out of a will to survive. I had become the one who ran the show: the protector, the peacemaker, the referee, the judge, the general. I was nine years old.

Many nights when his father abandoned him at the movies, that nine-year-old, who was still learning to read and write, had to get his little sister and himself home. Underneath the big-screen excitement of James Dean and Marilyn Monroe was a little boy's fear and worry. Sometimes when we stood in the dark streets not knowing what to do, my sister would cry, and, although I wanted to cry too, I had to make her think I was in charge of the situation. I was scared and mad because of the cold and dark empty streets. Sometimes the police would take us home, and other times we walked the three-mile trek in the dark, with dogs barking and chasing after us.

In high school I wrote and directed the church Christmas play, single-handedly designed and built the sets, and acted in the role of lead character. I didn't know it at the time, but doing everything gave me immense control and a sense of stability that served as an antidote to the instability of my home life. Paradoxically, accolades from teachers, neighbors, and relatives who admired and rewarded my disguised workaholism only drove me further into self-misery, feelings of inadequacy, and an addiction to work that would stalk me into adulthood.

Schoolwork helped me feel good about myself, and, later, the work world gave me the same sense of what I thought was fulfillment. It provided an escape so that I didn't have to deal with many feelings buried since childhood. I covered my pain with a cheery smile and hard work, both of which concealed the problem, kept me disconnected from people and intimate relationships, and gave me something intimate with which I could connect safely. Work also gave me a sense of total control of my life. I had found my drug of choice. I transformed my long hours of college study into long hours of work: weeknights, weekends, and holidays.

By the time I was forty, work addiction had invaded every tissue of my body. I was hooked. I was a chain-smoking, caffeine-drinking, one-man production line. Like an alcoholic, I felt restless and became irritable when I went more than a few days away from my desk. Even when lounging on a tropical beach, all my thoughts centered on my next project.

I hid my work as my father had hidden his bottle. I slept off work highs in my clothes, just as my father slept off his alcoholic binges in his clothes. As an adult, I came to realize that I had cultivated the use of work to conceal emotion and my true self instead of expressing them. Believing my family's problems were unique and shameful, I strove to gain control and approval by excelling in school and the world outside my home.

Gloria Steinem

On the surface, there seemed to be no similarities between Bryan's childhood and my own. Unlike his father, mine had been a kindhearted and gentle man who took care of me more than my mother did. Because her spirit seemed to have been broken before I was born, she was often a figure lying on the couch, talking to unseen voices, and only able to make clear that she loved me and my sister. There was no violence in my house, and I grew up with the sureness that my parents were treating us as well as they treated themselves. That not only satisfied my need to feel loved and therefore lovable, but also the sense of fairness that seems innate in children.

Nevertheless, as I read Bryan's feelings, I felt deep parallels. He had felt ashamed of his home and parents—and so had I. A house filled with dirty dishes, stacks of unwashed clothes, and a "crazy" mother had made me fantasize about a normal home where I could invite my friends. He had adopted cheerfulness and competence in school as a way of concealing the shame of sad feelings and "differentness"—and so had I.

I realized that Bryan had turned to the more rational and controllable world of first school and then work as a way of escaping emotions he did not want to feel—and so had I. I had even denied my need for vacations and periods of introspection, just as he had done. Though I had been lucky enough to find feminist work that was a direct way of helping myself and other women—and an indirect way of helping my mother—I had sometimes carried on these efforts at the expense of my own writing, and as an anesthetic to buried childhood emotions.

Only when I, like Bryan, was forced by one too many episodes of burnout to uncover those childhood sadnesses did I begin to see work as an irreplaceable part of my life, but not the whole of my life. And only then did I begin to focus on what I could uniquely do instead of trying to do everything—thus beginning to be far more effective as a worker.[12]

As Ross became his mother's surrogate husband, as I became my sister's father, as Katie became her mother's husband and her brother's mother, and as Gloria Steinem became her mother's mother, we forfeited our childhoods in return for the adult jobs of overresponsibility and overdoing. Workaholic kids grow into adults who believe that they cannot count on anyone else and that their very emotional, financial, and physical survival requires them to do everything themselves. These traits serve workaholics by providing them the psychological insulation of certainty and security that they manufactured to survive childhood.

Workaholics are damaged by these traits because their refusal to ask for help and their inability to delegate put them at risk for burnout. Paradoxically, the insulation of parentified children becomes their isolation, because, as adults, it is difficult for them to become fully involved in intimate relationships. They tend to be suspicious and unforgiving of people who procrastinate or who fail to follow through on commitments. Having renounced their own childhood need for care to attend to the designated family member, they pay a price in adulthood, where they carry forward a pattern of subjugation of self by attending to their work.

Suggestions for Clinicians

Workaholic kids are able to detach themselves emotionally from their stressful surroundings through the escape that their achievements and accomplishments provide. Along with this self-distancing comes a greater sense of emotional insulation, independence, and a more objective understanding of what's going on around them. Their early family misfortunes, instead of destroying their intellectual and creative potential, help motivate them, and in adulthood they become high achievers in their careers.

Caution with Labels

Clinicians have often overlooked workaholic kids because they are high functioning. It is important that professionals exercise caution in labeling children who appear to be high functioning, since the resilience of workaholic kids is also the source of their deeper feelings of inadequacy and poor self-esteem. Clinicians are advised not to discount the workaholic child simply because he or she appears to be functioning better than less competent children in the family. Workaholic children may, in fact, be in greater need than those who can reveal their vulnerability. The invulnerability may be a disguise for an inner misery that workaholic children are compelled to hide. Clinicians can be the best resource for these overfunctioning children by making sure that, while developing their talents and skills, these kids also get a chance to balance their personal lives to the maximum.

Mourning a Childhood Lost

The workaholic's defenses are strong. The unresolved hurt and pain of a lost childhood are buried under piles of ledgers, sales reports, and computer printouts. Here is where inner work —family-of-origin work—can help. It pinpoints how and why work became a haven in a dangerous world. And self-nurturing techniques give clients ways other than overwork to soothe themselves. When this work is done in the presence of the workaholic's partner, it can give the relationship some breathing room, as the spouse sees clearly that the work compulsion has ancient roots and is not a personal rejection of him or her. Once the childlike vulnerabilities have been uncovered, I teach clients ways to access their own nurturing abilities to consciously protect and nourish the childlike part that had been left behind. It also has been suggested that psychotherapy organized around the completion of mourning allows clients to master the consequences of role reversal in childhood.[13] Clinicians can help clients come to terms with the losses of their childhoods by helping them complete a delayed mourning process. Missing out on a magical and joyful childhood and one free of adult concerns is good reason to grieve. As clients recognize the parent's failure to nurture, emotionally protect, and provide a strong, wise, and loving figure for them, they uncover the feelings of anger, bitterness, sadness, despair, and sorrow that they have internalized. As they respond in time to the realization that their childhoods are lost forever to them, clients often travel through predictable stages of grief and loss that parallel the loss experienced by people mourning the death of a loved one. In a way, the period of mourning, from several months to several years, can be thought of as a grief process for the lost childhoods. Using the grief framework of the physician Elisabeth Kubler-Ross, clinicians can help clients see their progression through the stages of mourning and their emotional movement forward.[14] This grieving process can help clients remove their uptight, rigid, and inflexible masks and embrace that spontaneous, playful, and joyous child within—a part of themselves that they have disowned.

Inner-child work and the learning of self-parenting and nurturing skills is an integral part of the recovery process for careaholics and workaholics. Deep within each workaholic and each careaholic's heart is a wounded child whose needs are neglected. It is difficult for workaholics to access those inner feelings, and their barriers are difficult for psychotherapists to penetrate. Through the self-parenting process, clients learn to give to their inner child what they never got as children. This experience, in turn, leads them to allow others to give to them. Clinicians can encourage grief work around the loss of the safe and secure childhood. Supporting clients as they work out their anger, sadness, and hurt and get in touch with their playful inner child by learning to relax, play, and have fun is a worthy therapeutic goal.

Helping Clients Develop an Intimate Relationship with Themselves

While clients may believe that care and attention for themselves is selfish, wasteful, and counterproductive, the fact is the more they take care of themselves, the more they have to give and the more efficient they can be. Balancing the need to stay busy with a rich internal life can heal stress and burnout. Encourage clients to get to know themselves, to be their own best friends, and to treat themselves with the same respect and kindness with which they treat others. Have them think of themselves as a bank account. If they're always making withdrawals, they're headed for emotional bankruptcy. To stay "open for business," they need to make deposits in their personal accounts. Have them set aside fifteen minutes to an hour each day for themselves, and call it *internal time* or *daily deposit time.* They can use it in any way they choose—to go within to check with themselves, to collect their thoughts, to stay in touch with who they are, or to nurture themselves. Any of the following activities can help them get in tune with themselves: writing feelings down in a journal; listening to soft music with eyes closed, letting all thoughts go; reading daily devotionals; getting a facial, massage, or manicure; grooming themselves; soaking in a hot bath; going for a walk; or relaxing by a fire or on a cool screened porch. Whatever they decide to do, have them block all work-related thoughts or to-do lists as they try to enter their minds. They may go through withdrawal or feel boredom, restlessness, or depression at first. They may just want to sleep because of tiredness, and that's okay, too. It is natural for the body and the mind to resist attention when they're not used to getting it. Encourage clients to feel the boredom and restlessness, instead of medicating it with something to do. Have them sleep, walk, sit, and stare into space—whatever feels right. Have them recognize the symptoms and experience them and be aware of what their thoughts, feelings, and body say to them. Remind them to take it gradually, one step at a time.

Learning to Slow Down

By slowing down, workaholics can accomplish more and do a better job. In the process, they gain self-respect and admiration from coworkers. Clinicians can help clients make a conscious effort to slow down the pulse and rhythm of their daily lives by intentionally eating, talking, walking, and driving slower. Clinicians can help clients explore ways to prevent rushing by building time cushions between appointments and scheduling extra time to get to various destinations.

Meditation is a highly effective way to slow down and feel calm. The purpose of meditation is to quiet the mind so that the individual can hear what is already there. Scientific research has shown that meditation slows down heart rates and brain-wave patterns. It has a positive effect on the immune system so that certain life-sustaining hormones are secreted. Scientists have discovered that adults who meditate each day live longer than adults who do not.[15] Clinicians can suggest many types of meditation that can help workaholics unwind from work highs: relaxation exercises, yoga, quiet reflection, daily inspirational readings, prayer, or guided meditation. The following meditation exercise can be guided by the clinician or given to clients to help them slow down on their own:

In a quiet and comfortable place, close your eyes and get comfortable. Clear your mind of cluttered thoughts, and focus on your breathing. Inhale and exhale a few times. Let your body become completely relaxed from head to toe. Continue breathing and relaxing until you are in a totally relaxed state.

When you are relaxed, visualize yourself going through your day at a slow pace. Go through your daily routine from the time you get out of bed until the time you go to sleep that night. See yourself getting out of bed, having breakfast, getting dressed, and going to work.

Now see yourself at your workplace. Take yourself through your daily routine, all the while slowing yourself down. See yourself eating slower, driving slower, and doing one thing at a time. See the events of the day happening vividly, and imagine the smallest details of each one. Release any images you have of hurrying. Notice how you begin to feel as your routine slows down. How do others around you feel?

Pay close attention to your body. What does it need that it hasn't been getting? Pay attention to your mind. What does it need that it doesn't get? Pay close attention to your spiritual needs. What have they been missing? Next, think of how you can nurture your body, mind, and spirit.

Conclude your meditation by imaging going to bed at night. How do you feel as you drift off to sleep?

Don't be discouraged if you initially feel discomfort or even anxiety. Remember, you're changing habits that took a lifetime to form. Giving yourself attention and slowing down takes time, practice, and patience. Repeat this exercise as often as you feel the need. Each time you complete this meditation, notice how your feelings begin to change with practice and you feel more comfortable with taking a slower pace and nurturing yourself.[16]

Living in the Present

Clinicians can help clients become more aware of their preoccupation with the future to the exclusion of the present. In one exercise clients come up with ways they can begin living in the now and resisting the mind's attempts to preoccupy them with tomorrow or next week. Clinicians might suggest that clients rediscover things in their world that they take for granted or ignore and that they look at people and things around them as if they are seeing and enjoying them for the first time. Here is another meditation that can help clients slow down by staying in the present:

The next time you go to your workplace, imagine you have entered it for the first time. Look at the people and things around you as if you are seeing and appreciating them for the first time. Notice the entranceway, the architecture of the outside and inside of the building, and the people at their work stations. What's in the hallways and hanging on the walls? Notice the textures and colors of the wall, ceiling, and floor. Smell the flowers on someone's desk. Look at how your colleagues are dressed and the colors of their clothing. Notice who conforms and who marches to the beat of a different drum. Pay attention to the sounds you hear. Notice the smells in the air.

Be mindful of your coworkers' faces. Do they look happy or sad? Ready to embrace the day or wishing they were back home in bed? Are they smiling or frowning? Who has wrinkles and worry lines, and whose face is stress-free? Do people in this work environment touch or keep their distance? Do they affirm one another or put each other down with sarcasm and cutting remarks? Are they pulling together as a team or working against one another and coming apart at the seams? Pay close attention to as many sights, sounds, smells, tastes, and textures as you can. Look in people's eyes, behind their facial expressions, and into their hearts, where their true humanity resides. What do you see? What do you feel? What unseen baggage are your colleagues carrying with them into the workplace? How can you set the excess baggage aside and experience the true human being that lies beneath the surface? As you experience your workplace, you discover that the little things that you haven't noticed before are actually the most important things of all.

Participating in Life's Celebrations

Many workaholics refuse to break for birthdays, holidays, or even funerals, which has the effect of reinforcing their feelings of inadequacy: "I don't deserve to indulge myself." Clinicians can help clients reestablish the rituals and celebrations in their lives that have fallen by the wayside. Rituals are the glue that bind people together. Without them, we can feel separate, isolated, and disconnected from life. Taking time out to acknowledge rituals helps people realize the passage of time and the markers on the road of life. A child's recital or graduation or a loved one's birthday is a marker of time that needs acknowledging. Rituals can help workaholics to appreciate the here and now—"what is," rather than "what will be." Have clients evaluate the value they put on birthdays, graduations, anniversaries, reunions, and weddings in their lives. Emphasize the importance of taking time to recognize and celebrate their accomplishments and those of their loved ones and friends with vigor and enthusiasm.

Family-of-Origin Work

Family-of-origin work is essential for clients to fully understand work addiction. Clinicians can help clients understand their childhood family roles (e.g., hero, mascot, lost child, scapegoat) and how these roles functioned as survival responses to a dysfunctional family system.[17] A family systems approach to treatment can help workaholics examine more deeply their family-of-origin wounds that led them into work addiction. It is important to examine the etiology of the depression, anxiety, and anger that often drive the work addiction and to help clients find constructive outlets for the expression of these feelings. Drawing a *genogram*—a diagram of the family tree—can help clients to understand the intergenerational nature of addictions and to trace the origins of their own low self-esteem, difficulty with intimacy, perfectionism, and obsessive control patterns.

Origins-of-Work-Addiction Exercise

Clinicians can administer and discuss the following worksheet to help clients to probe more deeply the origins of their work addiction and to see how it serves them today:

Instructions:

1. In column 1, list what you are usually doing when you are overworking.
2. In column 2, record the purpose that work addiction serves.
3. In column 3, identify what you think the hidden fear is that the work addiction covers up.
4. In column 4, describe where the hidden fear comes from.

1. Overworking I do a lot of . . .	*2. Function because it makes me feel . . .*	*3. Fear to hide my fear of . . .*	*4. Childhood wound that comes from . . .*
Sample Responses:			
working to make money	in control of the future; secure	not having enough money	the message that resources are limited and will soon run out
taking on extra work	important, worthy	not being good enough	the belief that nothing I ever did was good enough
caretaking	needed	being unloved/ unimportant	the belief that I'm unlovable or that I'm not worth much

Now complete the table for yourself.

1.

2.

3.

4.

5.

6.

7.

8.

9.

10.

SELF-CARE PLAN

Write a self-care plan that will enable you to meet each of the needs that you listed in column 2 in a more balanced, healthy way than the ways you have used in the past to try to meet them (column 1).

7

Spouses and Partners of Workaholics

Americans generally spend so much time on things that are urgent that we have none left to spend on those that are important.

—HENRY WARD BEECHER

Renee

Having shared the past ten years of our lives together, I wanted to contribute to Ross's case,[1] because I feel spouses and families are all affected by the workaholic. Maybe a good way to start is to describe an average day.

The day normally starts the afternoon before. Upon arriving from the office, Ross walks straight to his study, checks the fax machine, opens his briefcase, then goes straight upstairs to take out of the closet the clean laundered shirt, pants, tie, and jacket for the next morning.

I find myself walking after him from room to room while he's in his own world, preparing, thinking, worrying, trying to talk to him, be it about his day, my day, or other issues about our family life. He does not stop until he's showered and had dinner. Almost certainly dinner will be interrupted at least once or twice with calls from the office.

He will read to unwind for a little while, and then he's off to bed. The only real conversation we have is the one about what has happened in his day. I often find myself asking him about his work just so I can have his attention. Our evening passes with him checking the fax machine at least every half hour. TV makes him "nervous," probably because he can't sit still and engross himself in anything outside his work. On a good day the children may have ten minutes of his time having a bit of play together. They do not demand much of him as they haven't shared with him their needs.

Our day starts very early, because Ross is full of energy. He will call me on an average of four or five times a day from the office. A lot of energy goes through our home, often nervous energy. There is no such thing as kicking our shoes off and having a carefree afternoon or weekend. Ideally for Ross every minute has to be planned. But plans are not always kept as he may have to travel, or he's too tired. An ideal evening on a weekend is a dinner at our home surrounded by people who are so impressed by Ross and his success, where he talks to them about his business success or entertains them with his jokes (he does have a great sense of humor). There is not much room for real friends, as very few people get to know him. There is not much time to spare either, because every minute of his day is dedicated to "building the business."

The start of every day is a walk to the fax machine before anything else. If the phone goes quiet, he will make it ring by calling people, generating work, expanding the business, following up on things. There is never a moment or an interest in developing a hobby or a set time to spend with his family. Our time with him is dictated by a lull in the business. Holiday time is virtually nonexistent, as it is usually linked to a business trip. Regardless of where we are in the world, we are dictated to by the business's time zone. We cannot go anywhere unless there is a phone and a fax machine available for his use.

On an emotional level, he's always in control. He knows how to manage people; he comes home and manages us.

And when it does not work, he's angry, very angry. There is little room to allow our emotions to flow in our household. When I express an opinion or stand up for what I believe, and it does not fit with Ross's "timing," as he calls it, our whole marriage is put on the line. There is no such thing as having a "fight" and forgiving and forgetting. It has to be days of sulking, pain, and disappointment and then a resurfacing of it again and again.

Often, when the day comes to a close, I wonder if many people live alone like me—always coming second-best to work. I don't say it in anger. It's just that I am watching a man who is capable of so much more love and sharing, who wants more out of life. And yet he walks up to the bedroom to prepare his clothes for the next day, rather than leave his business outside the door and take his children and wife in his arms.

Married to the Job

Renee's picture of the pain of living with a work-addicted husband follows a pattern common among partners of workaholics, who feel alone and isolated. She may have felt alone, but she is not alone: in 2001, I studied a random sample of 326 women members of the American Counseling Association, asking them to fill out questionnaires on their partner's work habits and the state of their marriage.[2] The 22 percent who reported being in workaholic marriages also reported far more marital estrangement, emotional withdrawal, and thoughts of separation and divorce than those whose partners were not workaholic. The workaholic husbands worked an average of nine and a half more hours a week than nonworkaholic husbands, and only 45 percent of the women married to workaholics were still married, compared to 84 percent of the women married to nonworkaholics. The spouses of workaholics also felt more helpless: they were more likely than the partners of nonworkaholics to report that external events controlled their lives.

In 2006 I repeated this study with a random sample of 272 men members of the American Counseling Association, asking them to rate their wives' work habits and the state of their marriages.[3] I found that the more husbands perceived their wives as workaholics, the more likely they were to say the women worked longer hours and to report their marriages as having greater incidences of marital estrangement and negative feelings. Together, these two studies suggest that the strength and cohesion of a marriage is associated with the presence or absence of a spouse's workaholism.

You have seen how the childhoods of workaholics predispose them to being more object focused than people focused. You also have seen how the workaholic mind-set is outer directed, geared almost exclusively toward task completion, to the point of neglecting oneself and the emotional needs of one's loved ones. This chapter illustrates how the workaholic neglect can negatively impact spouses and partners of workaholics. Has your partner failed to appear at family gatherings too many times because of work? Has your partner promised to spend more time with you and not delivered because work comes first? Has he or she said, "I'll quit tomorrow," but tomorrow never comes? Or has your partner stood you up or kept you waiting because of work? If you answered yes to these questions, your partner may be suffering from work addiction.

A woman said her workaholic husband had been away from his family for so long that he had grown a beard and mustache. When he showed up at home after six months, his two children didn't even know who he was. A workaholic mother was so chained to her job at the bank that on school holidays she took her three children to work with her, leaving them in her car in a parking deck. Her rationalization for her actions was that she had to get a report finished and that she went down to check on her kids every hour. Another workaholic husband arrived home after a hard day's work. When his wife asked about their son, whom he had taken to work for the day, the husband exclaimed, "Oh, my God! I forgot and left him at work!" The common theme in all these real-life examples is the emotional and/or physical absence of the workaholic from intimate relationships.

Often left with the responsibility of holding the family together, the mates of workaholics feel alone as partners *and* parents. They feel unimportant and minimized, even innately defective, because they get so little attention from their workaholic partners. They often harbor feelings of anger, resentment, sadness, and guilt. They live under a distinct set of unwritten and unspoken rules, dictated by the work habits of their loved one: Handle everything at home. Don't put expectations on me, because I have enough on my plate at work. Put me at the center of your life, and plan the household and family and social life around my work schedule. I'm depending on you to do your best, be perfect, and not let me down. Some partners have described the intimate, isolating times within the confines of the house and family as maddening. In rare cases, it has led to violence, as Edward Walsh reported:

> In February 1972, Earl D. Rhode, 28, a bright executive climbing the ladder of success, fell victim to a national aberration—workaholism. He returned to his suburban home in Washington, D.C., one evening after a long day at the office, with a briefcase bulging with work. The executive secretary of the Nixon administration's Cost of Living Council rested on the living room couch as his wife approached and then calmly put a bullet in his head. Then she killed herself. A newspaper story quoted neighbors as saying she had been complaining about her husband's seven-day workweek.[4]

Although most workaholics die from stress-induced illnesses, this rare case exemplifies the frustration that partners feel. Many say that life with their mates is a living nightmare, because they have little support from the mental health system, outside family, friends, and, least of all, the workplace. Their partners are perceived by society as superachievers and good providers. So what do they have to complain about?

Emma from New Jersey called me in anguish to say that her husband is doing a replay of ten years ago, when he left the relationship because of alcoholism. Now, after his successful recovery and the reestablishment of the marriage for another ten years, Emma says it's déjà vu. "Same story, different drug," she said, "but now it's work addiction that takes up 90 percent of his time. He eats, thinks, and breathes work. My marriage is going down the tubes again, and the therapists are saying, 'So what? He likes his job.'"

Barbara, the wife of the founder of Workaholics Anonymous, said, "Our lives revolve around the workaholics we married—around making excuses to friends why our spouses aren't at parties, making excuses to our children why daddy can't make birthday parties and baseball games."[5]

The biggest complaint partners have is neglect. A housewife said,

> I'm tired of sloppy seconds. After my husband finishes working, there's nothing left over for me and the kids. He's so tired, he just collapses in front of TV or falls asleep on the floor of his study in his clothes, with computer printouts covering him like a blanket.

Work, Work Everywhere, Not Any Time to Think

Families that include a workaholic have higher divorce rates than those that do not. A survey by the American Academy of Matrimonial Lawyers cited preoccupation with work as one of the top four causes of divorce. It makes sense that workaholic families would experience problems similar to those of alcoholic families, because of the similarity between the two addictions. A group of four hundred physicians was polled regarding their observations of workaholics as marital spouses. What follows is a summary of their responses:[6]

1. Workaholics devote an inordinate amount of time and effort to work for the following reasons, in descending order of frequency: inferiority feelings and fear of failure, compulsive defense against strong anxiety, need for approval, fear of personal intimacy, and sexual inadequacy.
2. Workaholics tend to choose spouses with more dissimilar than similar personalities.
3. Workaholics have higher than normal expectations for marital satisfaction.
4. Workaholics are much more demanding of achievement in their children.
5. The workaholic's typical approach to leisure time is to fill it with work activities.
6. The workaholic's usual style in marital fights is the avoidance of confrontation or passive-aggressive maneuvers, such as silence and sulking.
7. Workaholics are more likely than others to engage in extramarital affairs, while their spouses are less likely to do so.
8. Workaholics engage in marital sexual relations less frequently than other couples.
9. Workaholics are more prone to alcohol abuse than their nonworkaholic peers.
10. The most frequent sexual problems in workaholics, in descending order of frequency are emotional detachment, lack of sexual desire, routine and unvarying practices, inhibition of arousal, and inhibition of orgasm.

Sometimes partners feel jealous, even suspicious that an affair is taking place because of the spouse's long and late hours away from home. *Exec* magazine surveyed the work habits of three thousand men, and one-third reported having been accused of having an affair because of the long hours they had put into their jobs.[7] The survey also found that spending excessive time at the office can wreak havoc on family life. Eighty-six percent said their personal relationships were marred by work-related stress. Similar findings were reported in a survey by *McCall's* magazine, in which 80 percent of the readers said their husbands worked too much.[8] The phrase "wedded to work" illustrates this condition, and it knows no gender boundaries. Spouses of workaholics are not always wives. Where women are addicted to work, men become the suffering partners, as Elizabeth confessed:

> I remember my ex-husband saying to me, "I feel so lonely. You're here in this house and I feel so lonely." At the same time he was saying that, I felt lonely, too. And we couldn't come together. Work was what was filling us up, and he wanted me to fill him up, and I couldn't.

Another feeling frequently expressed by partners of workaholics is reflected in Eric's comment: "I feel like one of her employees and that the only way to be close to her is to join her in her work." And this is exactly what many do. Tears in her eyes, Valerie expressed her struggle with intimacy and work addiction this way:

> People think that the workaholic doesn't love them, and that's absolutely not true. It hurts me more than anything to think that my friends and family would think they're not important to me. Work addiction is like alcoholism, and workaholics have unfulfilled needs that they're trying to fill. It is sometimes uncontrollable. It just takes me over and carries me away. So family and friends need to be patient and need to educate themselves. That will help them understand the person they're with and care about. Work addiction is self-destructive, but it's also destructive to the people around you, if you're not careful.

Audrey, sixty-five years old, came to therapy because of a lingering unhappiness in her thirty-year-old marriage to her then-retired husband, Paul. She even had begun to question if she had ever loved him as she looked back over their marriage. For as long as she could remember, Paul had been unwilling to participate in family talks and casual pastimes, consumed instead by his engineering job, which provided them with a comfortable living and sent all five children to college. Paul had lapsed into "vital exhaustion," the withdrawal from family relationships.

Today, when Paul's now grown children visit, they still complain to Audrey about their father's sequestering himself in his workshop instead of sitting around and interacting with the family. Audrey, in turn, finds herself relaying the annoyances to her husband and feeling her resentment rise along with that of her children. She has started to realize that a large portion of time with her grown-up kids has been spent ganging up on and complaining about Paul. Unknowingly, for a lifetime, she has been caught between Paul and their five disenchanted children, trying to mediate, keep peace, and patch the brittle father-child relationships. She is tired and wary after carrying the family burden for so long. She has wept years of tears for the guilt she feels in creating the family divide and for not being able to repair it. She has cried for the pain she saw in Paul's confused face when he asks why the kids never seem to want to hug, kiss, or spend time with him. She has grieved for the hurt and resentment her sons and daughters still carry, evidenced by their stiffness and awkwardness when giving their father obligatory goodbye hugs. But, most of all, she has mourned the loss of an image of a family that never was and perhaps will never be. Table 7.1 presents a complete portrait of partners of workaholics, based on case studies and interviews.

Difficulty with Intimacy: When Your PalmPilot Is Your Best Friend

Workaholics tend to be what family therapists call minimizers in their couple relationships.[9] Minimizers withhold and minimize their feelings and are emotionally detached and withdrawn. In a marital argument they tend to be tight-lipped, cold,

TABLE 7.1
Portrait of the Partners and Spouses of Workaholics

- Feel ignored, neglected, closed out, unloved, and unappreciated because of the workaholic's physical and emotional remoteness
- Believe they are carrying the emotional burdens of the marriage and parenting, which brings a feeling of loneliness and aloneness in the relationship
- View themselves as second choice behind work, because family time is dictated by work schedules and demands, which come first
- Perceive themselves as extensions of the workaholic, who must be the center of attention
- View themselves as controlled, manipulated, and sometimes rushed by their partners, who "call the shots"
- Use attention-seeking measures to get their partners to see them or give in to conversations and activities around work in order to connect with them
- View the relationship as serious and intense, with a minimum of carefree time or fun
- Harbor guilt for wanting more in the relationship, while their partners are applauded by colleagues and society for their accomplishments
- Have low self-esteem and feel defective, in some way unable to measure up to their partners, who are often put on a pedestal
- Question their own gratitude and sanity when faced with the accolades bestowed on their workaholic partner

noncommunicative, and unfeeling. Intimate feelings are difficult because emotions are frozen. Constant work keeps workaholics numb, their feelings buried in the deep freeze, and emotionally disconnected from loved ones. When workaholics enter intimate relationships, there are bound to be problems. They handle relationship issues by wishing they would go away, putting them off, or ignoring them altogether. They preserve their own space by keeping their thoughts and feelings to themselves, making it difficult for their partners to know what they think or feel.[10] When workaholics share with their partners, it is more often about their work or logical and rational thoughts rather than feelings. Requests for closeness feel to workaholics like demands that would distract them from their goal-directed work. They often feel hounded by well-meaning loved ones who say, "Why don't you just cut back?" They don't understand that this is not as easy as it sounds.

Workaholics and their spouses or partners are often caught in the pursuer-distancer interaction style, which can be described as the "workaholics are from Mercury and their partners are from Jupiter" syndrome. I observe this phenomenon in couple therapy with 90 percent of the couples I see. This is an interactional dynamic that clinicians can almost count on between workaholics and their partners. Workaholics and their partners are coming from two totally different emotional worlds in which workaholics want distance and their spouses want closeness. So partners of workaholics pursue their mates for emotional closeness and affection, while workaholics (who are threatened by this closeness) retreat by throwing themselves into work or making themselves emotionally unavailable through preoccupation with work. The more partners pursue, the more workaholics flee. This interaction, which becomes circular, was shown in the Smith family by the stereotypical—but true—nature of Dorothy's "nagging" and Jack's withdrawing (see chapter 4).

Partners of workaholics, more than anyone else, feel the shield that their loved ones use to protect themselves from closeness and intimacy. The barriers are hard to penetrate, and workaholics have few or no friends. Their tools of trade are their best friends, because they don't have to worry about disappointing their faxes, falling short of their computer's standards, or hurting the feelings of their day-at-a-glance. They immerse themselves in their jobs, which are structured, predictable, and controllable and which are safer for them than immersing themselves in close, personal, and intimate relationships. Workaholics who excel at work but not at home in personal relationships are likely to spend more time in areas where they feel most competent. And these behaviors are encouraged and supported by our culture, which deifies the remote, controlled, rapid-fire-paced image of men as ideal (see chapter 2). Daniel Goldstein is a case in point:

> "What a week," Daniel Goldstein says to his secretary as she turns out the lights in his advertising agency.
>
> "What's so different about this week?" she wonders. Sunday through Tuesday, he flew over 10,000 miles. The rest of the week he spent on the phone nonstop. Now, he wants a fifth phone in

> his office because talking on four phones at once isn't enough. In total, he clocked over 70 hours.
>
> She puts on her coat, ready to leave. "Go ahead," he tells her, "I've got one more thing to do . . . see you Monday."
>
> Nervously, he sifts through his in-box. At the bottom, he finds what he's looking for: a 200-page proposal that needs extensive revision. It's not due for another month, "but what the hell," he says to himself, "It'll give me something to work on this weekend." Sure, his wife won't be happy. So what's new? Anyway, she's gotten pretty good at leaving him alone.[11]

Workaholics treat their relationships like they treat their jobs, because that's what they're best at doing. They use the same control, hard-driving perfectionism to relate to family members that they do with coworkers. Dictating and organizing, workaholics run their households like a work camp, and spouses often say they are treated like employees on work detail. A teenage son's ballgame must be scheduled; a partner is expected to share intimacy on command.

Workaholics tend to forget, ignore, or minimize important family rituals and celebrations, such as birthdays, anniversaries, or children's recitals. They may feel they cannot stop long enough to participate fully, because such events require total immersion of their time and energy. While accomplished in their chosen fields, they can be inept at home and in the social world because those are not their areas of expertise. They may appear helpless with small things and lacking in common sense. Learning to set a digital watch or to assemble a children's toy can be maddening because it takes precious moments away from what seem to be more important work tasks. They may have few social skills and few interests outside work, often remaining silent in social conversations that do not pertain to their work interests.

This sense of lostness or helplessness among workaholics when they are not working is especially noticeable during vacations, holidays, and retirement. On their trip across Europe, Wendy handled all the details of the plans. She kept Tim's wallet and passport and arranged their daily trips to museums, tours, and sightseeing. In Russia she computed the change ratio from dollars to rubles and made the actual exchange. Tim dutifully followed her lead from Scandinavia to the Mediterranean, almost as if this were an unspoken bargain. I call this the "Let's Make a Deal" syndrome: "I'll traipse all over the world with you and indulge your every whim, but I expect you to let me work without interruptions or complaints." In this way a tacit contract gets played out in ways that couples don't usually realize. Some workaholics bargain to win release from family obligations by telling a spouse, "I'll go with you to the wedding next weekend if you'll keep the kids out of my hair today and tomorrow so that I can finish the sales report." Promises to cut down on work or spend more time with family are more often broken than kept. As the weekend approaches, there's more work to be done, accompanied by an apologetic refrain: "Sorry, honey. Looks like you and the kids will have to go without me."

Helplessness is also observed among workaholics during retirement. Japanese wives use the derogatory term *nure-ochiba* (a wet fallen leaf) to refer to retired workaholic husbands who do not know what to do with themselves when they are not working and who hang around the house expecting their wives to be in charge of their spare time:

> They follow their wives around, like unwanted, wet fallen leaves which are stuck to the bottom of one's shoes. Thus, competencies developed at work are not necessarily transferable to a post-retirement lifestyle. The wife has lived all these years without her work-immersed husband's support, and has achieved emotional independence and ego-identity. She possesses appropriate skills for social survival and networking. On the other hand, the husband may lack such skills. He is like a fish out of water, becomes dependent upon his wife, while the latter feels annoyed with him who constantly disrupts her routine and demands her attention.[12]

Concealment and Deceit in the Couple Relationship

Workaholics do not tolerate obstacles to their working. If someone stands in their way, they take either an aggressive approach of blowing up or a passive-aggressive approach of sneaking their stash. Work goes everywhere the workaholic goes, regardless of what family or friends say: in briefcases or luggage, under car seats, in glove compartments, in car trunks, beneath spare tires, in dirty laundry bags, stuffed inside pants or inside skirt, and, in one case, hidden in a secret compartment of another person's suitcase, unbeknownst to that person.

Sometimes workaholics cave in to their partners' demands by concealing their work in an effort to please and to avoid criticisms, much like an alcoholic who hides beer bottles.[13] They may hide memos or files in their suitcases, pretend to rest while their partner goes off to the grocery store, or feign going to the gym and working out at the end of the day in order to sneak in an extra hour or two at the office. Mildred dealt with the stress and anxiety caused by her husband's expectation that she be home with him by five by telling him she had enrolled in an aerobics class after work. Her husband was thrilled that she was finally taking an interest in activities outside work. The truth was, however, that Mildred was working two hours overtime, changing in her office from business outfit to aerobic garb, tousling her hair, and dampening her tights with water—all to convince her husband that she was coming around.

In his book *Working,* Studs Terkel describes how the broadcast executive Ward Quaal concealed his working from his family:

> I get home around six-thirty, seven at night. After dinner with the family, I spend a minimum of two and a half hours each night going over the mail and dictating. I should have a secretary at home just to handle the mail that comes there. I'm not talking about bills and personal notes, I'm talking about business mail only. Although I don't go to the office on Saturday or

> Sunday, I do have mail brought out to my home for the weekend. I dictate on Saturday and Sunday. When I do this on holidays, like Christmas, New Year's, and Thanksgiving, I have to sneak a little bit, so the family doesn't know what I'm doing.[14]

Kate's work obsession became her weekend lover. She lied to her family so that she could rendezvous with work at the office:

> I'd tell my family that I was going shopping on a Saturday and I'd end up in my office working. Or I'd tell them I was going to my girlfriend's house. After calling my girlfriend's and not finding me, they'd call the office and say, "I thought you were going to Dottie's." I felt like I'd been caught with my hand in the cookie jar.

Workaholics may comply with pressures to curb work by the "white-knuckling approach"—going through the motions of a cocktail party or Caribbean vacation, child's ballgame or recital. Although present in body, in their heads they are often back at the office working. The spouse of a workaholic described her husband's inability to let go and enjoy himself:

> It's really difficult to pull him away from any of his work activities. He gets really anxious when he's not working, and then I feel guilty if I try to get him to do something with me other than work. I wind up feeling as if I have deprived him of something.

Concealment serves the purpose of lowering tensions in the couple relationship. But when the truth is revealed, partners often feel betrayed and mistrustful, and couple relationships suffer brutal, sometimes irreparable damage because of the deceit. Once workaholics have entered the lying and concealment stage, it reflects their desperation and their inability to say no. Professional help is often required at this juncture for workaholics and their partners.

Suggestions for Clinicians

Clinicians can provide counseling for couples whose marriages have been damaged by work addiction. Change, however, does not come easy or fast for workaholic couples, and change is necessary for all family members if the damage is to be repaired.

Preparing Families for Change

Expectations of change in workaholics require that family members, who have built a pattern of reactions to their loved one's work addiction, be prepared to change as well. They may have gotten into the habit of complaining or being cynical about the compulsive working, and workaholics may have withdrawn into "vital exhaustion." Clinicians who work with couples to restructure the family system must be prepared for resistance on both sides. The parent who has single-handedly raised the kids, for example, may become resentful when suddenly their work-addicted partner decides to take a more active role in parenting. Reversing these types of patterns can evoke anger and hurtful feelings of "where were you ten years ago?" and can lead to turf battles. Family members may be sending the workaholic mixed signals by complaining about his or her absence and, as movement back into the family system occurs, complaining about his or her attempts at integration. Family members also need to be made aware of the double bind they create by complaining about the work addict's overworking in one breath and making unreasonable financial demands in another. In some cases, they must be willing and prepared to sacrifice financial advantages in return for less time spent working and an increased presence and participation by the workaholic in the family.

Several clinical approaches can be taken to help workaholics and their loved ones who, not unlike alcoholic families, are entrenched in denial. Outwardly, workaholic families appear immune from the effects of the hard-driving, compulsive behaviors. Workaholics in particular mask their anxiety, depression, or fear of not being in control by demonstrating resiliency, perfectionism, overresponsibility, or self-reliance to the point of having difficulty asking for help. Family members often are reluctant to come forward for fear of being branded "ingrates" for the material rewards generated by the workaholic lifestyle. Typical workaholic families dance around this huge "elephant in the living room" without acknowledging its presence, which builds tension and resentment. By helping couples identify and express their feelings about the problem, it is possible to reduce tension and reactivity and set the stage for further work.

Working with the Pursuer-Distancer Dynamic

During the therapeutic process, clinicians need to be aware of the troublesome pursuer-distancer dynamic and to take steps to help couples identify and correct it. Naming the pursuer-distancer interactional style in therapy sessions helps couples recognize it and gives them something concrete to work on in their daily interactions. Helping couples understand the transmission of their respective roles from their families of origin also helps them take responsibility as a couple for their relationship, instead of blaming each other.[15]

Workaholics often distance themselves during therapy sessions, at which time clinicians can gently prompt them to invest more of themselves to effect change. The family therapist Stephen Betchen cautions clinicians not to enlist or enable pursuers to play cotherapist, which often unconsciously happens. When clinicians and pursuers align, workaholics feel ganged up on and withdraw even more. Because pursuers do both their relationship work and that of their spouse, Betchen recommends the following approach:

> Clearly, the pursuer is the overfunctioning, overresponsible spouse, and I often tell her that she overworks her relationship. I let the underresponsible distancer know that when he abdicates responsibility in his relationship, he is more likely to be

controlled by his spouse—something I know he is deeply concerned about.[16]

When working with couples affected by work addiction, I have observed that the more one spouse pursues, the more the other retreats. I often use this analogy with clients: "When it's hailing [the pursuer], the turtle pulls its head in his shell [the distancer], and as long as it's hailing, the turtle is not going to stick its neck out." To break this cycle, I suggest that the pursuing spouses consciously and deliberately pull back or take a vacation from working the relationship and that workaholics take more responsibility for their part by pursuing. Each party must embrace part of the role of the other. Pursuers can change by ceasing to offer unsolicited advice, no longer expecting distancers to join them at social events, no longer pushing for physical contact, or ceasing to constantly ask distancers if they love them. Distancers can learn to express their intimate feelings, create romantic dinners with candlelight and flowers, invite the pursuer to special social events, and initiate conversations by asking their partners about their day.

The effect of having pursuers withdraw is that it gives distancers the psychological space they need to take more initiative in the relationship. As distancers increase their interest in and attention to the relationship, pursuers ultimately get the closeness they have been seeking, and the couple is able to meet at an emotional halfway point. Other clinical evidence documents that distancers move closer to their partners when pursuers reduce their pursuing.[17]

Nourishing the Overworked Relationship

The typical twenty-first-century couple relationship is overworked. After spending all day at the office, couples spend evenings cooking meals, attending to children, and, in some cases, preparing work for the next day. Busyness and doing infiltrate the relationship to the point that intimate relationships are replaced with business relationships: discussing financial concerns, hassles of the job, headaches with the kids, problems with day care or school, juggling family schedules and children's activities, and preparing meals for the next day. Eventually, these overworked relationships start to show the same signs of stress and fragility as the individual workaholic: irritability, tension, and exhaustion. In problematic relationships, couples may have shut down completely and not talk at all, in which case television or late-night work often becomes a replacement for companionship.

Relationships must have attention to stay vital. Workaholic families need help in learning to negotiate boundaries around the amount of time they spend working together, talking about work, or discussing family business or scheduling issues. These boundaries must be tailored to the unique schedules and lifestyles of each couple. One possibility is to eliminate work after a set evening hour and to carve out a set time every evening (without television) for intimate conversations about non-work-related matters. Mealtime is a great time to put these boundaries in place; another possibility is to set aside the time immediately after the partner arrives home, as Renee and Ross did. Two days after I received Renee's story (which introduced this chapter), I received a fax from her husband, Ross, which explained the new boundaries he had set:

> Good afternoon, Bryan. Renee's letter to you made me think again. I am working at small things, like leaving the briefcase in the car when I arrive, spending the first half hour with her alone. In other words, I'm giving her the time she needs. There is no doubt that when I do this, she is indeed very happy. It is when I don't that there is chaos. I must give her time, and I am working at this. It is tough to break those lousy habits, but I will get better at it, I promise. Warm regards, Ross.

Couples can learn that work does not have to dominate their conversations but that they can discuss work frustrations and successes as all healthy couples and families do. Boundaries also can be set around making weekend working the exception rather than the rule and barring work from vacations. Establishing appropriate boundaries around work is essential in today's society to protect the fragile intimacy in relationships. One way clinicians can guide couples through a couple-care plan to achieve balance in their relationship is to use the procedures for the self-care plan outlined in chapter 3. Using the categories of (1) couple relationship, (2) family, (3) play, and (4) work, couples can separately and together compute REMAINDER scores for each area and then name three or four activities or goals for each area that they can use to bring healthier boundaries and greater balance to their relationship. The content of the couple-care plan can make for lively discussion and invigorate an otherwise neglected or overworked relationship.

Helping Partners Learn to Communicate

As the family unit tries to change its dynamics, additional goals may be to work on effective problem solving, better communication, more clearly established family roles, greater affective responses, more affective involvement, and higher general family functioning—all of which are often problem areas within the workaholic family system.[18]

Tension builds in families that have refused to acknowledge and discuss their problems, and angry outbursts may occur over trivial events that have nothing to do with the real problem. Clinicians can help families talk about the problems and communicate how they feel by providing a communication structure such as active listening or the couple's dialogue, the framework used in Imago Relationship Therapy to ensure that listening, understanding, and empathy are reciprocal.[19] Imago Relationship Therapy is an excellent approach not only to build communication among couples but also to help couples understand how their family-of-origin experiences get recast in unconscious ways, causing problems in their current relationship.

By facing the problems and getting their feelings out in the open, families can reduce tension and address the real source of conflict. Treatment issues must address intimacy problems as they are manifested in the present family and social functioning of the workaholic. The most common clinical observation is the psychological shield workaholics hide behind to avoid closeness with their families. It is important to help workaholics identify when and why they dissociate and to learn to stay in the present and to communicate with loved ones. Clinicians can facilitate the process for partners of workaholics, helping them to express their feelings of isolation, abandonment, anger, resentment, guilt, hurt, and sadness to the workaholic. The mates can share their hopes and dreams and disappointments for the relationship. They can share their fears that the partners in the relationship are drifting apart. They can share how it feels to be kept waiting or stood up and what it's like living with a stranger who escapes in work. With the right help, partners of workaholics can have compassion for the difficulty their companions have in controlling the compulsion to overwork without making themselves doormats to the abusive work style. Bibliotherapy resources for family members are often helpful in this regard (see chapter 10).

Interventions

Clinicians can assist family members in interventions when work addiction becomes life threatening. Forgetfulness, chronic fatigue, grouchiness, mood swings, and physical ailments related to stress all indicate that the body is burning out. Families can lovingly share their concerns for their workaholic's health and encourage him or her to consult a physician. They can ask the addicted family member to go with them for counseling and, if the addict refuses, get help for themselves through a support group or continued individual therapy.

In severe health cases, a family intervention might be appropriate. Family interventions with workaholics are conducted similarly to those used with alcoholics. The workaholic is lovingly confronted by family, friends, and significant colleagues (e.g., employers, supervisors, or employees) under the supervision of an experienced family therapist. Each person tells the workaholic how it feels to watch him or her deteriorate and explain what he or she plans to do (threats are never used) about the relationship unless the workaholic gets personal help with the problem.

8

Children of Workaholics

My child arrived just the other day, came into the world in the usual way, but there were planes to catch and bills to pay; he learned to walk while I was away.

—HARRY CHAPIN

Charles

My father had two loves: work and bourbon. He also, of course, loved his two sons, but we learned at an early age that being close to our father required entering his world of ambitious interests and endless cycles of working, drinking, sleeping. Our house ran on our father's energy. When the phone rang, as it frequently did just as we sat down to an already delayed, late-evening family dinner, it was usually a graduate student or colleague calling for my father. "Oh, damn!" he'd say as he jumped to his feet and raced from the dining room into his study. Sometimes I would groan as he made his quick exit, but usually my mother, sister, and I would just sit in silence, staring and continuing to eat until he returned with the latest tale of upheaval in the department or of the almost nervous breakdown his advisee was having over an oral comprehensive.

My father's life seemed exciting, passionate, and important. By comparison, everyone else's life seemed less so.

Childhood pleasures like the state fair, shooting basketballs through a new goal, picnics, going fishing or to the pool, learning to ride a bike without training wheels, or carving the Halloween pumpkin were all scheduled around Dad's work and often were simply endured by him in a state of irritation or, worse, exhaustion after long hours "at the office." It was clear from the start that family life and "traditional" family activities came second and were actually rather trivial compared to the adult world of work, politics, ambition, collegiality. Even vacations to the beach involved taking along favored graduate students. If students couldn't come with us, my father would make contacts with colleagues and former students in a nearby town to come visit. Over shrimp and beers, they would give him the latest scope on the local school system or reminisce with him about his early years as a bachelor high school chemistry teacher in this same nearby beach town.

My father's (and thus also my mother's) friends were his students and former students. I realize now that his mentoring of these young, admiring professionals occupied his time and energy and left me, his oldest son, competing with handsome, bright male graduate students for his love and attention.

When he brought home his favorite students or colleagues to drink and "talk shop" late into the evening, he was at his best: happy, lively, and eloquent. As a small boy on these nights of discussion and drinking, I would run rambunctiously in and out of the living room where he was holding forth and in childish ways would compete for his audience's attention or, perhaps, actually for his attention by asking questions, making noises, or hiding and jumping out from behind the sofa to scare everyone. Usually Dad would just give me a hug and then firmly direct me out of the room to find Mom (who was sequestered in her bedroom) so that she could give me a bath and put me to bed, usually well past the designated hour. These were the fun nights in the house filled with my father's business company, their laughter, their serious and meaningful conversation. I remember nights like these throughout my entire childhood and adolescence.

As I grew older, I learned to sit quietly and listen, watching Dad as he related to his students and colleagues. If I was quiet and didn't interrupt I could stay in the same room with him, and this was very important to me since it was often the only contact I would have with him for days at a time except when he would sleepily drive me to school (almost late) the following mornings. As I grew still older, I learned to enter into these conversations about philosophy, politics, child development, educational curriculum, John Dewey, Martin Buber, and other topics of interest to my dad, and thus topics I too attempted to read about and understand. I did my ninth-grade English project on existentialism. I learned to make strong percolated coffee and serve it to him in his study when he would write until two, three, or four in the morning. My bedroom was next door to his study, and I loved to try to stay awake reading as late into the night as his light was still on, and I would get out of bed, go to his study door, and see him sitting, focused intensely, at his desk, wearing his black horn-rimmed glasses. It seemed as if I was constantly interrupting him and distracting him from something very important.

My father was always "at work," whether at the office, hovered over his desk at home, or entertaining his students and "talking shop." When I was very little I would beg him to play with me in the evenings when he would come home from his office without his students. "Daddy's tired," he'd say as he slumped in a chair. I would grab his arm and pull him to get up to play cowboys with me, which at times he would agree to begrudgingly, and then, in a less than enthusiastic tone, he would respond to my piercing war cries with a distracted "bang, bang." Even then I remember feeling mad at him for being so tired and disinterested in my childhood fantasies and dramas.

I was always the little warrior in our family. I raged and cried at canceled camping trips, at my father's out-of-town consulting jobs, which took him away for days, and at his sleeping till noon on the weekends when I wanted him up to be with me. At a very young age I would follow him to his university office on Saturdays and Sunday afternoons to play alone in the science lab with the hamsters and gaze at anatomy books while he labored in a nearby office. It was lonely, but it was a way to be near him, so I always behaved and was trusted fully to take care of myself and not interrupt him too often. When he'd take a coffee break, we'd walk to the soda shop across the street, and I'd get a vanilla ice cream cone and, in our return to the office, would ask him to "Watch!" as I balanced myself walking along the ivy-covered stone wall lining the sidewalk. I was happiest when I was with my dad, even if it meant learning the importance and priority of his work over my childish whims and wishes.

When I cried and yelled at him for "always working," my little brother just sucked his fingers and watched quietly. Mom was depressed and often in her bedroom, or even hospitalized for extended periods with what later in the sixties was diagnosed as manic depression. Manic depression, I now muse, was an appropriate illness to have in my family. If she was to have a mental illness, manic depression certainly complemented her husband's waxing and waning energies. Dad's work cycles of all-night writing binges, teaching, and long hours with students at home or at the office were always followed by periods of intense exhaustion when he would sleep for long periods or sluggishly mope around the house, relax with his bourbon, and sleep more.

Dad had his first heart attack at forty-two. In my fifteen-year-old eyes he seemed so old, even fragile. His doctors told him to quit smoking his four packs per day, stop drinking caffeine, and stop eating the New York strips he loved to cook and serve generously to his protégés during those late-night sessions after bourbon rendered them ravenous at ten o'clock without dinner. His doctors also told him to exercise more, work less, reduce stress, and consume no more than two alcoholic beverages daily. In other words, at forty-two my father was told to change just about every aspect of his life that had so much been the source of his greatest success and pleasure: hard working, hard drinking, smoking, and late-night talking and dining. Although then, in my usual fashion, I was so angry at him and his failed attempts to reform himself, I realize now how very sad it was to watch his feeble efforts to smoke less, drink less, and be with his students less.

In the year before he died, I remember he would sometimes spend an entire weekend in bed or in a recliner reading a novel. In my early twenties, when I would return to my parents' home for visits, the students didn't come to the house as much, and I didn't hear anymore about his dreams of starting experimental schools or becoming president of a university. He was at home more, less busy, quieter, sadder. I didn't realize then what was happening. I thought he was just getting older—after all he was almost fifty. He died at fifty-one of a coronary after a full day at the office. My grandmother, his mother, said my father would have wanted it that way—to have worked fully every day of his life until he died. I was twenty-four when he died. I'm now forty-two, and fifty-one doesn't seem all that old.

Sometimes I go to professional baseball games and watch the fathers with their sons and daughters. The kids are so excited, and the fathers buy them things, hold them on their laps, and talk to them about the game, pointing, whispering in little ears, and them jumping up, arms waving, with loud joyous cheers. I don't really like ballgames now. I find them boring, no fun, a waste of time. But when I was a child, I wanted so much for my father to take me to ballgames like other dads. But he was either too busy or too disinterested in sports and the heroes like Mickey Mantle and Roger Maris whom I, as an eight-year-old, adored. Who knows? Maybe if he had taken me to some of those games before the age my stodgy boredom set in, I would know how to enjoy baseball now.

When I watch those children with their dads at ballgames, I get a glimpse of what it means to have lost the moments childhood offers us all, however so briefly, to know pure excitement over something simple and playful. My father worked through most of my childhood. And he hasn't been around for any of my adulthood.

Carrying the Legacy of the Pretty Addiction

In 1983 Janet Woititz wrote a small book that became a bestseller, *Adult Children of Alcoholics*. The book sold millions of copies and started a movement among legions of adults who had grown up in homes with alcoholics and who had been affected in ways of which they had been unaware. During the 1980s, a lot of research on adult children of alcoholics was published, and it showed this population to be at risk for a variety of problems.[1] Parental alcoholism was linked to low self-esteem in children and higher external locus of control, depression, and anxiety in adults. Adult children of alcoholics were awakened to an insidious legacy that was influencing their adult mental health, their intimate relationships, and, in some cases, their careers. The Woititz book, credited with starting the recovery movement of the late 1980s and early 1990s, opened the door for a flood of other popular books on codependency, dysfunctional families, and the inner child.

This chapter is about the other side of this story that has yet to be told—the pretty side of addiction that looks so good on parents and that is also becoming on their children. Despite the abundance of studies on children of alcoholics, the research on children of workaholics is slim. Clinical reports suggest, that, while attempting to medicate emotional pain by overworking, workaholics suffer some of the same symptoms as alcoholics.[2] My own clinical studies suggested that children who live in workaholic families are negatively affected and that work addiction can be destructive to children, who may experience coping problems similar to those of children of alcoholics.[3]

But near the turn of the century, still not one scientific study had been conducted on children of workaholics. So my research team at the University of North Carolina at Charlotte set out to study workaholics and their families in the same ways researchers had studied alcoholics and their families. We began by launching the first study on adult children of workaholics by giving a battery of tests to 211 young adults (average age twenty-four).[4] Using the WART, we asked them to rate their parents on workaholic tendencies. On the basis of the ratings, parents were grouped as either workaholics or nonworkaholics. Then we asked the young adults to rate themselves on depression, anxiety, and locus of control. Adult children of workaholic fathers had statistically higher levels of depression and anxiety and felt that events outside themselves controlled their lives, compared to adults from homes where fathers carried an average workload.

We concluded that children who grow up with workaholic fathers carry their psychological scars well into adulthood. These scars manifest as an outer-directed reliance on others for decision-making and a lack of inner confidence associated with greater anxiety and depression than are found in the population at large. These results match similar findings among adult children of alcoholics, compared to adult children of nonalcoholics.[5]

Although our sample was a select group of university students, two other studies followed on the heels of our research and replicated our findings with two different populations. One conducted at the California Graduate Institute surveyed a sample of 107 working nurses.[6] The other, conducted at the University of South Australia in 2000, tested 125 first-year university students.[7] Both studies found that children of workaholics, compared to children of nonworkaholics, had significantly higher depression and anxiety levels, more incidences of obsessive-compulsive tendencies, rated their families as more dysfunctional, and were at higher risk for workaholism themselves.

In 2000 I wanted to see if there was a difference in the psychological adjustment between children of workaholics and children of alcoholics. So I tested 207 young adults (average age twenty-five) at the University of North Carolina at Charlotte. Those who reported growing up with a workaholic parent had higher depression levels (as measured by the Beck Depression Inventory) and higher rates of parentification (as measured by the Jurkovic Parentification Questionnaire) than a control group of adult children from alcoholic homes. And children of workaholics reported that parents worked significantly more hours than did parents of children of alcoholics.[8]

These statistics match the stories I have received from readers far and wide who described patterns of failed marriages and anxiety and depression with no obvious causes—adults who seemingly came from picture-perfect childhoods.

Unlike alcoholic families, where children can point to the bottle as a source of their discontent, however, in workaholic families there is no tangible cause for the confusion, guilt, and inadequacy. If Dad drank too much, the child could point to the bottle; if Mom was strung out on pills, the drugs might explain her unusual mood swings. But the American work ethic prohibits children from faulting their parents for hard work or from viewing workaholism as a bad thing. So the logical conclusion that children of workaholics draw from their childhoods is that "something must be wrong with me." After all, workaholic parents are usually highly successful and responsible and may even hold leadership positions in the community. Their overachieving is sanctioned by society, the community, and, often, the church. So why should the family member complain about an upstanding contributor to society? Acknowledging the existence of a problem can bring up guilt and disloyalty; after all, the family has it so good because everything is so perfect. Children of workaholics often silently reprimand themselves for being the unappreciative "bad guy" who has nothing to complain about.

Charles and millions of other adult children of workaholics carry the legacies of this pretty addiction into their adult lives. Karen is another example of the many adults I have seen in my practice who suffer from having grown up in the best dressed of addictions. Her first marriage ended on a bright sunny day while she was vacationing in Yosemite National Park. Relishing the sunshine on her face, the smell of the clean fresh air, and the breathtaking natural beauty, she turned to share the experience with her husband, who was on his cellular phone to Argentina, grunting and kicking the dirt, because he had just lost a huge business deal. The loneliness of this marriage paralleled the loneliness she had felt with her father, a physician who was physically and emotionally absent during her early years.

Now, as she and her current husband sat before me, her second marriage was on the rocks, partly for the same reasons. Huge tears flowed down her cheeks faster than she could dab them away. Her guilty conscience said that she should stay in the marriage and make it work (even though she didn't want to) and sacrifice her needs, although another part of her was screaming to figure out who she was. After all, she'd spent her entire life pleasing everybody else. How selfish of her to entertain the idea of pursuing her own happiness. From the age of five, she had been taught that performing, being perfect, and accommodating the needs of others was her life's work. Never mind what she wanted, needed, or felt. Play the role, achieve, produce. Both husbands had been emotionally vacant, and she felt disconnected and emotionally sterile living with them. The distance felt so familiar to her because it echoed the same painful loneliness she had felt growing up with her workaholic father.

This scene is repeated over and over again in therapists' offices around the country. There is no label for it. There are millions of adult children of workaholics who are confused and in pain but don't understand why. Many are unaware that their parents were workaholics or that parental work addiction, insinuating itself into their lives at an early age, continues to play a role in their adult mental health. They are fumbling badly in relationships, are self-critical, anxious, depressed, and willing to accommodate whomever they are with at the moment. Most of what we know about children of workaholics is based on case studies and a handful of clinical observations. Although embryonic, the information we glean from case studies is insightful. Table 8.1 presents a picture of adult children of workaholics, painted from this small body of literature.

"Daddy Gone": Growing Up with a Workaholic Parent

Case studies indicate that workaholics are physically and psychologically unavailable to their kids, that they generally do not take an active role in their children's development, and that their offspring become resentful of the emotional absence.[9] According to the management consultant Marilyn Machlowitz, "It is easier for him [the workaholic] to be a mentor than a parent, because there is more distance. I have heard workaholics talk in glowing terms about students and subordinates and yet never speak with such delight about their own offspring."[10]

In interviews, adult children of workaholics revealed that they had four major concerns regarding their parents' work addiction.[11] *Preoccupation* was the most significant concern. The second was *haste*—their parents were always rushing around. The third was *irritability*; parents were so deeply involved in their work that it made them cross and cranky. Related to the fact that the children felt that their work-addicted parents took work too seriously and lacked humor was the fourth concern, parental *depression* about work. All four signs were present in the case of Charles.

Desperate for love and attention, Charles pulled every antic his child's mind could dream up to get his father to notice and spend time with him. Those futile quests, leaving him feeling

TABLE 8.1
Portrait of Adult Children of Workaholics

Adult children of workaholics tend to be:

- Outwardly focused conformists
- Self-critical
- Self-disparaging people who feel unworthy and incompetent for not being able to meet others' expectations
- Depression prone
- Approval seekers striving to make up for self-inadequacy
- Performance-driven perfectionists who judge themselves by their accomplishments, rather than by their inherent worth
- Overly serious people who have difficulty having fun
- Prone to feelings of disloyalty and guilt for acknowledging a problem in their picture-perfect family, which, on the surface, has provided them with everything
- Angry and resentful
- Prone to generalized and performance anxiety
- Unsuccessful in adult intimate relationships
- Chameleons with an undeveloped sense of self

lonely and angry as a child and empty as an adult, is a common refrain among children of workaholics. Tom said, "The second words I learned to say were, 'Daddy gone.' That indicates to me that I was missing my dad at a very young age, and it shocks me that I am doing the same thing to my kids."

Children like Charles, hungry for attention from their psychologically absent parent, complain about their parents' mental absenteeism. But their natural way of handling the disappointment is to defer their emotional needs by joining in the workaholic pattern to get their parents' approval. This involves working alongside the workaholic parent or accompanying him or her to the workplace in hopes of stealing a few moments of attention. Charles remembered going with his father to his office just to be in his company.

At thirty-five, Nell smuggled memos and contracts into her dying father's hospital room. "It was the only way I could be with him," she said, fighting back tears. "The only time he'd pay attention to me was around the subject of his work."

Desperate for connecting with the unavailable workaholic parent, children unwittingly enable the working parent by helping them. Nell's father died working, a pen in his hand. Now she lives with the guilt of hastening his death.

High Expectations

When workaholics do actively parent, it is often to make sure that their children are mastering their perfectionist standards. Workaholic parents push achievement and accomplishment over unconditional acceptance of their offspring. Their love and approval are unwittingly doled out on the condition that a standard is reached—one that, from the child's perspective, is often unattainable.

Children of workaholics feel loved conditionally and believe good performance is necessary first. Because of a perpetual fear of failure, children of workaholics sometimes suffer from performance anxiety in the challenges they face at school, in work, and even in relationships. Perfectionism is a lifelong and haunting companion.

Being good, doing well, becomes the standard to which children conform. Cindy's workaholic mother ran the household by the motto "Your best is always better yet." Cindy's mother believed that no matter how hard you work, you could work harder, earn more, do better. Marsha shudders at the memory of traveling home after her high school graduation—not just because there had been a late spring snow and it was cold outside but because of her mother's chilly attitude toward her. Despite the fact that Marsha had been honored for having the second-highest grade-point average among two thousand students, her mother had been distant and unenthusiastic all day long. As tires crushed the icy road beneath them, Marsha's mother broke the ice inside the car: "Why couldn't you have been number one?" she demanded.

The message many children of workaholics introject is, "I cannot measure up" or "I need to be someone other than who I really am." Expectations are often out of reach for children of workaholics, who internalize their failure as self-inadequacy. The anecdotal literature suggests that many children of workaholics carry the same best-dressed legacy of their workaholic parents: they become other directed and approval seeking as they try to meet adult expectations. Others go the opposite direction: they see measuring up as hopeless, give up trying, and act out their frustrations, anger, and hostility. These children become underachievers or conduct problems at school, where they displace their anger and aggression.

These clinical observations are supported by the scientific research, which reports that family environments in which parents hold high achievement expectations or evaluate their children's performance compared to others tend to promote the development of such Type A behaviors as competitiveness, aggression, and hostility, as well as losses in self-esteem and perceived control.[12] Moreover, an unsupportive family climate and a lack of positive familial affiliation have been linked empirically with children's anger and hostility.[13]

Four hundred physicians, polled on their views of workaholics, supported the clinical reports.[14] Asked if workaholics are more or less demanding of achievement in their children, 88 percent of the physicians responded "more demanding." As a result of these demands and workaholics' perfectionism, the psychiatrist Anthony Pietropinto suggests, children of workaholics learn that parental love is contingent on their perfect performance. They often react with resentment and may become hostile and rebellious. He suggests that family conflict is inevitable in workaholic families and that workaholics regard their spouses and children as extensions of their egos.[15]

Children of workaholics learn to measure their worth around what they do rather than by who they are. Expectations are so out of reach that children feel doomed to fail. When they ultimately do fail, they internalize the experience as a lowering of self-worth. They feel incompetent, as if nothing they do is good enough. They often feel inherently defective for being unable to meet parental expectations, and they feel like failures even when they succeed.

Sammy, a twenty-two-year-old college student, decided to become a physician's assistant but wouldn't tell his workaholic father, who he feared would think of him as a loser because he didn't go all the way and become a physician. After all, when, at fifty-two, his father qualified for a self-endurance test in the National Guard, he didn't just qualify for his age group; he trained hard until he qualified along with the younger men in the thirty-five-year-old age category. Sammy was right. His father, who thought Sammy didn't have his sights aimed high enough, was disappointed in his son and said so. Devastated, Sammy carried the shame and guilt of letting his proud father down.

The Making of a Chameleon

To compensate for the emotional deprivation, children of workaholics learn to conform and become approval seekers as they search for the acceptance they have never gotten. Early in childhood, they learn that doing "right," which is often doing what others want, is more important than being who you really are. They learn to mold their attitudes, emotions, and behaviors around the wishes of others, usually the dominant workaholic parent, much like Dana describes in her own upbringing in the next section of this chapter.

Children of workaholics feel that they push their true selves aside and pursue their quest to measure up outwardly by becoming whomever and whatever it takes to get the approval they crave. Somewhere along the way, they lose touch with who they are on the inside and become a chameleon who is viewed as accomplished and is held in high regard.

Having been extensions of their workaholic parents' egos, adult children of workaholics develop an outward focus (or an external locus of control), an undeveloped sense of self, and a lack of differentiation. Simply put, this means they become other centered and externally referenced. Research indicates that those who perceive themselves as being "at effect" instead of "at cause" in their own lives tend to be more pessimistic and to respond more negatively in general to the vicissitudes of life. As a result, they are at risk of being victimized by life rather than empowered by it and of entering into adult codependent relationships.

It's impossible to be perfect when it comes to human relationships, so children of workaholics either shun intimacy altogether or become enmeshed to the point of reinventing themselves to accommodate to their partners. On the inside they feel trapped in a lifelong legacy of personal emptiness, disappointment, and depression, much of which hits home in the adulthoods of children of workaholics. They often become involved in long-term relationships with people whom they are always trying to please, who are emotionally distant, and whom they are always disappointing. In other words, they become intimately involved with someone who reminds them of their workaholic parent.

Case studies of adult children of workaholics confirm that, in order to gain parental attention, they learned to gauge their emotions and behaviors by the expectations of their high-achieving parents, trying to please them—often an impossible task, as George described:

> Everything I did as a kid was based on accomplishment and goals. I tried hard and got awards for everything: outstanding academic scholarship, top awards in band and choir, captain of the football team. But the one award I never won was my dad's love and attention. He was always working. Oh, yeah, he would come to my games and criticize what I did wrong. He *always* looked for a better way to do things. His way was the right way. What about all those things I did right? "I'm proud of you" would have been nice. I just wanted him to play catch with me or hit me on the head with a pillow and say, "How ya doing?" To this day it's hard for me to sit in a room without having a project or a product. I guess something in me is still trying to grab my dad's attention.

Because they must be perfect to receive love, they try to please, even if it means being someone they're not, and they often do not think for themselves or venture outside a safe comfort zone for fear of ridicule. They learn to gauge their emotions and behaviors by the actions of their workaholic parents in order to please them, an impossible task. When the workaholic is working or emotionally absent or fails to keep promises because of job commitments, the children are unhappy. When the workaholic is present and accounted for, children are happy. In short, they learn to dance to the beat of their workaholic parent's drum, instead of their own.

Dana and Pat

Dana and Pat illustrate how children are negatively affected when workaholic parents sacrifice intimacy and warmth by putting more value on the children's performance than on their unconditional worth as human beings. Being in control, being perfect, doing what others want you to do, and measuring your self-worth by what you accomplish—these are important aspects of the personalities of children of workaholics. The way to self-esteem is to be good, to be right, to do well, and never to fail. Dana felt herself caught in this no-win cycle:

> When my dad got angry, he got cold and sarcastic. I didn't know how to deal with it. I would have rather been beaten. My response was to be crushed inside and not to react in a way that would let him know that I was hurt. I ate a lot to keep it inside and became overweight to deal with my stuffed feelings. It was also a form of rebellion for me, because my eating was an issue with my dad, who'd say, "Oh, you're having more potatoes?"
>
> My dad was such a workaholic that he got his thank-you notes out the day after Christmas. He does it right and holds those same standards for everybody. If he could do it, then everybody else ought to be able to do it and should do it. Wasting time was not allowed in my family, and both of my parents were always busy and doing.
>
> There was little open conflict in my family. Everybody was always trying to do everything right—anticipating anything that could create trouble before it happened. We operated from the avoidance of conflict. My dad didn't get angry; he got sarcastic. I

learned very early that the consequences of wrongdoing around my house was freeze time, an awful, tangible chill! I'd rather been beaten. It was worse than a slap across the face. I always feared that if I didn't meet my parents' expectations, they would withhold their love and abandon me emotionally. That had a big effect on my self-esteem. The way to have self-esteem was to be good, to be right, to do well, to be perfect. I never felt a sense that my parents were people to talk to or to turn to when I was in trouble. I didn't feel loved and accepted, even though I know my parents were well intentioned. They were always the last people on earth I wanted to have know my business, because there was no history of that kind of intimacy. There was a focus on the belief that "you are what you do."

When I was a child, my dad gave me a dollar every time I read *How to Win Friends and Influence People,* and I really internalized that book. It emphasizes the people-pleasing stuff—tuning in to others and making them feel important. Underneath all that manipulation is the need to control how others feel about me. That's how I can feel okay about myself. Today, at age fifty I still struggle with whether it's okay for me to be different from others. It's been okay for other people to be different from me, but the issue of my being different from them is based on a security within myself that I'm okay even if others don't like me. Being accepted and understood has been one of my own coping devices, being a good girl, a good daughter, doing all the things you're supposed to do. If I wanted Chinese and you wanted Mexican, I was willing to give up my wants. It still kills me to be a disappointment to someone or to let them down in any way. It's a carryover from worrying about what people will think if I don't meet their standards. And I still have a terrible fear of abandonment. I, too, often laid myself open too much and too soon and ended up hurt and resentful in my adult relationships, with a lot of self-doubt about not being smart enough on how to discriminate who to trust and how much.

There is no obvious dysfunction to point to as a reason for my discontent, emptiness, and frustration. My parents were avid churchgoers, civic leaders, a good family who worked hard to send us to summer camp. They wanted to be Ozzie and Harriet, and they tried real hard to be. They were so perfect that the logical conclusion was that there must be something wrong with me for wanting to have intimate, feeling conversations and relationships and for feeling like I wasn't loved or accepted. If I had children, the biggest thing I would hope to do would be to promote an atmosphere of intimacy, of being the kind of mother who would want to hear how your day went and to talk more about how I felt and how my children felt.

After her first therapy group, it was Dana who introduced hugging into her family, followed by saying "I love you," which she still has to say first today, if it is said at all.

Pat, age forty-three, also remembers how difficult it was living up to her workaholic mother's expectations. After sharing her memories with me, Pat felt like Dana and admitted having feelings of guilt and disloyalty for saying anything negative about what onlookers would call perfect parents and a perfect childhood.

In some ways growing up with a smart, hard-working mother was hard. I have never felt like I could measure up to her success in either of the domains of running a family or having a career. And while I have never competed directly with her, I know that working extra, extra hard and being successful is the only real way to feel good about my efforts.

Mom worked about fifty to sixty hours a week as a journalist since I was eight months old. She is a wonderful writer and quite famous in our small home town. There is no question that she would have been a contender on large newspaper staffs if she had not chosen to work in the small town where her husband joined her father's small business. Everyone in town knows, loves, and respects my mother, probably because she puts as much energy into her work as she does into her family. She goes the extra mile with each story she writes. I have felt a lot of pressure around this idea of "doing the best I can," because I am capable of doing a lot (and doing a lot well), but the notion of "the best I can" is a heavy load. I can think of only two times in my life when I did the best I could. In all of the rest of life, I work hard, but I never feel like I'm really successful, because I could have done more. I believe that my mother's way of being, more than any words she has ever said, has caused me to feel this way.

I often felt saddled with responsibilities as a teenager to help care for my three younger brothers and sister, because Mom covered a lot of meetings at night. With a family of seven, I had to do the dishes and help get the children to bed. I was a conscientious student, and I remember how nervous I often felt because it would get so late before I could get started with my homework. When I worked near my mom, she would call me and tell me to meet her at her car to go to lunch. Many times I would wait at her car for long periods of time and get furious, because I had "punched the clock." She would say that she had gotten a call or had run into someone, and I was supposed to just understand that that's how her work was. What I understood was that, for that moment, her commitment to me was less important than her commitment to work. On family vacations, she was exhausted, and I would worry about her. We went to the beach every summer, and I remember that we would all try to give her a break and let her sleep on the beach. And she would finally relax. But as a child, it was scary that we had to take care of her when we were so used to her taking care of us.

Suggestions for Clinicians

Clinicians are called on to work with children of workaholics with a variety of needs. There is almost always unfinished business in family relationships, on the part of the parents, their children, or both. Clinicians may work indirectly with children through their workaholic parents who are struggling to alter their lives to accommodate their families. In other situations, clinicians may work directly with young children or, retrospectively, with adult children of workaholics.

Repairing Relationships with Children

Workaholics' self-care plans usually address how they can put more thought, care, and time into their often-neglected relationships with their children. This is an important area for clinicians to explore with workaholic clients, because there is almost always unfinished business with children, whether they are twelve or twenty.

Realistically, most clients do not have the luxury of quitting their jobs to mend family relationships. But achieving an understanding of the nature of the parent-child relationship and setting goals to repair tense and broken relationships are essential parts of the workaholic's individual psychotherapy. Sound advice comes from an interview with Bill Smith, who suggests that workaholics use the tools of their trades as a way to revive closeness:

> Write a love note to your son or daughter or wife telling them how much they mean to you. Pull out your DayTimer and make appointments to meet with your children one by one. No one on their deathbed wishes they'd spent less time with their family.[16]

Clients benefit from knowing that relationships are a good investment of their time. Clinicians can assess the client's view of relationships and, where appropriate, help the client set aside time to rebuild relationships and focus on the people he or she is with at the moment. These activities might include taking long walks and having heart-to-heart talks with loved ones who have been neglected and planning time together with children, to whom they give their undivided attention. Clinicians can explain to clients the importance of saving newspaper reading or work until children are asleep. Helping children with homework, playing board games, scheduling weekday or weekend family outings, or conducting family projects are examples of quality time. Preparing meals together and having pleasant mealtime conversations (without television) gives families a chance for healthy communication. Clinicians can help clients see the importance of taking an active interest in their children's lives by listening to what they have to say and finding out what they have been up to during the week and by becoming more aware of how they interact with children. Everybody has bad days, but they can try to avoid coming home in foul moods or unloading their anger on their kids. It is important for them to focus on the positive things children do, rather than harping on the negative.

As I mentioned in an earlier chapter, practicing daily rituals is the glue that holds the family together. This glue is lost in workaholic families that forgo the bedrock ritual of nightly dinners. Family members become virtual strangers when they lose track of who is doing what and how each one is feeling about his or her life. Research backs the idea that rituals keep loved ones stabilized and help them fare better amid the chaotic juggling of each day's diverse activities. Families that eat on the run or in shifts—instead of sitting down together—are not as close as families that make it a point to eat together. Households where holidays are observed and birthdays and anniversaries recognized and celebrated have stronger relationship bonds than homes where life's markers are ignored. Rituals such as a family dinnertime provide an anchor for families caught in the whirlwind of today's fast-paced society. They help heal tensions and teach kids the importance of togetherness and of having plans and seeing them through. Rituals provide stability and dependability and make members feel they have something to count on. Families that value and practice rituals generally have less anxiety and fewer signs of stress related to burnout. Clinicians can explore with clients what rituals they can put back in their lives to restore feelings of togetherness and to heal tensions in their relationships.

Working with Internal Parts

One of the most effective approaches to helping workaholics rebuild relationships is Internal Family Systems (IFS) Therapy, proposed by Richard Schwartz.[17] This approach helps people get in touch with their true self that the workaholic part has eclipsed. Most workaholics have highly developed manager parts —the part of the character that brings home the bacon, focuses on goals, and exercises the virtues of strength, persistence, decisiveness, self-denial, and determination. IFS shows clients how to lead their lives from a more calm, centered, confident, and compassionate place.

Reese, the forty-six-year-old president of a large computer company, for example, had built a business from the ground up with determination and perseverance that had taken him from poverty to great wealth. But his workaholic part's singular focus on goals had led to communication problems that made disgruntled employees leave in droves, left his wife fed up, and produced teenaged children who, feeling they could never reach their father's impossible standards, used drugs and got into trouble at school. Labeled the tyrant workaholic at work and the Nazi parent at home, he had a genuine desire to change.

I encouraged Reese to continue to value his determination and hard-working parts but also to get in touch with his wise, creative inner elder who helped him slow down, see the magic of process, stay in the present moment, smell the flowers, and enjoy each instant of life as he moved toward his accomplishments. The Wise Elder helped Reese to control less and delegate more, trusting in the creativity of his employees to find their own ways to get the job done.

I also helped Reese get in touch with his Compassionate Self which allowed his caring and love to flow, as well as passion and commitment. Compassionate Self helped Reese be more accepting of all people, especially his employees, wife, and children. It helped him recognize human frailty when his workers made mistakes or revealed weaknesses. It listened, showed genuine appreciation for his employees' hard work, and praised them for good work, as his workaholic part had often failed to do. Compassionate Self also pulled out his PalmPilot, scheduled date nights with his wife, and carved out special moments to be with his children.

Reese also made contact with his Clown—the fun-loving and playful part of the self that restores the lost joy and freedom that workaholics forfeit in order to complete tasks. The Clown helped Reese see the lighter side of life at home and work and helped him enjoy laughing and being with people. He started planning trips with his family and instituted birthday celebrations and employee picnics to boost morale at work. He became less serious about financial security, less perfectionistic, less explosive, and more lighthearted.

Young Children of Workaholics

Professionals who work with children often fail to assist those who come from workaholic homes, because, as we have seen, these children appear to be immune to the effects of the parent's hard-driving approach, competitiveness, and perfectionism. As adults, these children are usually well liked and accomplished, and they excel in their careers. Low self-esteem, anxiety, or depression are often masked by resiliency, overresponsibility, and exaggerated self-reliance. Clinicians can look underneath the veneer to see if young and adult children of workaholics are driving themselves for approval, and they can provide the following tips to workaholic parents or directly apply them to help children of workaholics:

- Be on the lookout for "overly competent" children who appear to be functioning at their maximum. It is important to mention that not all successful or competent children are suffering in the way described in this chapter. Clinicians need to scrutinize for an *overdeveloped* sense of accomplishment, responsibility, and perfectionism and to make sure these children get as much attention as other children who may have an easier time of showing their needs or asking for help.

- Insist that children of workaholics do not sacrifice or forgo potential benefits derived from activities, experiences, or interactions because they are too busy putting others' needs before their own.
- Avoid being overly critical, comparing the child to others, overencouraging or setting unattainable goals, and overcommitting the child to activities without evidence of a natural interest or consent.
- Continue to present children of workaholics with challenges that match their developmental abilities, but help them learn not to take on too much. Avoid having unusually high expectations and burdening these children with adultlike responsibilities, even when they are eager to accept and capable of accepting them.
- Let children know that it is okay to relax and do nothing. Reassure them that they do not always have to be producing to please someone else and that it is acceptable to please themselves, which can include doing nothing.
- Encourage children in their successes and enjoy their accomplishments with them, but let them know that it is acceptable to fail and that they do not have to be perfect in everything they attempt. Encourage adults around these children to let children see them fail and handle it in a constructive way.
- Affirm children, and provide them with unconditional support for who they are, regardless of their achievements. Let them know they are valued even when they are not producing and that they are accepted regardless of whether they succeed or fail. Be there for a big failure or letdown. Help children understand and accept that success is built on failure.
- Encourage children to identify their true feelings and to

express them often in conversations or through creative outlets.

- Provide children with guidance when they must make significant and difficult decisions that parents have left up to them, such as how and where to spend their after-school time.
- Provide children with opportunities for noncompetitive games so that they can enjoy the sheer fun of play and enjoy their childhood with other youngsters their age, rather than spend all their time with adults in adult activities. Welcome laughter, giggling, even silliness by building in funny stories or experiences during the day, and suggest activities that are creative and here-and-now to balance out the focus on product and future-oriented activities.

Adult Children of Workaholics

Children of workaholics often grow into adults who are envied by everyone: responsible, achievement oriented, able to take charge of any situation. At least that's how they appear to the outside world. Inside, they often feel like little kids who can never do anything right, holding themselves up mercilessly to standards of perfection.

Clinicians can screen for work addiction in the families of origin of all clients during the intake process, just as they do for alcoholism and other addictions. When identified, this information can be used in implementing a therapeutic plan for clients. In cases where adult clients identify living or having lived with a workaholic parent as the presenting problem, clinicians can help them learn how to avoid enabling parental work addiction. They can inform clients of the potential damage of joining in the compulsive work habits out of their need to spend time with their parents and of bringing them work to do when they go to bed sick. They can help the clients refuse to make alibis for their parents' absenteeism or lateness at parties or family get-togethers and let their parents be responsible for explanations. They can stress the importance of not enabling workaholics by refusing to assume their household chores, return phone calls, fulfill family obligations, or cover for them in a business meeting or social gathering. It is important for them to understand that building their lives around the workaholic's busy schedule only sets them up for further hurt and disappointment.

Clinicians can help adult children of workaholics to lower their perfectionistic standards to more reachable goals and to delegate tasks in the office or at home. They can also help clients to be less self-critical and to strengthen their inner, nurturing voice and teach them to affirm themselves for who they are and not just for what they do. Providing unconditional support for themselves as individuals—not just measuring their worth by what they produce or achieve—can be a major step forward for individuals who have spent their lives measuring their value by the standards and approval of others.

Clinicians can teach stress-relief exercises or refer adult children of workaholics to workshops or special classes where they can learn yoga, meditation, and other relaxation techniques to help them live more in the moment. They can learn to develop flexibility by building in spontaneous, spur-of-the-moment activities and welcoming fun and laughter, perhaps by deciding to go to the beach at the last minute or walking barefoot and umbrellaless in a summer rain shower. Encourage clients to deliberately do something imperfectly—to go for a week without making their bed or to find a process-oriented activity or hobby that they cannot measure by a standard of perfection that lets them be imperfect—such as painting their feelings on canvas or engaging in activities that permit them to make and learn from their mistakes (e.g., growing plants or learning new dance steps).

9

Work Addiction in the Company

The rung of a ladder was never meant to rest upon, but
only to hold a man's foot long enough to enable
him to put the other somewhat higher.

—THOMAS HUXLEY

Mary

To see me now, you'd never guess that I was once a rabid workaholic. I wear sweat pants and flannel shirts, and my big decision of the morning is whether to do the dishes before or after I feed the horses. I'm in recovery, and though the workaholic in me lurks just under the surface, I have learned to say no as well as yes, and I have learned to protect my family from my problem. Though my sense of worth has been built on being "needed"—perhaps as yours is—I stopped using my job as my main way of feeling good about myself, no matter what the cost. This is how:

Once, I was like the rest of you. Up at 5 A.M. for a little uplifting reading before the day began, in the office at 6 or 6:30 to run the company, Racing Strollers (now called the Baby Jogger Co.). My husband, Phil, and I were trying to juggle the dual demands of growing the company and raising a family, and we reasoned that if we staggered our shifts, our kids would have minimal time in day care. So I would come home by 3 or 4, take a few phone calls, work after dinner, and make a to-do list before going to bed, at 9.

See, if you're an entrepreneur, you are certainly a workaholic, and if you're a workaholic, you're operating out of some weird neurotic need. The curse of the workaholic is that you live for being needed. You're so important. You have to be at all the meetings because people might make a bad decision without your presence to show them the error of their ways. What if there's a crisis? Nobody's as good as you are in a crisis, right? With your wily, ratlike cunning, only you know just what to say to that customer, banker, or vendor.

And working long, hard hours is so delicious. Somewhere in the depths of your mind there's a buzzer saying that your family needs you, too, but when a phone call comes in at 5:15, you just can't hang up. I was the worst of hog-all-the-fun managers. I must have made fifty decisions a day. What our marketing plans were. What kind of pencils to buy. When I finally realized that I needed to delegate, I still made that initial decision: "Okay I'm not going to give this manager the answer. I'm going to ask for the solution." But in deciding that, I still did a preemptive strike.

I thrived on the constant decisions. I was good at decisions, so I became like a computer program that anyone in the company could gain access to. "Computer, this part is breaking, what should we do?" "Computer, we need goals, what should we do?" "Computer, we need a price increase; what should we charge?" Wouldn't you love to have a software program that could answer all your questions? Wouldn't you use it constantly? And that's what we did, only Mary's Tiny Brain was the software site. And that's how all my entrepreneurial friends are: they love problems, they get juiced by solving them, and, by God, if they don't have the answer, they have to hustle to find someone who does.

When folks asked how I did it, I thought to myself, "Well, everyone else's lives are so slow. I thrive on a little stress, and, besides, this is how we self-actualized, high-achiever types get so much done, unlike the poor slobs who are schlepping along." Sigh. What a jerk I was. A caring, sympathetic jerk, but still an egomaniac. Is this the entrepreneur's lament? Is the only way to get our businesses up and running to go crazy for a few years? Business is what we're good at, and it's fun to know the answers. But if we are good at this, how do we ever learn to shut up and let other people surge ahead? How do we get some rest without getting rid of the thing we love, our business?

Eventually, things caught up with me. My marriage fell apart, and though I blamed Phil for not being interested in me or the marriage, I realized later that, as I sped along the fast track, I had made an unconscious choice of the company over our marrriage. I picked up another clue when our business hit the black hole of Calcutta, financially speaking. It happened because when I felt I was approaching utter burnout, I finally started to delegate. Unfortunately, I delegated some of the wrong things, like reading the financials line by line. So our business got into the pits, and we spent two years dragging ourselves out. By the time we were safe, I was totally sick of making decisions. I wanted to sleep for a million years.

I knew something had to change, but what? Now, I didn't wake up one glorious day and leap out of bed, saying, "Praise the Lord! I'm cured, and now I'm going to put my family first." First I had several years of saying I wanted to work less—maybe a forty-hour week. Notice I said that I wanted to change. I didn't actually change for quite a while.

Finally, two years ago, I took a month off. I had become so tired. My professional advisers all told me I shouldn't take the time, that things would fall apart without me, that we weren't strong enough yet. But I went anyway. It was February. I stayed home, slept late, and watched the snow come down. My kids loved my cooking, something none of us realized I had any talent for. Someone had once taught me how to do vacations right, and during that month I followed all the rules: I took no phone calls and no faxes, and if there was an emergency, it had to be routed through a senior manager who would protect me from trivia. Basically, I said, "Don't call me unless someone dies." It was the most peaceful month.

By the end of the month I had unwound, and I decided to look at Racing Strollers in a new way. I was tired of pushing, tired of always comparing our company with some other company and falling short in my own estimate. I had always thought, "Yeah, we did Okay, but look how much more we could do if we only worked harder!" But finally, I learned to say, "Screw it, I don't care if we ever grow again. We can be just a nice little company, like a fine Swiss watch company." We could stand still and keep on making a good living. I wanted time. Free time started to seem more precious than money. I looked around and saw friends in high-powered jobs who were working on Sundays. They had lots of money but no possibility of enjoying it.

I quietly started to train my successor, Colette, without really telling her why. Eventually, I told her that I hoped she would be president one day, and we started to make the transition. It was so hard to tell my managers. Finally, one day our friend and adviser Spike said to me, "What are you waiting for? Colette's ready, you're ready." I promptly burst into tears—not about wanting my job, but because of my intense relief at being able to let it go, into safe hands.

I can't say it's been easy. The first few weeks were horrible. All of my social life and all my friendships were at the office. It was pretty boring at home. Gradually, I made new friends and started finding life outside work. I was a little bit jealous for a while. Colette is kind and funny, with a mind like a steel trap. Everyone thinks she is tough, and everyone loves her. What if you train your successor, and he or she is better in your job than you were? I decided to thank my lucky stars, and Colette kindly reassures me that she still needs my advice.[1]

Thank God It's Monday (TGIM)!

Everything you have read about workaholics up to this point is carried over into the workplace: their rigid thinking, their compulsive work habits, their ways of relating to people, even their families of origin. In this chapter I show how—because the workplace is often a replication of the family of origin—some adults who have a higher tolerance for stress and chaos and who seek out high-stress jobs unwittingly reenact unresolved issues in the form of rampant work addiction.[2] I also show how the work environment can breed workaholics and how, after a certain point, these work habits and patterns hurt not only the workaholics but also the company.

While many of us dread facing a new workweek after a relaxing weekend, workaholics, having white-knuckled it through, cannot wait to get back to the office on Monday morning. While some workers have the Monday-morning blahs, workaholics are revved up and ready to go. As a general rule, workaholics are not team players, and their need to control makes it difficult for them to solve problems cooperatively and to participate in give-and-take situations. They believe their approach and their style are best, and they cannot entertain less perfect solutions. Spontaneity is diminished and creativity stifled when the narrow view of one workaholic prevails. Because of these problems, some management experts have gone so far as to say that the best advice for any workaholic is to work alone or only with other workaholics.[3]

Workaholics feel different from their coworkers because excessive work isolates them and sets them apart. They feel that colleagues do not understand the significance of the volume of work they accomplish. In addition, workaholics as a group, because of their diverse work styles, do not always understand each other. Savoring workaholics, for example, drive relentless and attention-deficit workaholics nuts because they feel restrained in their productivity (see chapter 3). While relentless workaholics are task focused and high in completion, savoring workaholics make sure there's another high-pressured project so that they can work day and night, deliberately or unwittingly creating more work to do. Dennis, an administrator and a savoring workaholic, said,

> I have a tendency not only to do what's on my job description but to create new duties and responsibilities to make it better than what the other administrators are doing. Down the road I get mad at myself for taking on more than was expected of me or more than I'm being paid to do. Always doing more than is asked of me, I end up despising the job and everybody around; I have created a situation by taking on extra tasks that I don't need to do.

The Emperor Has No Clothes

While I was conducting research on workaholics and family dynamics, organizational psychologist Gayle Porter at Rutgers University was studying the impact of workaholism on the job. Her findings in the workplace paralleled those of my own research with families. In the new millennium, while corporate America failed to underscore problems resulting from workaholism and extolled its virtues, Porter continued to emphasize how workaholism leads to inefficiency and erodes trust throughout the organization.[4] She insists that it is not uncommon for workaholics to generate a crisis but also to get attention and praise for resolving it:

> During a crisis, everyone's attention goes to its resolution. Rarely is time taken to reexamine the history of decision points at which the crisis might have been averted, but the cost of meeting crisis conditions is significant. All organization members should be concerned about the possibility that someone in their midst may contribute to or create crisis. Indeed, managers focus on praise for those who function well during that time. The same person could be playing both roles, and this person may be a workaholic.[5]

Porter also describes how, eventually, the amount of effort savoring workaholics put into their jobs exceeds their level of productivity:

> The important distinction, when talking about addictive behavior maintenance, is that a workaholic seeks to maintain a high level of involvement in the work even when the task could be accomplished with less involvement. This is the person who convinces himself that working on Saturday is necessary and spends time carefully lining up tasks that would not be completed without doing so. In comparison, another worker exerts extra effort during the week, asks for help, or finds more efficient ways to approach the task in order to have the weekend off. Both accomplish the required task. However, the first worker has devoted more of the week to doing so. To some, that person would appear to be more involved in the job, or appear to be the harder worker, but the motive was not to do better, only to keep doing.[6]

It is this tunnel vision, this detailed and self-absorbed approach to work, that creates problems for savoring workaholics. Because of their sense of time urgency, workaholics, regardless of their work type, can take the most inefficient avenue for completing tasks. Because they overcommit and spread themselves too thin, attention-deficit workaholics are headed in many different directions at once. Their compulsions to push themselves and to impulsively jump in over their heads without planning and forethought make it hard for them to complete projects in a timely manner. Muriel, a health care administrator, gained a reputation for taking something, going with it, and then having to go back and clean up her tracks:

> An idea would come to me and I'd say, "This is great!" And I'd jump in and go with it. I'd have it moving and be way ahead of everyone else. Everybody else sat back and took it all apart and thought the details through, and I was way ahead of them. Our billing procedures were behind because we were working so far

> ahead of ourselves. It took us two years to clean up the billing mess.

As workaholics continue to overinvest in their jobs, fatigue sets in, and rates of errors and accidents increase. Thus, many workaholics are less efficient than their coworkers who put in fewer hours planing and working toward a job goal.

In contrast to the workaholic, the optimal performer has warm, outgoing relationships and a good collaborative sense and is a master at delegating. A nationwide study of fifteen hundred persons in numerous career fields revealed a major difference in the success of workaholics compared to that of optimal performers.[7] The investigator, Dr. Charles Garfield, concluded that workaholics are not the high-level performers that management perceives them to be. He found, in fact, that workaholics hurt the company because they are addicted to the process of working, not to getting results. They tend to be motivated more by fear and loss of status than by high-level motivation and creative contribution, and they are more reluctant to take the necessary risk in the organization to achieve positive, creative outcomes. Table 9.1 shows the characteristics that distinguish optimal performers from workaholics.

Garfield found that the career projectories of workaholics are predictable: they tend to be flashes in the pan. Like shooting stars, they burst on the scene, are viewed as "up and coming," rise quickly on the basis of their big splash, and level off, consumed with managing the details of their careers. The leveling-off stage tends to appear at midlife, concurrently with cardiovascular disease, psychosomatic disorders, alcoholism, drug abuse, and marital problems.

Work Environments That Promote Work Addiction

Workaholics and work addiction could not survive without the workplace. The corporate atmosphere encourages work addiction by perpetuating a work ethic promoting loyalty to the com-

TABLE 9.1
Portrait of Optimal Performers in the Workplace

Optimal performers are:	Workaholic are:
Good collaborators and delegators	Unable to delegate or work as a team; work best alone
Socially gregarious	Employees with few or no friends
Employees who enjoy the process and outcome of work	Employees who work for the sake of working
Motivated by intrinsic needs and creative contributions	Motivated by fear and loss of status
Efficient; see the whole picture as well as the steps toward the goal	Inefficient; they get bogged down with details
Creative risk takers who stretch beyond customary bounds	Reluctant to take chances to achieve creative outcomes
Masters of self-correction; when they make mistakes they try to learn from them	Unable to tolerate mistakes; they try to avoid them or cover them up

pany at the personal expense of its employees. A 2006 global survey by *World Business* revealed that 49 percent of workers said overwork was encouraged and applauded by their company. More than 70 percent said they worked weekends, and 14 percent admitted they'd be proud to be called a workaholic.[8] Workaholics are often attracted, consciously or unconsciously, to these types of work environments because they are looking for a lot to do. So companies must take some responsibility for enabling and promoting work addiction. Many companies operate from top to bottom through a workaholic structure. In contrast to slogans that condemn drug use like "Just Say No" or "Just Don't Do It," the message that rings loud and clear—some times subtle, sometimes direct—in the workaholic organization is "Don't Go Home Without It." As I travel far and wide and in my own clinical practice, I hear more stories of corporate threat. One woman told me the subtlety of the threat: "Oh yeah, I could take all of my earned vacation. But if I do I won't have a job when I get back. They may say it's okay, but believe me it isn't!" Other workers say they are afraid to take lunch breaks for fear of how they'd be perceived by management. There comes a point where these work environments hurt employees, whether or not they are workaholics. Organizations that actively recruit workaholics and promote work addiction tend to attract more workaholic types. Nonworkaholic types, however, do not fare as well in these jobs. Many organizations have stripped management layers in order to remain competitive and now make a habit of employing four people to do the work of five.[9]

The philosophy of one major U.S. bank in 2007 was, *We expect you to change tires going eighty miles an hour.* An executive at this bank told me that at meetings six or seven managers sit around a table discussing issues, each one constantly checking her Blackberry as it goes off. The group consensus is that to survive in this culture employees can no longer afford to just focus on one thing at a time. Multitasking is an essential lifeboat to keep from drowning in a sea of work.

Gayle Porter fears that the combination of excessive corporate demand and wireless technology carries the risk of company exploitation of workers who feel they must be available 24/7.[10] If career advancement depends on 24/7 connectivity, it becomes more difficult to distinguish between worker choice and employer manipulation. The advent of wireless technology raises many questions about the future of corporate responsibility: Have organizations set their expectations so high that addiction-level work involvement is a requirement for the job, and can employers be held liable for employees' addictions to wireless technology?

Another example of corporate excess is the disappearance of company picnics, which used to be a family affair. Replacing them are what is proudly heralded as "power picnics"—the traditional company picnic serving double duty to get more work squeezed in during the annual event. During 2006, Chicago's Windy City Fieldhouse—which hosts company picnics—reported a 20 percent increase in company events with an added work dimension such as two-hour brainstorming sessions before the celebration.[11] Companies are making sure they get a greater bang for their buck, that every dollar spent contributes to the company's growth. This shift in corporate emphasis has begun to show up in sobering ways: "As PowerPoint presentations replace softball, the guest lists are changing. Business partners, vendors and potential customers are being invited and families are getting nixed."[12]

Are you overworked? Micromanaged? Downsized? Or are you overworking, micromanaging, or downsizing others? Today, nonworkaholic employees are under the gun to work more because of downsizing, fear of losing a job, or job insecurity resulting from takeovers. Employers foster work addiction by limiting neither the hours employees work nor the amount of work they take home, by discounting the importance of family, and by applauding those who work tirelessly rather than those who have balanced lives. Some companies send mixed messages to employees (a trait of the workaholic personality). They say they don't want workaholics, but they scrutinize time records or put subtle pressure on employees to log more hours. An alarming 46 percent of professional workers claim they have too much stress and pressure in their jobs.[13]

Some companies have been accused of deliberately manipulating the darker sides of worker consciousness for profit. They set tight deadlines that are impossible to meet, hint at nonexistent competitors, and tell employees that clients are dissatisfied, even when they are not. This corporate tactic creates paranoia, stress, and a prolonged adrenaline rush among the workforce; employees never know for sure which crises are real and which are fabrications. In their book *Corporate Abuse,* Leslie Wright and Marti Smye use the label "cultures of sacrifice" to refer to those organizations that manifest crises as a ploy to keep pressures on employees to produce:

> In a culture of sacrifice, people are driven by feelings of responsibility to the company. This is particularly true for those who link loss of performance with loss of self-esteem. These people become the company workaholics. Workaholics get caught up in a never-ending mission to gain control by devoting more and more time to work, to the exclusion of virtually everything else. If they slow down or relax, they worry they will be seen as

> slackers or incompetents. In their quest to be "good enough" they draw themselves and others into a working frenzy that focuses on quantity rather than quality, aggressively pushing the company and fellow workers to the point of collapse.
>
> Failure is inevitable in this culture. These companies operate on the assumption that the company is more important than its workers, and they are prepared to sacrifice excellent workers to prove the point.[14]

Anne Wilson Schaef and Diane Fassel charge that businesses encourage the denial of work addiction and actually promote it as acceptable and preferable because it seems to be productive.[15] They suggest that corporate America functions as an individual active addict by denying, covering up, and rewarding dysfunctional behaviors among its employees. They further say that dysfunctional managers and those in key corporate positions negatively affect the organizational system and the employees of that system by perpetuating work addiction at every level. They offer six characteristics of companies that promote work addiction on the production line, in boardrooms, or in sales meetings. These characteristics are especially noticeable in the health care industry and in the helping professions, where the human element is overshadowed by the details of the workload.[16]

1. *The mission of the organization is denied, ignored, or forgotten.* Workers are so preoccupied with being productive that they forget why the organization exists. Workers lose sight of the overall mission of their work because they are pressured by the economics of the business.
2. *Corporate survival reigns supreme.* Corporate survival is the top priority, and workers are viewed as commodities to be used up and then discarded. Stress management is offered to keep the workers productive. The business survives as employees drop like flies.
3. *Profit is the driving force of the workaholic company.* Fassel and Schaef say that businesses seek short-term, immediate

gratification instead of deferred, long-range solutions, results, and profit. The integrity and the mission of the organization, as well as the mental health of employees, are better served by a long-term focus at the expense of immediate profit.

4. *The workaholic environment is self-centered and has no boundaries or respect.* Employees with workaholic jobs are expected to carry bulging briefcases of work home on weekends or are forced to glue themselves to their faxes, computers, and beepers on weekends and holidays, in order to perform adequately. That's because the workaholic environment has no boundaries. It does not respect and honor the personal lives of workers. It is selfish, greedy, and demanding. Workers are always at the disposal of the organization, regardless of their personal or family needs. Still, the workaholic organization makes employees dependent on it through perks and benefits. It buys the loyalty of its workers, even though many are miserable and morale is low. Quitting does not appear to be a viable option.
5. *Crisis management is the norm in workaholic organizations.* Crisis shifts the focus of the organization away from emphasizing the needs and welfare of its employees to solving the crisis. When businesses are organized to respond to problems without forethought, they are perpetually putting out fires. This keeps employees hyped, adrenaline flowing, attention focused on the needs of the organization, and the emotional and mental health needs of employees on the back burner. There is less attention devoted to long-term planning; when it does exist, it is often gratuitous.
6. *Intimacy does not exist in the workaholic environment.* Employees are cogs in the corporate wheel. The environment is cold and impersonal. Socializing and close relationships are minimized or even discouraged. The workaholic organization operates on the premise that employees are dispensable, like machine parts, and, once used up, will be replaced by someone else.

Workaholics are attracted to and thrive in jobs that have any or all of these six characteristics. They insinuate their way into the rank and file of management positions in these companies and perpetuate work addiction at every level, as the opening case illustrates. Efficient workers, however, are less willing to sacrifice their whole lives for unreasonable work demands and in some cases are making drastic changes in their work lives, such as downshifting into less stressful jobs and simplifying their personal lives. Businesses, too, are taking a stand against work addiction and are structuring more humane working environments. George A. Schaefer, chairman of Caterpillar, Inc., is one example of a corporate head who insists that his employees lead balanced lives:

> I don't want workaholics working for me. . . . One of my predecessors called that "living on the square." . . . One side of the square represents our work life, one our family life, one our spiritual life, and one our community life. I believe we're healthier, happier—and more productive—if we live on all sides of that square.
>
> I doubt that such people [workaholics] can be effective managers over a lifetime. I question whether they've learned how to delegate, if they've sought ways to become more efficient, if they've learned how to set priorities.[17]

Do you work in a job that promotes work addiction or one that nurtures its employees? See table 9.2 for a test that allows you to evaluate your workplace for work addiction.

The Boss from Hell

Does your boss wail at the clock and shake a fist at the heavens because there's never enough time to do everything? Is your boss someone who rushes around moaning about the shortage of time and creating crises for everyone in his or her work path? Is your boss the sort who sets short deadlines and overloads you

Table 9.2
Corporate Abuse: How Would You Grade Your Job?

Are you in a win/lose work culture? Do you work in a job that promotes work addiction, stress, and burnout? Or are you fortunate enough to work in a company that considers human factors and nurtures its employees? Test your workplace to see how it rates on corporate abuse by answering yes or no to the following questions:

____ 1. Is your job rapid paced, with little time to casually talk with coworkers or supervisors?
____ 2. Does your work environment feel cold, sterile, or devoid of the human touch?
____ 3. Does your work environment thrive on crisis, chaos, and pressure?
____ 4. Do you work for a company that emphasizes production and profit above the welfare and morale of its employees?
____ 5. Does success in your company hinge on your putting in overtime on weekdays, weekends, or holidays?
____ 6. Do you think your company fosters work addiction?
____ 7. Are you constantly in a hurry and racing against the clock on your job?
____ 8. Is it necessary to juggle many activities or projects at one time in order to keep up in your job?
____ 9. Does your company put you under the gun with short notice of high-pressure deadlines?
____ 10. Have you had any stress-related illnesses caused by this job?
____ 11. Do you work for a company that puts the welfare of its employees above profit and production?
____ 12. Does your company have a nurturing attitude toward workers who show concern for family and personal time or who experience stress and burnout?
____ 13. Is your job relaxing, even paced, warm, and friendly?
____ 14. Do you feel like a human being more often than a commodity on your job?
____ 15. In your job, can you limit the amount of work you bring home and have weekends and holidays for yourself and loved ones?
____ 16. Do you think your company has a long-term, vested interest in you as a human being, as opposed to a short-term interest?
____ 17. Does your company promise birthdays, holidays, celebrations, or socializing as an integral part of the work schedule?
____ 18. Do you work with colleagues who are cooperative and supportive and with whom you can communicate?
____ 19. If you have a problem in your job, can you talk with someone who has a listening ear and who will offer you support?
____ 20. Does your job give you personal satisfaction, meaning, or purpose?

SCORING:
Start with 60 points. Subtract 2 points for each yes answer to questions 1 through 10. Add 2 points for each no answer to questions 1 through 10. Subtract 2 points for each no answer to questions 11 through 20. Add 2 points for each yes answer to questions 11 through 20.

YOUR JOB'S REPORT CARD:

Scores	*Grade*	*Interpretation*
Below 60=	F	Poor; a workaholic's paradise; high corporate abuse, stress, and burnout
60 to 69=	D	Below average
70 to 79=	C	Average
80 to 89=	B	Good
90 to 100=	A	Excellent; nurturing and supportive atmosphere; although work-addiction-free, a workaholic could find a way to foster his or her addiction even in this environment.

with more to do than is humanly possible? If so, your boss could be a workaholic.

Andrea worked for a major East Coast newspaper. Her boss, she says, was a workaholic who routinely awakened employees in the middle of the night and on weekends to get an obscure fact from the West Coast for a next-morning deadline. "Naturally everything was closed, so there were times when I ended up calling Tokyo at 3:00 A.M. to get the information he wanted," she said. "It was always one crisis after another!"

Workaholics are often rewarded for their attempts to change and control other people by being promoted into management positions. Although many bosses are blatant in fostering work addiction, some are much more subtle. Their overresponsibility, poor communication skills, and inability to express feelings usually make them ineffective managers. Managers who are out of touch with their emotional lives are likely to be insensitive to the needs and feelings of their subordinates. If they are uncomfortable expressing feelings, they are less likely to provide positive feedback, praise, and appreciation. Instead of seeking advice, asking for input, or showing vulnerabilities, workaholic bosses tend to rule with an iron fist, using intimidation as a defense against their own insecurities and unwittingly undermining, rather than supporting, subordinates to reinforce their own, more powerful position. They tend to pressure employees to match their own inhuman standards, long hours, and frantic pace. Everybody under the manager's supervision goes nuts and feels miserable as morale nosedives and burnout skyrockets.

Working under a workaholic boss can be a nightmare. I've been there, done that, and I have the tee-shirt to show for it. So have countless millions who become anxious at the thought of facing a new week with their work-addicted managers, supervisors, or employers. Table 9.3 presents a picture of the workaholic boss.

Alcoholics like nothing better than a drinking buddy. Workaholics feel contempt for slackers, preferring instead to surround themselves with people who can match their crisis-oriented pace. Workaholic supervisors and managers spread work addic-

TABLE 9.3
Portrait of the Workaholic Boss

- Constantly watches over employees' shoulders to monitor their work, because of refusal to delegate
- Is constantly pushing and hurrying employees to the point that they feel undue stress and burnout
- Makes unreasonable demands in terms of work hours, workloads, and deadlines
- Has unpredictable, erratic moods, so employees never know what to expect
- Creates a climate of frenzy, urgency, and tension without respect for the feelings or personal lives of employees
- Manages time inefficiently because of overscheduling and overcommitting
- Judges himself or herself and employees without mercy as they struggle to hit impossible targets
- Tends to be overly critical and intolerant of even the most minor employee mistakes

tion by setting impossible and incredibly high goals and by pushing their employees to replicate their own frenetic work patterns, often against the employees' natural work pace:

> One of ITTs former presidents set a companywide precedent for work weeks of sixty hours or more and more late-night meetings. Some CPA firms send a memorandum to all their employees just before tax season reminding them that a fifty-hour workweek is considered the minimum. These pressures impose feelings of guilt on all executives who do not work the same number of hours others are working. As a result, employees feel insecure about their jobs unless they spend Saturdays at their desks.[18]

Workaholic bosses are overly critical, overly demanding, and unable to tolerate mistakes. Workaholic bosses become roadblocks to productivity and quality in the workforce, causing disharmony, absenteeism, tardiness, mistrust, and conflict. Their leadership style lowers productivity and morale and destroys team playing and creative brainstorming in the workplace. Judith shared the difficulty she had working under Susan, her sales manager at a multimillion-dollar computer company:

> Susan's addictive work habits as district sales manager make it unbearable for her sales representatives, myself included. At forty-seven, Susan gets up and goes to work by 7:30 and doesn't

get home until eight or nine o'clock. She generally works at home for another couple of hours before she comes to bed. Frustrated at her work addiction, Susan's husband took a job traveling because his interests and needs were not being met in their relationship. Her obsession and constant driving leave no time for family life, and her social life includes only people within the company.

She will not leave the sales representatives alone to do their jobs. Instead, she is burning herself out trying to keep her hands in everything they do. She cannot delegate and let it go and wait until a task is accomplished. There is nothing else in Susan's life but work. Her business associates have never known her to take a day off without leaving one of them an electronic message. Most of her employees are frustrated. She's constantly concerned that things go like she wants them to go. She's too much of a perfectionist. She's always breathing down our necks by telephone or electronic messages. She's afraid that nobody's going to do the job as well as she would do it if she were there. So she keeps her hands in everything.

The morale of the sales reps is rock bottom. The sales force doesn't function as a team. Their spirits are shattered, and they are constantly frustrated that they are not accomplishing enough in a time frame to satisfy Susan's desires. The staff's frustration levels rise and fall in response to Susan's unpredictable behaviors.

Some of my fellow workers try to respond to everything she wants, and they're getting as crazy as she is, just constantly working. If you're buried in the middle of two or three things and she starts this routine, I've seen people come into the office with bloodshot eyes, completely drained. They look as if they haven't slept in three or four days. It's really rough.

It's sometimes Jekyll and Hyde because it's tough to read which way she'll go immediately. She's constantly flying off the handle and jumping down people's throats, venting frustrations of her own. If you're under the pile (that is, you've got too much to do and you're really suffering), she helps you build up a frus-

> tration level and get buried in your pile of work. Then she will pounce on you, too. When she notices we're covered up with things to do, she starts harping on what we're doing and picking on a selected victim. Everybody always knows when they get on her list. She starts looking over our shoulders. She sees us as getting buried and not responding like she would, then she jumps us. Rather than helping take the load off, she puts more stress on us.

No matter how hard employees try to please, they never satisfy the perfectionist standards and end up feeling resentful. They get very little positive feedback for their work efforts, which rarely are good enough to match the boss's expectations. The workaholic's mood can swing from high to low in a workday or workweek. Working for a supervisor, manager, or foreman who has adrenaline highs and irritable and restless withdrawals can be trying. As the moods of the boss swing from high to low, employees try to satisfy him or her by swinging back and forth as well. Many workers, like Judith, have compared the mood swings of company bosses to a Jekyll and Hyde personality. Employees are never sure what to say or do. They waste enormous amounts of energy trying to second-guess their employers. Workers become frustrated and exhausted from trying to match their behaviors to the boss's mood.

Willa, who is an office manager for a prominent attorney, said her boss is a "grouchaholic" with giant-size mood swings:

> One day he's happy, the next day he's snappy. He works day and night and hardly ever talks to the other people in the office. He comes in, walks into his office, shuts the door, and stays there all day long. Everybody walks around on eggshells and has learned to steer clear of him for fear of becoming the target of his anger. The tension is so thick, you could cut it with a knife. When he's grumpy, I feel like I've done something wrong and spend half the day worrying and feeling guilty because maybe it's my fault, or I try to get him out of his bad mood. Although

> part of my job is to inform him of problems that need to be addressed for the good of the business, I am afraid to tell him some critical things he needs to know because I'm afraid he'll blow up at me. When I do have meetings with him, I have to measure each word to make sure I don't use the wrong approach or sound too negative, because if I do, it will set him off.

Workaholic managers are notorious for making and breaking promises because the unrealistic deadlines they set cannot be met. So a new plan is substituted. The work climate is unpredictable and inconsistent, just like the climate in an alcoholic home. Apprehension, fear, and insecurity are normal reactions for employees in unpredictable job positions.

Many problems befall employees as a result of the stresses and strains of their work-addicted environments. Emotions run the gamut from fear, anger, confusion, guilt, and embarrassment to sadness and depression. In order to cope, subordinates guess at what their bosses want and often find themselves making stabs in the dark. Emotionally battered and bruised, many workers limp through their careers. Poor self-esteem, lack of control over their careers, poor coping skills, and problems in interpersonal relationships all result as they attempt to meet dysfunctional demands from the powers that be. Work output that ordinarily would go into quality production is instead consumed by workers' efforts to cover their tracks, lies, and deceptive practices. Many workers get revenge by passive resistance. One man said that his way of getting back at his boss is to do as little as possible and that his productivity would increase dramatically if he worked under someone else.

Instead of benefiting companies, workaholics are costing them money in terms of personal injury lawsuits, workman's comp, and medical insurance claims—all related to the stress and emotional burnout of work addiction. Workaholic employees cost businesses $150 billion a year because of absenteeism, diminished productivity, and stress-related illnesses such as high blood pressure, heart disease, abdominal problems, and a host of mental health problems such as depression and anxiety. Heart disease caused by job stress alone is responsible for an annual loss of 135 million workdays. Workers' compensation costs rose from $23 billion in 1982 to $60 billion in 1990, due to increased claims for psychological and mental stress. Milton Bordwin provides a real-life example:

> Francis C. Dunlavey was an insurance claims adjuster with Kemper in Iowa. A merger of his employer with another insurance company brought changes: a revision of claims handling procedures, different managerial personnel, and, most troublesome, an increase in workload. Also, his supervisor made unrealistic demands and constantly downgraded him with unfavorable evaluations.
>
> Dunlavey reacted to all this by putting in overtime, working from 6:30 A.M. to 6:30 P.M. plus several hours on the weekends. Eventually, Dunlavey became afflicted with major depression, and his doctors were of the opinion that stress on the job was the cause.
>
> Dunlavey's claim was allowed by the industrial commissioner and affirmed by the Iowa District Court. In January 1995, the Iowa Supreme Court agreed. It found that Dunlavey's depression was a "personal injury" under the workers' comp statute and that it arose from his work.[19]

Changes in the Workplace

In the past, the corporate world believed that having ranks of workaholic employees would guarantee greater production. But corporations are finding they can achieve more creative results and greater revenues from a more balanced workforce. Salespersons who have achieved balance in their lives, for example, are more likely to attract potential clients than are obsessed, high-pressure salespeople, who are more likely to turn clients off and drive them away.

How can corporate America take all the problems of work

addiction and convert them into dollars and cents? That is the question that is being asked more and more. Many businesses are refusing to hire known workaholics. Finding cost-effective ways to help employees balance career with family, recreation, and self-care needs are major concerns for employers nowadays. More employers are taking active steps to close the great divide between work and family responsibilities. Employee assistance programs (EAPs) have undertaken major new responsibilities for helping with work- and family-related issues such as stresses and strains that occur on the job. Continued assertive efforts by EAPs to recognize and treat work addiction will give employees seeking help a bona fide support system. These programs can be instrumental in drawing attention to and promoting support for those who need help. A plan of action for improving the work climate can be adapted to the company's unique needs.

More companies are starting to hire socially balanced employees and to support paternity leave, job sharing, and flextime. Workaholic bosses and employees are being channeled into stress-reduction classes, meditation workshops, and work-break aerobics. More bosses are telling employees, directly or indirectly, to slow down. General Mills is among a growing number of companies that insists workers use their vacation time. Susan's boss rejected one day she "took off" for vacation because she had left him electronic messages that same day. He told her, "You were not on vacation because you sent me a message, so take another day of vacation. Get away from the office and forget about work for a while."

Companies can raise employee awareness by establishing "healthy work" days, perhaps in conjunction with Earth Day, with posters and special seminars featuring the components of a healthy work environment. Organizations can present the information by using outside speakers so that all workers learn about the effects of work addiction on the job in a nonthreatening way.

Company administrators can assess the degree to which their organizations promote work addiction. Using the six characteristics of the workaholic company and the test in table 9.2 as criteria, company officials can objectively evaluate the work environment at their organization to determine what needs changing to improve the welfare of workers first and the profit of the organization second.

The removal of work addiction from the workplace can dramatically reduce burnout and stress, health problems, poor communication, and low morale, while saving business and industry billions of dollars a year and providing a better work climate for employees and a better product for consumers. Thus, employers, employees, and consumers all benefit.

Suggestions for Clinicians

Clinicians can begin by asking themselves what type of work environments they have established for themselves and their clientele. Is the atmosphere rushed and frenetic? Or is it serene and relaxed? Taking the test in table 9.2 can help professionals evaluate their own work space to see what kind of example they are setting. It is important for practitioners who work with workaholics and their families to provide positive role models and positive work environments.

The suggestions in the next section can help clients who are work addicts and those who are trying to survive in a workaholic company or under a workaholic boss.

Coping with a Workaholic Boss

Even though your clients may work for the boss from hell and they cannot fire him or her, they can take some action that will benefit them in the long run. Clients can individually and collectively, in cooperation with coworkers, deal with a workaholic boss in a number of ways:

- *Know where to draw the line.* Don't wait for your company to decide what's reasonable for you. Evaluate your job and life and decide what is reasonable for you. Decide how far you are willing to go to meet your boss's unreasonable demands. Be prepared to put your foot down when you believe your employer oversteps those bounds. There are many occasions on the job when you have a choice to stay late or work weekends. You may be reluctant to say no. But feeling overloaded and saying no without feeling guilty or disloyal is a healthy thing to do for yourself.

- *Keep your own balance.* Each of us is responsible for maintaining the balance in our own lives. Take ten or fifteen minutes in the middle of the day to walk or meditate to release bottled-up stress and become more clear-minded. Take an aerobics class, a meditation workshop, a stress-reduction class, or an exercise program during work breaks to combat stress and burnout. Striving for balance in your personal, social, and family life—although sometimes a tightwire act—will ensure greater harmony within yourself, at home, at work, and at play and make it easier for you to cope with a workaholic boss.
- *Avoid anger and impatience.* These are the traits of workaholics who are socially isolated and task focused. Remain tactful and diplomatic, even when you're frustrated. Talk with your boss and try to see his or her human side. Try to find an idea, pastime, or point of view that gives you common ground to connect with your boss so that you can stay objective and see the problem as bigger than just the two of you.
- *Schedule a meeting with your boss to find out his or her expectations of you and the expectations of your boss's boss.* Ask exactly what type of performance is expected of you to achieve an excellent review rating. According to some experts, 99 percent of the time work hours are not one of the factors.[20] This practice ensures that you will not be downgraded for not putting in extra hours. Make sure your boss also understands your point of view, the importance of your personal life, and your expectations concerning job demands. Make priorities, set goals, and schedule your time accordingly.

- *Reach out to coworkers who are experiencing similar problems with the boss.* Encourage support-group meetings before or after work or during lunch in designated places at the work site. By meeting together and talking about their problems constructively, workers can develop a rich support system to draw on in the job setting. When appropriate, schedule a group meeting with the boss and explain in a constructive way your concerns. Ask your boss for some feedback or ground rules so that all of you can be productive and avoid future problems.

Performing Optimally Instead of Workaholically in the Workplace

Flashy, dramatic bursts of working often draw attention from supervisors and colleagues, but consistency and moderation are the redeeming traits of optimal performers. Like the hare, workaholics make a big splash, crash, and then burn. Optimal performers, on the other hand, are like the tortoise. They plod along, showing consistent, high-level performance over time. Optimal performing doesn't contain the adrenaline highs, the ups and downs, or the stress of work addiction. The attention is slower coming for optimal performers, but the delayed gratification pays off in the end. The following tips can assist clinicians in helping workaholics learn the benefits of postponing temporary highs now for greater, longer-lasting rewards over their career projectories:

- *Don't let work dominate your life.* When you feel overloaded, don't cancel dinner with a loved one or your afternoon aerobics class. These are the very activities you need to help you maintain balance. Typically, workaholics think that staying at the office for two more hours is the answer to achieving results. But that usually makes them more tired and less clear-headed and often leads to more work. Maintaining outside interests or exercising daily brings a clearer perspective to your work and gives you more vitality to get out from under the work pile. Plan for spare time just as you would an important business meeting. Schedule time for doing things you like to do best.

- *Delegate and negotiate.* If you're the type who has trouble turning a project over to someone else, you must learn to delegate in order to perform optimally. Review your workload, and determine what part you can turn over to an assistant or coworker. If deadlines are too tight, negotiate them with your supervisor. Deadlines can almost always be modified, although workaholics cannot readily admit that. Develop a plan explaining the need for the extension, and suggest a revised time frame. Lesley Alderman offers this creative example of delegating when you're at a dead end: Tina, a production manager for a New York symphony orchestra, found herself working fifteen hours more a week without a pay increase. Instead of spending several hours watching symphony rehearsals, she put a college intern in charge with a cellular phone so that she could be reached in a pinch. Jeff Caselin, Merrill Lynch's senior biotechnology analyst, when swamped with sixty-hour workweeks, found a way around a hiring freeze to get his projects under way. He recruited a graduate student from Harvard, who helped him two days a week for free.[21]
- *Learn the art of prioritizing your workload.* Have your priorities clear and practical. Don't overplan. The clearer you are on what you want to accomplish and how you plan to accomplish it, the more focused and efficient and the less stressed you will be. Decide which aspects of your job are key, pay attention to the essentials first, and put the nonessentials on the back burner for now or farm them out to another employee.
- *Take charge of your technology.* More people are working in cafes, coffee houses, on airplanes, and at home, making the corporate work space dead zones of empty cubicles—a literal workplace ghost town.[22] Refrain from falling into the management trap of using the extra time that your

technology provides to do more work instead of taking a leisurely break. It is important that you are in charge of your fax, laptop, and cell phone and not let your technology be in charge of you. You can have the time-saving technology without becoming a slave to it. You can check your E-mail twice a day, for example, instead of every time it beeps. You can turn off your portable phones and Blackberry after a reasonable hour and put limits on when and where you choose to carry a fax or laptop—declaring off limits your Caribbean cruise or your trek through the Amazon jungle, for instance. On a daily basis I suggest to clients that they leave their laptops in the trunk of their car when they arrive home. Or at the very least put their technological tools away in a drawer after a reasonable day's work—just as you would put away ingredients and utensils after baking or put away carpentry tools after building shelves in your den.

10

Workaholics Anonymous and Other Resources

The way to do is to be.

—LAO-TZU

Further Readings

Books

Crowley, Katherine. 2006. *Working with You Is Killing Me: Freeing Yourself from Emotional Traps at Work*. New York: Warner Books.

Tips on extreme bosses, corporate culture, and how to protect yourself in the workplace.

De Graaf, John, ed. 2003. *Take Back Your Time: Fighting Overwork and Time Poverty in America*. San Francisco, Calif.: Berrett-Kochler.

How to avoid overscheduling and overworking and live a fuller, more well-rounded life. Chapters by Vicki Robin, Juliet Schor, and Bill Doherty.

Hobfoll, Steven, and Ivonne Hobfoll. 1996. *Work Won't Love You Back: The Dual-Career Couples' Survival Guide*. New York: W. H. Freeman.

How to keep your marriage intact when both partners work.

Loehr, Jim, and Tony Schwartz. 2003. *The Power of Full Engagement: Managing Energy, Not Time, Is the Key to High Performance and Personal Renewal.* New York: Free Press.

The authors suggest that the number of hours in a day is fixed, but the quantity and quality of energy available to us is not. This fundamental insight has the power to revolutionize the way we live.

Robinson, Bryan. 2008. *Heal Your Self-Confidence.* Deerfield Beach, Fla.: Health Communications.

A guide to a better and happier life for people on the fast-track who've lost touch with themselves and for anyone looking to develop more confidence at work, at home, at play.

Robinson, Bryan, and Nancy Chase. 2001. *High-Performing Families: Causes, Consequences and Clinical Solutions.* Washington, D.C.: American Counseling Association.

A look at families on the fast track and at what causes it and what are the consequences and solutions.

Robinson, Bryan, and Claudia Flowers. 2004. "Symptoms of Workaholism: Pop Psychology or Private Pain?" In R. H. Coombs, ed., *Handbook of Addictive Disorders.* New York: John Wiley & Sons.

Examines the symptoms and problems of workaholism, going beneath the pop-psychology allegations and exposing the intense private pain this addiction can cause for the workaholic as well as friends and families.

Robinson, Joe. 2003. *The Guide to Getting a Life.* Berkeley, Calif.: Berkeley Publications Group.

An impassioned manifesto about the need to take vacations for restoration of body and soul.

Schwartz, Richard. 2001. *Introduction to the Internal Family Systems Model.* Oak Park, Ill.: Trailhead.

Describes Internal Family Systems, one of the fastest growing approaches to psychotherapy, which helps folks heal by listening inside themselves in a new way to different "parts." It shows how clients can work with their "workaholic part," unburdening it and helping it function inside in a more balanced way.

Sotile, Wayne, and Mary Sotile. 1996. *The Medical Marriage: A Couple's Survival Guide.* New York: Birch Lane Press.
The first book to address the intimate lives of medical couples, it presents sound advice, dramatic case studies, and cutting-edge information on how to prevent careers from consuming a medical marriage and how to make it work in the twenty-first century.

Workaholics Anonymous. 2005. *The Book of Recovery.* Menlo Park, Calif.: Workaholics Anonymous World Recovery.
A comprehensive overview of workaholism from individual stories to a step-by-step guide to successful recovery to practical information on how to get meetings started.

Daily Readings

Breathnach, Sarah Ban. 1995. *Simple Abundance: A Daybook of Comfort and Joy.* New York: Warner.
This book helps readers create a manageable lifestyle as well as live in a state of grace. It takes readers through the year with 365 daily readings on how to live an authentic life.

Covey, Stephen. 1994. *Daily Reflections for Highly Effective People.* New York: Fireside.
Provides daily reflections on how to attain professional success and personal fulfillment. Brings you closer to inspirational effectiveness in your career.

Larranaga, Robert. 1990. *Calling It a Day: Daily Meditations for Workaholics.* New York: Harper & Row.
365 daily meditations to help workaholics bring balance into their lives.

Lazear, Jonathon. 1992. *Meditations for Men Who Do Too Much.* New York: Fireside.

365 daily meditations to help men on the fast track slow down and take care of themselves.

Lazear, Jonathon, and Wendy Lazear. 1993. *Meditations for Parents Who Do Too Much.* New York: Fireside.

A brief time-out to recharge your batteries and meet the challenges of parenthood. How to slow down, pay attention to your children, and give them the guidance they need in today's hectic, pressure-cooker world.

Monaghan, Patricia. 1994. *Working Wisdom: A Guide to the Art and Strategy of Success at Work.* San Francisco, Calif.: HarperCollins.

A strategy manual in the tradition of oracles that provide fast, savvy advice to help people skillfully master work challenges.

Pollar, Odette. 1996. *365 Ways to Simplify Your Work Life.* Chicago: Dearborn Financial Publishing.

The author presents ideas that bring more time, freedom, and satisfaction to daily work.

Schaef, Anne Wilson. 1990. *Meditations for Women Who Do Too Much.* New York: HarperCollins.

Especially for women, 365 daily reminders of how to slow down and consider what's really important in life.

Audiovisuals

Videotapes

Interview with a Workaholics Anonymous Member.

This thirty-minute videotape shows an interview with a member of WA and the wife of a workaholic. Order from Workaholics Anonymous, P.O. Box 289, Menlo Park, CA 94026-0289.

Married to the Job.

Taped by the Canadian Public Broadcasting Company, this

thirty-minute video shows real-life people dealing with work addiction. Portions of a Workaholics Anonymous meeting in Los Angeles are shown. Order from Workaholics Anonymous, P.O. Box 289, Menlo Park, CA 94026-0289.

Overdoing It: When Work Becomes Your Life.
A thirty-minute documentary in which seven people give heartwarming stories that portray the consequences of work addiction—inner misery, family neglect, broken marriages and relationships, physical problems, and, in some cases, death. Hosted by Dr. Bryan Robinson, this film shows why people become workaholics, how the addiction has affected their lives, and where they sought help. Available on VHS only. To order, call 1-800-582-9522 or write WTVI Video, 3242 Commonwealth Avenue, Charlotte, NC 28205.

Audiotapes

Being and Living with a Recovering Workaholic.
An audiotape that describes what it's like living with someone with work addiction. To order, write Northern California Workaholics Anonymous Intergroup, c/o Mandana House, 541 Mandana Blvd., Oakland, CA 94610.

Workaholics Anonymous Interview.
An audiotape of an interview with the founder of WA, Dan G. To order, write Northern California Workaholics Anonymous Intergroup, c/o Mandana House, 541 Mandana Blvd., Oakland, CA 94610.

Support Organizations

Workaholics Anonymous
www.workaholics-anonymous.org
Workaholics Anonymous, World Service Organization, P.O. Box 289, Menlo Park, CA 94026-0289. A twelve-step support group that has chapters nationwide. The purpose of WA is to help people to stop working compulsively. Startup packets for

beginning new chapters of WA can be obtained from the address given.

Center for Self-Leadership

www.selfleadership.org

The Center for Self-Leadership, P.O. Box 3969, Oak Park, IL 60303. The Center for Self-Leadership was established in August 2000 to promote and expand the training, consulting, clinical, and research activities of Internal Family Systems (IFS). IFS involves helping people heal by listening inside themselves in a new way to different "parts"—feelings or thoughts—and in the process, unburdening themselves of extreme beliefs, emotions, sensations, and urges that constrain their lives. The unburdening of work-addictive parts, in particular, gives people more access to self, our most precious human resource, and they are better able to lead their lives from centered, confident, compassionate places.

Imago Relationships International

www.imagotherapy.com

160 Broadway, East Building, Suite 1001, New York, NY 10038. Telephone: 800-729-1121. The Institute for Imago Relationship Therapy was founded in 1984 by Harville Hendrix. It offers face-to-face learning opportunities, including national and international workshops for couples and singles, and products that teach the dynamics of the love relationship in achieving personal growth. The Institute's mission is to transform marriages and relationships and to improve parenting. The Imago Relationship Therapy approach is one of the best approaches I know of for couples struggling with work addiction. Write or call to locate a Certified Imago Therapist in your area or for dates and locations of workshops for couples across the United States.

Beck Institute for Cognitive Therapy and Research

www.beckinstitute.org/

Beck Institute for Cognitive Therapy and Research, GSB Building, City Line & Belmont Avenues, Suite 700, Bala Cynwyd, PA 19004-1610. The Beck Institute was founded in 1994 as a natural outgrowth of the psychotherapy developed by Dr. Aaron Beck, known as cognitive therapy. The Center provides state-of-the-art psychotherapy and research opportunities and serves as an international training ground for cognitive therapists at all levels. Cognitive therapy lends itself to the treatment of work addiction, because workaholics tend to be more in touch with their thinking than their feelings. Many opportunities are available at this institute for clinicians who would like beginning or advanced training in cognitive therapy.

Workaholics Anonymous

History of Workaholics Anonymous

The first chapter of Workaholics Anonymous was started on the East Coast in April 1983 by a New York corporate financial planner and a schoolteacher who had been "hopeless" workaholics.[1] They founded WA in an effort to help others who suffered from the disease of workaholism and to stop working compulsively themselves. They were joined in their first meeting by the spouse of the planner, who started WorkAnon, a program of recovery for those in relationships with workaholics. At about the same time a nurse suffering from burnout on her high-stress job began one of the first chapters on the West Coast. Other chapters sprang up spontaneously and autonomously throughout the United States and other countries. In March 1990 representatives from various chapters in four states got together for the first time and officially formed the World Service Organization for Workaholics Anonymous.

The only requirement for membership in Workaholics Anonymous is a desire to stop working compulsively. There are no dues or fees for WA membership; it is self-supporting through member contributions. WA is not allied with any sect, denomination, politics, organization, or institution; does not wish to engage in any controversy; neither endorses nor opposes any causes. The primary purpose is to help members stop working compulsively and to carry the message of recovery to workaholics who still suffer.

The Tools of Workaholics Anonymous

WA has developed tools of recovery that supplement the suggested Twelve Steps. The tools are guidelines for living happily, joyously, and free from work addiction one day at a time. They include:

- *Listening.* We set aside time each day for prayer and meditation. Before accepting any commitments, we ask our Higher Power and friends for guidance.
- *Prioritizing.* We decide which are the most important things to do first. Sometimes that may mean doing nothing. We strive to stay flexible to events, reorganizing our priorities as needed. We view interruptions and accidents as opportunities for growth.
- *Substituting.* We do not add a new activity without eliminating from our schedule one that demands equivalent time and energy.
- *Underscheduling.* We allow more time than we think we need for a task or trip, allowing a comfortable margin to accommodate the unexpected.
- *Playing.* We schedule times for play, refusing to let ourselves work nonstop. We do not make our play into a work project.
- *Concentrating.* We try to do one thing at a time.
- *Pacing.* We work at a comfortable pace and rest before we get tired. To remind ourselves, we check our level of energy before proceeding to our next activity. We do not get "wound up" in our work, so we do not have to unwind.
- *Relaxing.* We do not yield to pressure or attempt to pressure others. We remain alert to the people and situations that trigger pressure in us. We become aware of our own

actions, words, body sensations, and feelings that tell us we're responding with pressure. When we feel tension, we stop to reconnect to our Higher Power and others around us.

- *Accepting.* We accept the outcomes of our endeavors, whatever the results, whatever the timing. We know that impatience, rushing, and insisting on perfect results only slow down our recovery. We are gentle with our efforts, knowing that our new way of living requires much practice.
- *Asking.* We admit our weaknesses and mistakes and ask our Higher Power and others for help.
- *Meetings.* We attend WA meetings to learn how the fellowship works and to share our experience, strength, and hope with each other.
- *Telephoning.* We use the phone to stay in contact with other members of the fellowship between meetings. We communicate with our WA friends before and after a critical task.
- *Balancing.* We balance our work involvement with efforts to develop personal relationships, spiritual growth, creativity, and playful attitudes.
- *Serving.* We readily extend help to other workaholics, knowing that assistance to others adds to the quality of our own recovery.
- *Living in the Now.* We realize we are where our Higher Power wants us to be—in the here and now. We try to live each moment with serenity, joy, and gratitude.

The Twelve Steps of Workaholics Anonymous

The Twelve Steps have worked for millions of people with a variety of addictions, including alcohol and other drugs, food, gambling, shopping, and addictive relationships. They can also help those who are committed to a program of spiritual recovery from a life of compulsive, uncontrollable, and harmful work habits. The steps are vehicles for healing work compulsions and establishing a more meaningful and fulfilling lifestyle.

The Problem

Workaholism takes many forms, among them deriving our identity and self-esteem from what we do; keeping overly busy; neglecting our health, relationships, and spirituality; seeing everything as work related; having no desire to do anything (work avoidance or burnout); procrastinating; postponing vacations and rest; doing unnecessary work; worrying; demanding perfection; avoiding intimacy; being controlling.

All these are ways we cope with the pain of having lost our sense of being and of not feeling good enough. Overscheduling our lives with activities is how we run from ourselves. We keep busy to blot out our feelings. We enjoy the adrenaline highs that come from intensity and rushing to meet deadlines. Maybe we are praised and promoted at work for being responsible and hard working. We may even be employed by a workaholic company that uses praise and promotion to encourage our addiction. Yet we have paid an enormous price for these "rewards." We have traded self-awareness for burying our pain in work. We have endangered our health and destroyed our relationships. We may have often felt, "Is this all there is?"

Because there are many misconceptions about workaholism, recognizing it may take a long time. It is both a substance (adrenaline) and a process (overdoing) addiction and is not limited to our paid work life. We can also be workaholic in hobbies, fitness, housework, volunteering, or trying to save the world. All of these activities may appear admirable, but if they mean self-abandonment due to incessant doing, they represent work addiction.

Since workaholism is a progressive disease, we become increasingly driven until we hit bottom. The bottom may come in the form of a serious health problem or an ultimatum from a partner, employer, or friend. At some point, "workaholic" is no longer a label we prize. We realize that we have to change.

To help us in our recovery, there are the twelve suggested steps of Workaholics Anonymous. Because our work addiction is so entrenched in our lives, the process seems overwhelming.

How much time will recovery take? We are already too busy! What do we do with our commitments and responsibilities?

The Solution

As our pain intensifies, we begin to gain willingness—willingness to admit that we are addicted to work, that our lives are unmanageable, and that our way hasn't worked; willingness not to have all our questions answered immediately or to expect a quick fix; willingness to say, "I'm sick. I want to recover and I need help." In Workaholics Anonymous, this admission of powerlessness is Step One. We have found it helpful to take this step and those that follow with others in WA.

From this initial willingness comes more willingness. Step Two tells us that a power greater than ourselves can restore us to sanity. This power can be God, a Higher Power, the Universe, the WA group—whatever is our source of strength.

Step Three involves making a commitment to turn our will and our lives over to God as we understand God. Letting our Higher Power guide us requires giving up control, not being irresponsible. Our will now becomes a tool to turn self-will into willingness. For those of us who pride ourselves on being self-sufficient and strong-willed, taking this step involves a new way of thinking.

In Step Four we make a written inventory of ourselves in relation to our workaholism. We include both our shortcomings and our assets. We ask a WA member for help on how to do Step Four. By taking a close look at ourselves, we become acquainted with the lovable person we truly are, the person we have lost in busyness.

Because many of us feel shame about how our work addiction has hurt ourselves and others, it is healing to do Step Five and talk to an understanding person. This person can be anyone we choose. When we share our secrets, we often find that others have had similar experiences.

Steps Six and Seven ask us to prepare ourselves inwardly to make amends to those we have harmed. In Step Eight we list those people, and in Step Nine we make amends, prudently. After these steps are completed, many of us discover that a great burden has been lifted, that we have a sense of freedom and peace.

Recovery from workaholism is not a cure but a lifelong process. We are granted only a daily reprieve contingent on our maintaining our abstinence and growing spiritually. In Step Ten, we continue the process begun in Step Four—gaining awareness of our feelings and taking responsibility for our words and actions. Taking Step Eleven strengthens our conscious contact with our Higher Power, begun in Step Two, by having us stay in touch through prayer and meditation.

Step Twelve tells us we can maintain and expand the spiritual awakening we experienced in doing all the preceding steps. We can do this by carrying the WA message of recovery to workaholics and by practicing these principles at work, at home, on vacations—everywhere.

The best way for us to keep from sliding back into old habits is to share about our WA recovery with others: "We can't keep it unless we give it away." We carry the message by being an example of a recovering workaholic in our daily activities, as well as by giving service in WA.

Following the steps brings us in touch with our inner wisdom and our spirituality. As we learn to accept ourselves as we are, we experience a new attitude toward work and activity. We enjoy our work more and find ways to work more effectively. When work has its proper place, we find time to have fun and to nurture our health, relationships, and creativity.

We welcome you to our program and wish for you the recovery, serenity, and self-enjoyment we have found.

The Twelve Steps of Workaholics Anonymous

1. We admitted that we were powerless over work—that our lives had become unmanageable.
2. We came to believe that a Power greater than ourselves could restore us to sanity.

3. We made a decision to turn our will and our lives over to the care of God as we understood God.
4. We made a searching and fearless moral inventory of ourselves.
5. We admitted to God, to ourselves, and to another human being the exact nature of our wrongs.
6. We became entirely ready to have God remove all these defects of character.
7. We humbly asked God to remove our shortcomings.
8. We made a list of all persons we had harmed and became willing to make amends to them all.
9. We made direct amends to such people wherever possible, except when to do so would injure them or others.
10. We continued to take personal inventory and when we were wrong promptly admitted it.
11. We sought through prayer and meditation to improve our conscious contact with God as we understood God, praying only for knowledge of God's will for us and the power to carry that out.
12. Having had a spiritual awakening as the result of these steps, we tried to carry this message to workaholics and to practice these principles in all our affairs.

The Signposts of Workaholism

1. We find it hard to love and accept ourselves. Work has become our means of gaining approval, finding our identity, and justifying our existence.
2. We have used work to escape our feelings. Thus, we have deprived ourselves of knowing what we truly need and want.
3. By overworking, we have neglected our health, relationships, recreation, and spirituality. Even when we are not working, we are thinking of our next task. Most of our activities are work related. We have denied ourselves the enjoyment of a balanced and varied life.

4. We have used work as a way to deal with the uncertainties of life. We lie awake worrying; we overplan and overorganize. By being unwilling to surrender control, we have lost our spontaneity, creativity, and flexibility.
5. Many of us grew up in chaotic homes. Stress and intensity feel normal to us. We seek out these conditions in the workplace. We create crises and get adrenaline highs by overworking to solve them. Then we suffer withdrawals and become anxious and depressed. Such mood swings destroy our peace of mind.
6. Work has become addictive. We lie to ourselves and others about the amount we do. We hoard work to ensure that we will always be busy and never bored. We fear free time and vacations and find them painful instead of refreshing.
7. Instead of being a haven, our home has become an extension of our workplace. Our family and friends are often our enablers.
8. We have made unreasonable demands on ourselves. We don't know the difference between job and self-imposed pressure. By overscheduling our lives, we become driven, racing to beat the clock, fearful that we will get behind, and binge-work in order to catch up. Our attention is fragmented by trying to do several things at once. Our inability to pace ourselves leads to breakdown and burnout. We have robbed ourselves of the enjoyment of working.
9. Many of us are perfectionistic. We have not learned to accept mistakes as part of being human and find it hard to ask for help. Because we believe no one can meet our standards, we have difficulty delegating and so do more than our share of work. Thinking ourselves indispensable often prevents our progress. Unrealistic expectations cheat us of contentment.
10. We tend to be overly serious and responsible. All activity must be purposeful. We find it hard to relax and just be; we feel guilty and restless when not working. Because we often make play into work, we rarely experience recreation

and renewal. We have neglected developing our sense of humor and rarely enjoyed the healing power of laughter.

11. Waiting is hard for us. We are more interested in results than process, in quantity than quality. Our impatience often distorts our work by not allowing it proper timing.
12. Many of us are concerned with image. We think looking busy makes people think we are important and gains their admiration. By surrendering our self-approval, we are alienated from ourselves.

The Psychometric Properties of the Work Addiction Risk Test (WART)

The Work Addiction Risk Test (WART) has been used clinically and in research. The test-retest reliability of the instrument is 0.83, and the coefficient alpha for the individual items is 0.85.[2] An internal consistency estimate of reliability (Cronbach's alpha) of 0.88 was obtained for the twenty-five WART items,[3] and the split-half reliability of the inventory with 442 respondents was 0.85.[4]

Face validity and content validity have been established for the instrument. Five major subscales have emerged: Overdoing, Self-Worth, Control-Perfectionism, Intimacy, and Mental Preoccupations/Future Reference.[5] A total of twenty psychotherapists, randomly selected from a state list, critically examined the twenty-five items on the WART for content validity. They were asked to identify twenty-five items from a list of thirty-five that most accurately measured work addiction. Selected test items had generally high content validity, with an average score of 89 out of a possible 100, and 90 percent of the psychotherapists scored 72 or higher.[6]

Concurrent validity was established on the WART in a study with 363 respondents.[7] Scores on the WART were correlated 0.40 with generalized anxiety on the State-Trait Anxiety Inventory[8] and 0.37 with the Type A Self-Report Inventory.[9] Moderate to low significant correlations were obtained on the four scales of the Jenkins Activity Survey—the most commonly used measure of Type A behavior—with 0.50 on the Type A scale, 0.50 on the Speed and Impatience scale, 0.39 on the Hard-Driving and Competitive scale, and 0.20 on the Job Involvement scale.[10]

Concurrent validity also was demonstrated between the WART and the Thinking/Feeling scale on the Myers-Briggs Indicator in a study with ninety participants.[11] A regression analysis revealed that WART scores correlated more with the T end of the Myers-Briggs scale than with the F end. In addition, WART scores were significantly higher for respondents who worked more than forty hours a week than for those who worked fewer than forty-one hours per week.

Notes

Notes to the Introduction

1. Bryan Robinson, "Work Abuse: Walking the Line at Work, at Home, and at Play" (unpublished manuscript, 2007).

2. Bryan Robinson, "Chained to the Desk: Work May Be the Great Unexamined Therapy Issue of Our Time," *Family Therapy Networker,* July/August 2000, pp. 26–37.

3. Heather Berrigan, "Is the Workplace the Real American Idol?" *Living Church Foundation,* 30 November 2003, p. 1.

4. Neil Chesanow, "Vacation for the Health of It," *Endless Vacation,* January/February 2005, pp. 31–32.

5. Stephanie Rosenbloom, "Please Don't Make Me Go on Vacation," *New York Times,* 10 August 2006, pp. E1–E2.

6. Po Bronson, "Just Sit Back and Relax: Why Do Americans Have to Work so Hard at Taking It Easy?" *Time,* 26 June 2006, p. 78.

7. Rosenbloom, "Please Don't Make Me Go on Vacation" (2006).

8. Robert Putnam, "You Gotta Have Friends," *Time,* 3 July 2006, p. 36.

9. Wayne Oates, *Confessions of a Workaholic* (New York: World, 1971).

10. Loren Stein, "Workaholism: It's No Longer Seen as a Respectable Vice," *A Healthy Me,* 25 March 2006, p. 2.

11. Emilie Filou, "Death in the Office," *World Business,* July/August 2006, pp. 19–22.

12. Bryan Robinson, Claudia Flowers, and Chris Burris, "An Empirical Study of the Relationship between Self-Leadership and Workaholism 'Firefighter' Behavior," *Journal of Self-Leadership* 2 (2005): 22–36. See also Richard Schwartz, *Introduction to the Internal Family Systems Model* (Oak Park, Ill.: Trailheads 2001), for a more detailed discussion of workaholism as an internal firefighter and the role it plays in the internal family systems model.

Notes to Chapter 1

1. Quoted in Tony Schwartz, "Acceleration Syndrome," *Vanity Fair,* October 1988, p. 180.

2. See chapter 10 for the psychometric properties of the WART.

Notes to Chapter 2

1. Daniel Seligman, "The Curse of Work," *Fortune,* 7 March 1994, p. 133.

2. Walter Kiechel, "The Workaholic Generation," *Fortune,* 10 April 1989, pp. 50–62.

3. Marilyn Machlowitz, *Workaholics: Living with Them, Working with Them* (Reading, Mass.: Addison-Wesley, 1985).

4. Ishu Ishiyama and Akio Kitayama, "Overwork and Career-Centered Self-Validation among the Japanese: Psychosocial Issues and Counselling Implications," *International Journal for the Advancement of Counselling* 17 (1994): 167–182.

5. These four levels of enabling are based on the four levels of ecosystems proposed by Urie Bronfenbrenner: microsystem, mesosystem, exosystem, and macrosystem. Urie Bronfenbrenner, *The Ecology of Human Development* (Cambridge, Mass.: Harvard University Press, 1979).

6. Marilyn Machlowitz, "Workaholics Enjoy Themselves, an Expert Says: It's Their Family and Friends Who Pay," *Psychology Today,* June 1980, p. 79.

7. Lars-Erik Nelson, "Republican Bills Invite Employers to Abuse Work Force," *Charlotte Observer,* 20 June 1997, p. 15A.

8. Owen Edwards, "Romancing the Grindstone," *Forbes ASAP Magazine,* 5 December 1994, p. S178.

9. Louise Sloan, "Office Junkie," *Out Magazine,* August 1997, p. 100.

10. See James Levine and Todd Pittinsky, *Working Fathers* (Reading, Mass.: Addison-Wesley, 1997).

11. See Gloria Steinem's foreword to Bryan Robinson, *Overdoing It: How to Slow Down and Take Care of Yourself* (Deerfield Beach, Fla.: Health Communications, 1992), p. xi.

12. See, for example, Diane Fassel, *Working Ourselves to Death* (San Francisco: Harper & Row, 2000, Bryan Robinson, *Work Addiction* (Deerfield Beach, Fla.: Health Communications, 1989), and Janet Woititz, *Home Away from Home: The Art of Self-Sabotage* (Deerfield Beach, Fla.: Health Communications, 1987).

13. Barbara Garson, "Work Addiction: Organizational Boon or Doom?" (unpublished manuscript, Garson and Associates, Atlanta, Ga., 1990).

14. Richard Weinberg and Larry Mauksch, "Examining Family of Ori-

gin Influences in Life at Work," *Journal of Marital and Family Therapy* 17 (1991): 233–242.

15. Anne Wilson Schaef and Diane Fassel, *The Addictive Organization* (San Francisco: Harper & Row, 1988).

16. See, for example, Bruce Matthews and Mark Halbrook, "Adult Children of Alcoholics: Implications for Career Development," *Journal of Career Development* 16 (1990): 261–268, and Woititz, *Home Away from Home* (1987).

17. Edward Walsh, "Workaholism: No Life for the Leisurelorn?" *Parks and Recreation,* January 1987, pp. 82–84.

18. See, for example, Fassel, *Working Ourselves to Death* (2000); Sandra Haymon, "The Relationship of Work Addiction and Depression, Anxiety, and Anger in College Males," *Dissertation Abstracts International* 53 (1993): 5401-B; Oates, *Confessions of a Workaholic* (1971); Robinson, *Work Addiction* (1989); and Janet Spence and Ann Robbins, "Workaholics: Definition, Measurement, and Preliminary Results," *Journal of Personality Assessment* 58 (1992): 160–178.

19. Bryan Robinson and Lisa Kelley, "Adult Children of Workaholics: Self-Concept, Anxiety, Depression, and Locus of Control," *American Journal of Family Therapy* 26 (1998): 223–238; and Bryan Robinson and Phyllis Post, "Work Addiction as a Function of Family of Origin and Its Influence on Current Family Functioning," *Family Journal* 3 (1995): 200–206.

20. Robinson, *Overdoing It* (1992).

21. Machlowitz, *Workaholics* (1985).

22. Jill Johnson Piper, "All Work and No Play Make Jack an Addict," *Memphis Commercial Appeal,* 8 October 1989, pp. E1–E2.

23. Robinson and Kelley, "Adult Children of Workaholics" (1998).

24. Bryan Robinson and Phyllis Post, "Risk of Addiction to Work and Family Functioning," *Psychological Reports* 81 (1997): 91–95.

Notes to Chapter 3

1. Robinson, Flowers, and Burris, "An Empirical Study of the Relationship between Self-Leadership and Workaholism 'Firefighter' Behaviors" (2005).

2. Bryan Robinson, *Work Addiction* (1989).

3. Oates, *Confessions of a Workaholic* (1971).

4. Diane Fassel describes work anorexics in her book *Working Ourselves to Death* (2000).

5. Gayle Porter, "Organizational Impact of Workaholism: Suggestions for Researching the Negative Outcomes of Excessive Work," *Journal of Occupational Health Psychology* 1 (1996): 70–84.

6. Fassel, *Working Ourselves to Death* (2000), p. 82.

7. Consult chapter 10 for a more detailed explanation of the psychometric properties of the WART, or refer to the following research studies: Claudia Flowers and Bryan Robinson, "A Structural and Discriminant Analysis of the Work Addiction Risk Test," *Educational and Psychological Measurement* 62 (2002): 517–526; Bryan Robinson, "Concurrent Validity of the Work Addiction Risk Test as a Measure of Workaholism," *Psychological Reports* 79 (1996): 1313–1314; Bryan Robinson and Bruce Phillips, "Measuring Workaholism: Content Validity of the Work Addiction Risk Test," *Psychological Reports* 77 (1995): 657–658; Bryan Robinson and Phyllis Post, "Validity of the Work Addiction Risk Test," *Perceptual and Motor Skills* 78 (1994): 337–338; Bryan Robinson and Phyllis Post, "Split-Half Reliability of the Work Addiction Risk Test: Development of a Measure of workaholism," *Psychological Reports* 76 (1995): 1226; Bryan Robinson, Phyllis Post, and Judith Khakee, "Test-Retest Reliability of the Work Addiction Risk Test," *Perceptual and Motor Skills* 74 (1992): 926; and Sandra Swary, "Myers-Briggs Type and Workaholism" (unpublished honors thesis, Georgia State University, Atlanta, 1996).

8. Wayne Sotile and Mary Sotile, *The Medical Marriage: A Couple's Survival Guide* (New York: Birch Lane Press, 1995).

9. Edward Hallowell and John Ratey, *Driven to Distraction: Recognizing and Coping with Attention Deficit Disorder* (New York: Simon & Schuster, 1994), p. 182.

10. Garson, "Work Addiction: Organizational Boon or Doom?" (1990).

Notes to Chapter 4

1. Bryan Robinson, "The Workaholic Family: A Clinical Perspective," American *Journal of Family Therapy* 26 (1998): 63–73.

2. Anthony Pietropinto, "The Workaholic Spouse," *Medical Aspects of Human Sexuality* 20 (1986): 89–96.

3. Barbara Killinger, *Workaholics: The Respectable Addicts* (New York: Fireside, 1992).

4. Robert Klaft and Brian Kleiner, "Understanding Workaholics," *Business* 38 (1988): 37–40.

5. See, for example, Nancy Chase, *The Parentified Child: Theory, Research, and Treatment* (Thousand Oaks, Calif.: Sage, 1998 and Gregory Jurkovic, *Lost Childhoods: The Plight of the Parentified Child* (New York: Brunner-Mazel, 1997).

6. Ishiyama and Kitayama, "Overwork and Career-Centered Self-Validation among the Japanese" (1994).

7. Reports of the entire research study can be found in these two

sources: Robinson and Post, "Work Addiction as a Function of Family of Origin and Its Influence on Current Family Functioning" (1995); Robinson and Post, "Risk of Addiction to Work and Family Functioning" (1997).

8. Ann Bailey," He Puts Work Ahead of the Family," *First for Women*, August 2003, p. 91.

Notes to Chapter 5

1. Diane Fassel and Anne Wilson Schaef, "A Feminist Perspective on Work Addiction," in Nan Van Den Bergh, ed., *Feminist Perspectives on Addictions* (New York: Springer, 1991), pp. 199–211.

2. Porter, "Organizational Impact of Workaholism" (1996).

3. Fassel and Schaef, "A Feminist Perspective on Work Addiction" (1991), p. 208.

4. Porter, "Organizational Impact of Workaholism" (1996).

5. Annmarie L. Geddes, "The Pitfalls of Being Addicted to Work," *Cleveland's Small Business News,* June 1995, p. 57.

6. Porter, "Organizational Impact of Workaholism" (1996), p. 74.

7. Dell Jones, "Go Home! Working Longer Hours Isn't Always Smarter," *USA Today,* 2 September 1994, pp. 2A–2B.

8. Norman Cousins, *Headfirst: The Biology of Hope* (New York: Dutton, 1989).

9. Deepak Chopra, *Perfect Health: The Complete Mind/Body Guide* (New York: Harmony Books, 1991).

10. Ishiyama and Kitayama, "Overwork and Career-Centered Self-Validation among the Japanese" (1994).

Notes to Chapter 6

1. See, for example, Fassel, *Working Ourselves to Death* (2000); Robinson, "The Workaholic Family: A Clinical Perspective" (1998); Robinson and Post, "Work Addiction as a Function of Family of Origin and Its Influence on Current Family Functioning" (1995); and Robinson and Post, "Risk of Addiction to Work and Family Functioning" (1997).

2. For an excellent discussion of emotional incest, see Patricia Love, *The Emotional Incest Syndrome: What to Do When a Parents' Love Rules Your Life* (New York: Dutton, 1990).

3. Rebecca Jones and Marolyn Wells, "An Empirical Study of Parentification and Personality," *American Journal of Family Therapy* 24 (1996): 145–152.

4. Jones and Wells, "An Empirical Study of Parentification and Personality" (1996).

5. Malcolm West and Adrienne Keller, "Parentification of the Child: A Case Study of Bowlby's Compulsive Care-Giving Attachment Pattern," *American Journal of Psychotherapy* 155 (1991): 425–431.

6. West and Keller, "Parentification of the Child" (1991), p. 426.

7. John Bowlby, "The Making and Breaking of Affectional Bonds," *British Journal of Psychiatry* 130 (1977): 201–210.

8. Quoted in Walter Scott, "Walter Scott's Personality Parade," *Parade,* 7 July 1996, p. 2.

9. Quoted in Gail Buchalter, "In That Moment, I Grew Up a Lot," *Parade,* 1 September 1996, p. 8.

10. Quoted in Buchalter, "In That Moment, I Grew Up a Lot" (1996), p. 10.

11. Gloria Steinem, *Revolution from Within: A Book on Self-Esteem* (New York: Little, Brown, 1992).

12. Gloria Steinem, from her foreword to Robinson, *Overdoing It* (1992), pp. ix–xii. Used with permission.

13. West and Keller, "Parentification of the Child" (1991).

14. In her book *On Death and Dying* (New York: Macmillan, 1969), Dr. Elisabeth Kubler-Ross proposed five stages of grief that the dying and their loved ones go through: shock, denial, bargaining, anger, and acceptance.

15. Associated Press, "Meditation May Help Prolong Life, Study Says," *Charlotte Observer,* 4 February 1990; and Cousins, *Headfirst: The Biology of Hope* (1989).

16. Robinson, *Overdoing It* (1992).

17. See Sharon Wegscheider, *The Family Trap* (Palo Alto, Calif.: Science and Behavior Books, 1979), for a comprehensive examination of family-of-origin roles. See also Bryan Robinson and Lyn Rhoden, *Working with Children of Alcoholics: The Practitioner's Handbook* (Thousand Oaks, Calif.: Sage, 1998), for these roles as they apply to children of alcoholics.

Notes to Chapter 7

1. Renee is the wife of Ross from chapter 6.

2. Bryan Robinson, Jane Carroll, and Claudia Flowers, "Marital Estrangement, Positive Affect, and Locus of Control among Spouses of Workaholics and Spouses of Nonworkaholics: A National Study," *American Journal of Family Therapy* 29 (2001): 397–410.

3. Bryan Robinson, Claudia Flowers, and Kok-Mun Ng, "The Relationship between Workaholism and Marital Disaffection: Husbands' Perspective," *Family Journal* 14 (2006): 213–220.

4. Edward Walsh, "Workaholism: No Life for the Leisurelorn?" *Parks and Recreation,* January 1987, p. 82.

5. Terri Finch Hamilton, "Women Susceptible to Working Whirl," *Grand Rapids Press,* 27 June 1991, pp. D1–D3.

6. Pietropinto, "The Workaholic Spouse" (1986).

7. Daniel Weeks, "Cooling Off Your Office Affair," *North West Airlines World Traveler Magazine,* June 1995, pp. 59–62.

8. Ann Herbst, "Married to the Job," *McCall's,* November 1996, pp. 130–134.

9. Harville Hendrix, *Getting the Love You Want: A Guide for Couples* (New York: Harper & Row, 1988).

10. Paul DeLuca, *The Solo Partner: Repairing Your Relationship on Your Own* (Point Roberts, Wash.: Hartley & Marks, 1996).

11. Eugenia Killoran, "Thank Goodness It's Monday: Workaholism," *Vantage Point,* November 1991, pp. 1–3.

12. Ishiyama and Kitayama, "Overwork and Career-Centered Self-Validation among the Japanese" (1994), p. 178.

13. Robinson, *Work Addiction* (1989).

14. Studs Terkel, *Working* (New York: Pantheon Books, 1974).

15. Stephen Betchen, "Parentified Pursuers and Childlike Distancers in Marital Therapy," *Family Journal* 4 (1996): 100–108.

16. Betchen, "Parentified Pursuers and Childlike Distancers in Marital Therapy" (1996), p. 103.

17. Thomas Fogarty, "The Distancer and the Pursuer," *Family* 7 (1979): 11–16; and Thomas Fogarty, "Marital Crisis," in P. Guerin, ed., *Family Therapy: Theory and Practice* (New York: Gardner, 1976), pp. 325–334.

18. Robinson and Post, "Work Addiction as a Function of Family of Origin and Its Influence on Current Family Functioning" (1995).

19. Hendrix, *Getting the Love You Want* (1988); and Harville Hendrix, *Getting the Love You Want: A Couples Workshop Manual* (New York: Institute for Relationship Therapy, 1994).

Notes to Chapter 8

1. See, for example, Virginia Kelly and Jane Myers, "Parental Alcoholism and Coping: A Comparison of Female Children of Alcoholics with Female Children of Nonalcoholics," *Journal of Counseling and Development* 74 (1996): 501–504; Phyllis Post and Bryan Robinson, "A Comparison of School-Age Children of Alcoholic and Nonalcoholic Parents on Anxiety, Self-Esteem, and Locus of Control," *Professional School Counselor* 1 (1998): 36–42; Phyllis Post, Wanda Webb, and Bryan Robinson, "Relationship between Self-Concept, Anxiety, and Knowledge of Alcoholism by Gender and Age among Adult Children of Alcoholics," *Alcoholism Treatment Quarterly* 8 (1991): 91–95; Robinson and Rhoden, *Working with Children of*

Alcoholics (1998); Sandra Tweed and Cynthia Ryff, "Adult Children of Alcoholics: Profiles of Wellness Amid Distress," *Journal of Studies on Alcohol* 52 (1991): 133–141; Wanda Webb, Phyllis Post, Bryan Robinson, and Lynn Moreland, "Self-Concept, Anxiety, and Knowledge Exhibited by Adult Children of Alcoholics and Adult Children of Nonalcoholics," *Journal of Drug Education* 20 (1992): 106–114.

2. Pietropinto, "The Workaholic Spouse" (1986); Robinson, *Work Addiction* (1989); and Gerald Spruell, "Work Fever," *Training and Development Journal* 41 (1987): 41–45.

3. See, for example, Bryan Robinson, "Children of Workaholics: What Practitioners Need to Know," *Journal of Child and Youth Care* 12 (1998): 3–10; Bryan Robinson and Jane Carroll, "Assessing the Offspring of Workaholics: The Children of Workaholics Screening Test," *Perceptual and Motor Skills* 88 (1999): 1127–1134; Bryan Robinson, "Adult Children of Workaholics: Clinical and Empirical Research with Implications for Family Therapists," *Journal of Family Psychotherapy* 11 (2000): 15–26; Bryan Robinson, "Workaholism and Family Functioning: A Profile of Familial Relationships, Psychological Outcomes, and Research Considerations," *Contemporary Family Research* 23 (2001): 123–135.

4. Robinson and Kelly, "Adult Children of Workaholics" (1998).

5. See, for example, Kelly and Myers, "Parental Alcoholism and Coping" (1996); Robinson and Rhoden, *Working with Children of Alcoholics* (1998); and Webb, Post, Robinson, and Moreland, "Self-Concept, Anxiety, and Knowledge Exhibited by Adult Children of Alcoholics and Adult Children of Nonalcoholics" (1992).

6. Sheri Navarrete, "An Empirical Study of Adult Children of Workaholics: Psychological Functioning and Intergenerational Transmission," Ph.D. diss., California Graduate Institute, August 1998.

7. Elaine Searcy, "Adult Children of Workaholics: Anxiety, Depression, Family Relationships and Risk for Work Addiction," Master's thesis, University of South Australia, January 2000.

8. Jane Carroll and Bryan Robinson, "Depression and Parentification among Adults as Related to Parental Workaholism and Alcoholism," *Family Journal* 8 (2000): 360–367.

9. Oates, *Confessions of a Workaholic* (1971); Robinson, *Overdoing It* (1992); and Bryan Robinson, "Relationship between Work Addiction and Family Functioning: Clinical Implications for Marriage and Family Therapists," *Journal of Family Psychotherapy* 7 (1996): 13–29.

10. Machlowitz, "Workaholics Enjoy Themselves, an Expert Says" (June 1980), p. 79.

11. Oates, *Confessions of a Workaholic* (1971).

12. Tina Harralson and Kathleen Lawler, "The Relationship of Parent-

ing Styles and Social Competency to Type A Behavior in Children," *Journal of Psychosomatic Research* 36 (1992): 625–634; and Patti Watkins, Clay Ward, Douglas Southard, and Edwin Fisher, "The Type A Belief System: Relationships to Hostility, Social Support, and Life Stress," *Behavioral Medicine* 18 (1992): 27–32.

13. Karen Woodall and Karen Matthews, "Familial Environment Associated with Type A Behaviors and Psychophysiological Responses to Stress in Children," *Health Psychology* 8 (1989): 403–426.

14. Pietropinto, "The Workaholic Spouse" (1986).

15. Pietropinto, "The Workaholic Spouse" (1986).

16. Weeks, "Cooling Off Your Office Affair" (1995), p. 63.

17. Richard Schwartz, *Internal Family Systems Therapy* (New York: Guilford Press, 1995); Schwartz, *Introduction to the Internal Family Systems Model* (2001).

Notes to Chapter 9

1. Mary Baechler, "I'm Mary, and I'm a Workaholic," *Inc.*, April 1996. Copyright 1996 by Goldhirsh Group, Inc., 38 Commercial Wharf, Boston, MA 02110. Used with permission of the publisher.

2. Matthews and Halbrook, "Adult Children of Alcoholics" (1990); and Woititz, *Home Away from Home* (1987).

3. Klaft and Kleiner, "Understanding Workaholics" (1988).

4. Gayle Porter, "Workaholics as High-Performance Employees: The Intersection of Workplace and Family Relationship Problems," in Bryan Robinson and Nancy Chase, eds., *High-Performing Families: Causes, Consequences, and Clinical* Solutions (Washington, D.C.: American Counseling Association, 2001), pp. 43–69; Gayle Porter, "Work, Work Ethic, Work Excess," *Journal of Organizational Change Management* 17 (2004): 424–439; Gayle Porter, "Profiles of Workaholism among High-Tech Managers," *Career Development-International* 11 (2006); Gayle Porter and N. Kakabadse, "HRM Perspectives on Addiction to Technology and Work," *Journal of Management Development* 25 (2006): 535–560.

5. Porter, "Organizational Impact of Workaholism" (1996), p. 82.

6. Porter, "Organizational Impact of Workaholism" (1996), p. 71.

7. Bill Billeter, "Workaholics Are Hurting the Company and Themselves," *Charlotte Observer,* 16 May 1981, p. 5C.

8. Emilie Filou, "Death in the Office," *World Business,* July/August 2006, pp. 19–22.

9. Lesley Alderman, "How to Tell the Boss You're Getting Worked to Death—Without Killing Your Career," *Money,* May 1995, p. 41.

10. N. Kakabadse, Gayle Porter, and D. Vance, "Employer Liability for

Addiction to Information and Communication Technology" (unpublished paper, Rutgers University, 2006).

11. Ellen Gamerman, "The New Power Picnics," *Wall Street Journal,* 12 August 2006, p. PG.

12. Gamerman, "The New Power Picnics" (2006).

13. Alderman, "How to Tell the Boss You're Getting Worked to Death" (1995).

14. Leslie Wright and Marti Smye, *Corporate Abuse: How "Lean and Mean" Robs People and Profits* (New York: Macmillan, 1996), p. 82.

15. Schaef and Fassel, *The Addictive Organization* (1988).

16. Fassel and Schaef, "A Feminist Perspective on Work Addiction" (1991).

17. John Sheridan, "Workin' Too Hard," *Industry Week,* 18 January 1988, pp. 31–36.

18. Klaft and Kleimer, "Understanding Workaholics" (1988), p. 39.

19. Milton Bordwin, "Overwork: The Cause of Your Next Workers' Comp Claim?" *Management Review,* March 1996, p. 50.

20. Klaft and Kleimer, "Understanding Workaholics" (1988).

21. Alderman, "How to Tell the Boss You're Getting Worked to Death" (1995).

22. Michelle Conlin, "Square Feet: Oh, How Square!" *Business Week,* 3 July 2006, pp. 100–101.

Notes to Chapter 10

1. Information on Workaholics Anomymous in this section is reprinted by permission of Workaholics Anonymous World Service Organization, Inc., © 1991 WA World Services, Inc.

2. Robinson, Post, and Khakee, "Test-Retest Reliability of the Work Addiction Risk Test" (1992).

3. Bryan Robinson, "The Work Addiction Risk Test: Development of a Self-Report Measure of Workaholism, *Perceptual and Motor Skills* 88 (1999): 199–210.

4. Robinson and Post, "Split–Half Reliability of the Work Addiction Risk Test" (1995).

5. Robinson and Post, "Validity of the Work Addiction Risk Test" (1994).

6. Robinson and Phillips, "Measuring Workaholism" (1995).

7. Robinson, "Concurrent Validity of the Work Addiction Risk Test as a Measure of Workaholism" (1996).

8. Charles Spielberger, *Self-Evaluation Questionnaire* (STAI Form X-2) (Palo Alto, Calif.: Consulting Psychologists Press, 1968).

9. James Blumenthal, Steve Herman, Leslie O'Toole, Thomas Haney,

Redford Williams, and John Barefoot, "Development of a Brief Self-Report Measure of the Type A (Coronary Prone) Behavior Pattern," *Journal of Psychosomatic Research* 29 (1985): 265–274.

10. David Jenkins, Ray Rosenman, and Meyer Friedman, "Development of an Objective Psychological Test for the Determination of the Coronary-Prone Behavior Pattern in Employed Men," *Journal of Chronic Disease* 20 (1967): 371–379.

11. Swary, "Myers-Briggs Type and Workaholism" (1996).

Index

Abstinence, establishment of, 25, 53, 81; in Workaholics Anonymous, 103
Acceptance, as tool of Workaholics Anonymous, 244
Achievement. *See* Productivity
ADD. *See* Attention deficit disorder
Addiction: as a model of family disease, 5, 88–89; workaholism as, 11–29, 243–250. *See also* Workaholics; Workaholism
Addiction to work. *See* Workaholism
Addictive Organization, The (Schaef and Fassel), 45
Adrenaline: as addiction, 48–49; effect on physical system, 127; as related to heart attacks, 127; as a rush for workaholics, 17, 73, 109, 219, 227; as self-medication, 74, 80; withdrawal from, 81
Adrenaline-seeking workaholics: and attention deficit disorder (ADD), 71, 80–81; treatment of, 80–82
Adult Children of Alcoholics (Woititz), 188
Advertisements for workaholics, 38–39, 45; as enabler of workaholism, 39–40
Al-Anon, 23, 101, 104; as substitute for unavailable WorkAnon
Alcoholics Anonymous: as a condition for continuing therapy, 29, 101, 109; hitting bottom, 5, 25
All-or-nothing thinking of workaholics, 121, 122
Alliances in workaholic families, 100
Amends, as part of Twelve Step program, 248
American Academy of Matrimonial Lawyers, survey on divorce, 195
American Idol, as applied to work addiction, 11–29
Anger, in workaholics, 47, 55, 127
Anxiety: in children of workaholics, 189–190, 192; in workaholics, 47, 53, 55, 99, 127; in the workplace, 229
Approval, need for: in children of workaholics, 196–201; in workaholics, 43, 46–47, 110–117
Art (case study), 106–110
Asking for help, as tool of Workaholics Anonymous, 244
Attention deficit disorder (ADD), and need for adrenaline, 73–75
Attention-deficit workaholics, 68, 69, 73–75, 80, 215

Balance: achieving, among workaholics, 15, 27, 52, 56, 154, 229, 233–234; benefits of work force having, 229–231; for clinicians, 29; as tool of Workaholics Anonymous, 244; in the workplace, 229–230
Ball, Lucille, 33
Barrymore, Drew, 144
Beck, Aaron, 131–133
Beck Institute for Cognitive Therapy and Research, 241–242
Becker, Boris, 123
Beecher, Henry Ward, 161
Behavioral signs of workaholism, 68

Bibliotherapy for family members of workaholics, 181
Binging on work, as symptom of workaholism, 65–66, 71–72
"Blackberrization" of our lives, 1–2
Blackberry, 1; love affair with, 3, 218
Bluetooth, 2
Blurred-boundary thinking among workaholics, 123
Bosses. *See* Managers
Boundary setting: with families of workaholics, 176–180; lack of in workplace, 221; workaholics and, 27–29, 81–82, 233–235
Bowlby, John, 144
Brenda (case study), 85–87
Brownouts, as symptom of workaholism, 66
Bryan (case study), 11–14
Bulimic workaholics, 68, 71–73, 79
Burnout: among workaholics: 46, 62, 108; reducing in workplace, 231
Burns, David, 131–133
Busyness, as symptom of workaholism, 63–64, 178

Campbell, Joseph, 137
Camus, Albert, 58
Cancer, increased risk of, and stress, 126–127
Careaholic workaholics, 76
Careaholism, 143–147; test for, 145
Career path of workaholics, typical, 216
Caring for oneself, learning how to, 154–155
Carnes, Patrick, 50
Caselin, Jeff, 234
Case studies: Art, 106–110; Brenda, 85–87; Bryan, 11–14; Charles, 183–188; Dana, 198–200; Glenn, 58–60; Margo, 30–32; Mary, 209–212; Pat, 200–201; Renee, 161–163; Robinson, Bryan, 148–150; Ross, 137–139; Smith family, 90–91; Steinem, Gloria, 150–151
Caterpillar, Inc., 222
Celebrations in life, learning to participate in, 158
Cell phones, using rather than being used by, 235
Center for Self-Leadership, 241
Chapin, Harry, 183
Charles (case study), 183–188
Childhood, lost: mourning for, 153–154; roots of workaholism in, 137–160
Children, workaholic, 139–147; helping, 152–160
Children of workaholics, 23–24, 183–208; concerns regarding their parents' workaholism, 192–193; parentification of, 95–96; portrait of, 193; support for, 104–105; tips for nurturing, 202–203, 205–208. *See also* Family members of workaholics; Workaholics
Circularity of blame in workaholic families, 91–93
Clinicians: addressing boundary setting, 27–29; confronting enabling behaviors, 101–102; developing self-care plans, 82–84; helping workaholics establish abstinence, 25–26; helping workaholics repair relationships, 202–203; initial screening and family contracts, 100; introducing the concept of work addiction as family disease, 100; matching counseling to workaholic type, 79–81; putting time cushions into work schedules, 26; referral to Twelve Step and Support groups, 102–105; screening for work addiction, 207; steps for breaking the workaholic cycle, 130–131; working with the pursuer-distancer dynamic, 177–178. *See also* Counseling
Coalitions in workaholic families, 92
Communication: helping partners learn skills for, 180–181; impaired among workaholics, 62, 224, 231; as tool of Workaholics Anonymous, 246
Compassion, as Self in Internal Family Systems Therapy, 204–205
Concealment in relationships of workaholics, 174–175
Concentration, as tool of Workaholics Anonymous, 243
Confessions of a Workaholic (Oates), 6
Contracts within families, rewriting of, as therapy tool, 100. *See also* Tacit family contract

Control: loss of, in workaholics' children, 196–197; need for, in workaholics, 47, 55, 99, 111, 128, 141, 213; as symptom of workaholics, 63–64, 139
Corporate Abuse (Wright and Smye), 198
Corporate survival, as ultimate value in workaholic companies, 220
Corporate world: and abuse, 219–223; as enabler of workaholism, 38, 216–222; as an individual addict, 220; traits of workaholic companies, 220–222; workaholics' work patterns hurt, 213
Cortisol, effect on physical system, 126–127
Counseling, matching with workaholic type, 79–81. *See also* Clinicians; Treatment for workaholics
Cousins, Norman, 126
Coworkers: dislike of workaholics, 117; reaching out to, 233
"Crackberry," 1
Crises: and addiction to adrenaline, 48–50; created by workaholics, 73, 214–215; as norm in workaholic organizations, 221
Culture: embedded beliefs about work, 40–42; as enabler of workaholism, 38–40; work trends in, 35–36
Cultures of sacrifice, 198

Daily deposit time, setting aside, 154–155
Daily rituals. *See* Rituals
Daily surroundings as enabler for workaholism, 37
Dana (case study), 198–200
Dass, Ram, 144
Daytimer appointment calendars, as help in boundary setting, 26, 28
Dean, James, 149
Deceit in relationships, 174–175
DeGeneres, Ellen, 123
Delegating authority: importance of, 234; inability to, 47, 53, 57, 64, 234
DeMello, Anthony, 128
Denial of workaholism: as a culture, 30–57; overcoming, 153–155; overcoming in family members, 99–105; in workaholics, 55–57
Depression: in workaholics, 5–6, 47, 53, 55, 99, 110, 127, 229; in children of workaholics, 189–190, 192; in workaholic workplaces, 228
Disease concept: of the workaholic's family, 88–89; introducing to family members, 100–101
Disenfranchised groups, seeking worth through work, 40–41
Divorce, as result of workaholism, 163–164, 166
Downsizing, 36–37, 43
Driven to Distraction (Hallowell and Ratey), 80
Dunlavey, Francis C., 229
DWW (driving-while-working mentally), 66
Dyed-in-the-wool workaholics, 71
Dysfunctional families of workaholics, 37, 54, 88–89, 99, 139, 158; in workaholic's childhood, 44. *See also* Family members of workaholics; Family systems model

EAPs. *See* Employee assistance programs
Economic Policy Institute, 2
Efficiency, diminished, in workaholics, 46, 214–217, 222, 224
Emotional bankruptcy and workaholics, 154
Emotional enmeshment in childhood and workaholism, 146; and children of workaholics, 197
Emotional unavailability and workaholism, 19, 92, 192, 224
Employee assistance programs (EAPs), 230
Enabling of workaholism, 22, 36–40, 42, 93–94; avoidance of, 101–102; by children, 193, 207–208; by corporate world, 38, 216–222; as a process explained by clinicians, 56, 57, 100; by societal system, 94–95
Endorphins, effect on physical system, 126–127
Euphoria. *See* Work highs
Exec, 167
External locus of control among workaholics, 47

Externalized thinking of workaholics, 125

Family and Work Institute, 2
Family hero, 47
Family members of workaholics, in recovery, 104–105
Family of origin, analysis of: in research on workaholism, 97–99; in therapy with workaholics, 153–154, 158–159; in workaholism therapy, 158–159
Family system, diagramming of, as therapy tool, 100
Family systems model, 5, 88–89, 158; improving communication in, 180–181; structural and dynamic characteristics of, 91–94; use by clinicians to prepare families for change, 176–177
Fassel, Diane, 45, 74, 112, 220
Feelings, learning to identify and accept, 134–135
Financial demands and enabling of workaholism, 37, 176
Firefighter, 7
Flexiplace, as enabler of workaholism, 38
Flextime, 15, 38, 39, 230
Fortune, 34

Gainfully employed myth about workaholics, 51
Garfield, Charles, 216
Garson, Barbara, 44
Gay men, seeking worth through work, 40–41
General Mills, employee policies of, 230
Genograms, as tool for understanding workaholism, 159
Glenn (case study), 58–60
Goldstein, Daniel, 171
Graham, Billy, 33

Hallowell, Edward, 80
Headfirst (Cousins), 126
Health problems of workaholics, 47, 53, and associated costs, 228–229, 231. *See also* Anxiety; Depression; Stress
Healthy Work Days, as employee awareness tool, 230
Heigh-Ho Syndrome, 117
Helpless thinking among workaholics, 124, 172–173
Higher Power, submission to, as part of Twelve Steps, 246–248; in Workaholics Anonymous, 103
High-powered couples, 78
Hitting bottom, 5–6
Hurry and workaholism, 127
Huxley, Aldous, 11
Huxley, Thomas, 209

I'll-quit-tomorrow myth about workaholics, 52
Imago Relationships International, 241
Imago Relationship Therapy, 180, 241
Impatience, as symptom of workaholism, 67, 125
Imposter myth about workaholics, 48–50
Imposter syndrome, 113–117
Inadequacy: among family members of workaholics, 104; workaholics' feeling of, 43, 152. *See also* Productivity; Self-worth
Innovators, as workaholic type, 74
Institute for Imago Relationship Therapy, 241
Interconnections between settings, as enabler of workaholism, 37–38
Internal Family Systems Therapy (IFS), 204
Internal time, setting aside of, 154–155
Internet, love affair with, 3
Interventions, in life-threatening cases of workaholism, 181–182
Intimacy: lack of in workaholic-enabling company, 221–222; workaholics' difficulty with, 47, 48, 55, 99, 169–173. *See also* Relationship problems; Spouses of workaholics
Inventory of self, as part of Twelve Steps, 246–247
Irritability, as symptom of workaholism, 66, 192, 227

Japan: work week in, 36; *Karoshi* in the workplace, 36; legacy of postwar economic ruin and workaholism, 52; *nure-ochiba,* 173; "seven-eleven husband" in, 96–97

Jekyll and Hyde: parenting, as root of workaholism in childhood, 140; personality of workaholic managers, 226–227
Jenkins Activity Survey, correlation with WART, 250–251
"Job makes me do it" myth about workaholism, 43

Kahn, Jeffrey, 6
Karoshi, in Japanese workplace, 36
Keary, Annie, 106
King, Larry, 33
Kipling, Rudyard, 30
Kubler-Ross, Elisabeth, 153

Lao-Tzu, 236
Laughter, effect on physical system, 127
"Let's Make a Deal" syndrome, 17
Leveling-off stage of career for workaholics, 215–216
Life-threatening cases of workaholism, interventions for, 81–82
Limitations, learning to accept, 135–136
Listening, as tool of Workaholics Anonymous, 243
Living in the now: as therapy, 157–158; as tool in Workaholics Anonymous program, 243

Machlowitz, Marilyn, 35, 38, 192
Managers: dysfunctional, 220; ineffective, 224; portrait of workaholic boss, 225; as workaholics, 116, 222–229, 230, 231–233
Managers as parts in Internal Family Systems Therapy, 204
Managing time among workaholics, 57
Margo (case study), 30–32
Marriage problems, due to workaholism, 6, 37, 22–24, 90–95, 100, 161–182, 190
Marshall, Penny, 4
Marx, Groucho, 111
Mary (case study), 209–212
Mauksch, Larry, 45
McCall's, 168; magazine survey of work habits, 168
McCarthy, Colman, 46
Media: as enabler of workaholism, 38–40; failing to take workaholism seriously, 7, 33–34, 38, 50
Medications for workaholics, 80
Meditation: as effective relaxation, 155; as relief from stress, 208, 230; techniques for, 156–158. *See also* Relaxation
Meetings, attendance as tool of Workaholics Anonymous, 244
Mental preoccupation and workaholism, 53
Merrill Lynch, 39
Messiah myth about workaholism, 47, 92, 124
Mind-body link, and health problems of workaholics, 126–127
Minimizers, workaholics as, 169–170
Monday morning, looking forward to, 213
Monroe, Marilyn, 149
Multitasking, 218
Myers-Briggs Indicator, correlation with WART, 251
Myths about workaholism, 30–57

Needed, workaholic's craving to be, 209–212
Needs of well rounded person, attending to, 82–84
Negative thinking: health repercussions of, 121–127; technique for overcoming, 127–129
Neuropeptides, effect on physical system, 126–127
Nure-ochiba, 173
Nurses: as adult children of workaholics, 189; workaholism among, 50

Oates, Wayne, 6, 71
Obsessive-compulsive tendencies among children of workaholics, 190
Obsessive thoughts, and workaholism, 19
Oprah, 34
Origins-of-addiction exercise, 159–160
Overcompensation in workaholics, 110–113
Overresponsibility in workaholics, 99, 224

Pacing, as tool of Workaholics Anonymous, 243
Parentification of workaholic's children, 95–96
Parentified children who become workaholics, 141–152
Parents, workaholic, high expectations of, 194–196
Parts, working with internal, 204–205
Pat (case study), 200–201
People-pleasing: among children of workaholics, 196–198; among workaholics, 135
People-pleasing thinking, among workaholics, 123
Pep talks, self-administered, 135
Perfectionism, as symptom of workaholism, 46, 47, 53, 55, 64–65, 75, 99, 111, 141, 227
Perfectionistic thinking of workaholics, 121, 122
Pessimistic thinking among workaholics, 124
Physical signs of workaholism, 68
Physicians, workaholism among, 50. *See also* Clinicians
Pietropinto, Anthony, 195
Pitt, Brad, 123
Play: attending to need for, 82–84; as tool of Workaholics Anonymous, 243
Point of view, restricted mind-sets due to, 117–121
Porter, Gayle, 115, 214–215, 218
Positive emotions: effect on physical system, 127; learning to have, 127–129
Powerlessness: admission of, as first of Twelve Steps, 247–248
"Power picnics," 218
Power struggles, in workaholic families, 93–94
Present, learning to live in, 157–158
Prioritizing: learning art of, 232, 234; as tool of Workaholics Anonymous, 243
Procrastination and workaholism, 68–69, 72
Productivity: optimum, versus workaholism, 233–235; as symptom of workaholism, 67, 71, 113, 114. *See also* Overcompensation in workaholics
Psychological aspects of workaholism, 3–6, 22–24, 43–44, 48–50, 106–136. *See also* Anxiety; Childhood, roots of workaholism in; Denial of workaholism; Depression; Productivity, Stress
Psychotherapeutic community. *See* Clinicians
Public's failure to take workaholism seriously, 6–7, 33–34
Puritan work ethic, 40, 47, 117, 190–192
Pursuer-distancer dynamic among couples, 26, 92, 170, 177–178

Quaal, Ward, 174–175

Racing Strollers, 209–210
Ratey, John, 80
Recovery: importance of sharing with others, 247–248; as life-long process, 247–248; as a movement, 188
Relationship problems: with children of workaholics, 192; repairing with children, 202–203; as symptom of workaholism, 19, 54, 65; technology as barrier to intimacy, 169–173; using the WART with, 78; in workaholic marriage, 163–166. *See also* Children of workaholics; Intimacy; Marriage problems; Spouses of workaholics
Relaxation: learning, 155–158; as tool of Workaholics Anonymous, 243. *See also* Meditation
Relentless workaholics, 68, 70–71, 79, 213–214, 227
Renee (case study), 161–163
Research on workaholic family system, 8, 22, 62, 97–99, 163–164, 189–190, 196
Research on workaholics in the workplace, 214–216
Resistance thinking of workaholics, 124
Restlessness, as symptom of workaholism, 66
Retirement, helplessness of workaholics in, 172–173
Revolution from Within (Steinem), 146
Rigid thinking among workaholics:

learning to overcome, 127–133; types of, 121–126
Rituals: daily, as glue that holds family together, 203; learning to participate in, 158; workaholics ignoring or minimizing, 172
Robinson, Bryan, 11–14, 148–150, 237
Ross (case study), 137–139
Rushing, as symptom of workaholism, 63, 111, 192

Savoring workaholics, 68, 69, 75–76, 81, 213–215
Schaef, Anne Wilson, 45, 112, 220
Schaefer, George A., 222
Schwartz, Richard, 204, 237–238
Screening, initial, of workaholic families, 100
Self: learning to care for, 82–84, 154–155; learning to validate, 133; taking inventory of, as part of Twelve Steps, 246–247
Self-assessment, learning to conduct, 246–247
Self-care, failing to perform as symptom of workaholism, 67–68, 123
Self-care plan for workaholics: development of, 82–84, 160; used in repairing relationships, 202–203; as used in Workaholics Anonymous, 103
Self-esteem, and workaholism, 15, 47, 55, 67, 104, 108, 111, 115, 116, 152; among spouses of workaholics, 105
Self-fulfilling prophecy and workaholics, 124
Self-victimizing thinking among workaholics, 124
Self-worth: low among workaholics, 129; workaholics' need to establish, 110–117
Seligman, Daniel, 34
Serious thinking among workaholics, 125
Selye, Hans, 126
Service to others, as tool of Workaholics Anonymous, 244
Shame: as basis for workaholism, 110; confronting, in Twelve Step program, 246
Sheedy, Ally, 33
Shields, Brooke, 145–146
Signposts of workaholism, 248–250
Simplifying workaholic life, 136
Slacker myth of workaholics, 51
Slowing down, as effective therapy, 155–156. *See also* Meditation
Smith, Bill, 202
Smith family (case study), 90–91
Smye, Marti, 219
Society: embedded beliefs about work, 40–42; as support for workaholism, 94–95
Sotile, Mary, 78, 238
Sotile, Wayne, 78, 238
Spiritual growth, as part of recovery process, 247
Spouses of workaholics: effects of workaholism on, 161–182; making unrealistic demands, 176–177; as part of addictive system, 91–96; portrait of, 170; support for, 104–105. *See also* Family members of workaholics; Intimacy; Relationship problems
Stability, human need for, 139–141
Stages of workaholism, 44–45
State-Trait Anxiety Inventory, correlation with WART, 250
Steinem, Gloria, 42, 146, 148; case study of, 150–151
Stepchild addiction myth about workaholics, 50–51
Stewart, Martha, 41
Stress: and addiction to adrenaline, 48–49; and health, 46, 126–127; in the workplace, 216–222. *See also* Anxiety; Burnout; Depression
Stress and workaholism, 19, 47, 219–220; and workaholic environments, 228; reduction of, at work, 230
Stress-induced illness: cost to businesses, 228–229, 231; and workaholism, 165, 228. *See also* Anxiety; Depression
Stress-related illnesses and workaholism, 53
Substitution of activities, as tool of Workaholics Anonymous, 243
Success, workaholics' need for. *See* Overcompensation in workaholics; Productivity

Superhero myth about workaholics, 46
Support groups: for employees of workaholic companies 233; for family members, 104–105; for workaholics, 242–250. *See also* Treatment *entries*
Symptoms of workaholism, 60, 63–68

Tacit family contract, 89, 100, 147
Tangible success, need for among workaholics, 112
Technology and workaholism: 1–2; as it affects relationships, 169–173; erasing the line between home and work, 38, 218; as glamour of work, 39; using, rather than being used by, 234–235; wireless, risk of in company, 218
Telephoning, as tool of Workaholics Anonymous, 244
Telescopic thinking of workaholics, 122
Terkel, Studs, 174
Thinking, in workaholics. *See* Rigid thinking among workaholics
Thoreau, Henry David, 10
Time: helping workaholics manage, 57; and urgency, 215–216
Time cushions in work schedules, 26, 28
Time urgency and workaholics, 215–216
Treatment for children of workaholics. *See* Children of workaholics; Clinicians
Treatment for spouses of workaholics, *See* Clinicians; Workaholism, helping spouses cope with
Treatment for workaholics: by connecting with their inner selves, 133–136, 154–155; with cognitive psychotherapies, 130–133; through family model, 99–102; with grief therapy, 153–154; by helping them communicate with their partners, 180–181; with learned self-care, 82–84; by matching therapy to workaholism type, 79–81; program, 102–105; with Twelve Steps, 247–248; with written exercises and behavioral techniques, 131–133. *See also* Counseling
Treatment for workers under workaholic bosses, 231–233
Triangulation in workaholic families, 96–97, 100
Trump, Donald, 69, 123
Twelve Step programs of Workaholics Anonymous, 101, 102–103, 247–248
Type A behaviors, 101, 195
Type A Self-Report Inventory, correlation with WART, 250–251
Typology of workaholics, 77

Underscheduling, as tool of Workaholics Anonymous, 243
United States: percentage of population estimated as workaholic, 50. *See also* Work ethic
University of North Carolina at Charlotte, research at, 9, 22, 97, 189–190
US News and World Report, 2

Vacation days: not taken by workaholics, 2–3; forcing employees to take, 230
Vital exhaustion, definition of, 176
Volunteering as workaholism, 51

Walsh, Edward, 165
Warning signs of workaholism. *See* Symptoms of workaholism
WART. *See* Work Addiction Risk Test
Wedded-to-work myth, 48
Weinberg, Richard, 45
Wilde, Oscar, 85
Windy City Fieldhouse, 218
Wishful thinking among workaholics, 125
Woititz, Janet, 188
Woodhull, Nancy, 15
Work: as anesthetic, 109; and baby boomers, 35; and technology, 36, 38, 39. *See also* Balance; Boundary setting
Work addiction. *See* Workaholism
Work Addiction Risk Test (WART), 20–22; for couples, 78–79; as self-help tool, 20–22; as used in research, 98, 189–190; psychometric properties of, 250–251
Workaholics: childhoods of, 137–160; children of, 183–208; feeling unappreciated, 61; health problems of, 5, 47,

53, 228–229; high expectations as parents, 194–196; jokes about, 34; as managers, 45, 222–229, 231–233; marginalized in their families, 96–97; mindset of, 122; minds of, 106–136; mixed messages from family, 37; portrait of childhood, 142; recovering, 242–250; rigid thinking of, 112, 114, 121–126; types of, 68–77; types of and matching clinical strategies, 78–81; versus optimal performers, 216–217, 233–235; work habits hurt company, 213; working impulsively, 74. *See also* Case studies

Workaholics Anonymous: history of, 242–243; jokes about, 33, 38; recovering member, 1, 111; spouse of member, 166; tools used by, 243, 244; studied for research, 97–98; Twelve Step program of, 103, 109, 244–245. *See also* Support groups; WorkAnon

Workaholism: and abstinence, 25, 53, 81; as an addiction, 5; best-dressed problem, 4; case study research on, 8; in the company, 209–235; debunking the myths, 8, 53; definition of, 6–7; as developmental phenomenon, 44–45; difficulty of recognizing, 7, 33–34, 38, 50; effects on children, 183–208; as a family disease, 22, 37, 54, 85–105; and family dysfunction, 22, 91–94, 97–99; as a firefighter, 7; helping spouses cope with, 104–105; intergenerational transmission of, 101; lack of acceptance in mental health field, 6–7, 9, 35; myths about, 43–53; origin of term, 6; recovery from, 242–250; rewarded by culture, 40, 43, 50; signs of, 60, 63–68; versus healthy working, 16–19; versus performing optimally, 233–235; worn as badge of honor, 33, 217. *See also* Health problems of workaholics

WorkAnon, 104; history of, 242–243. *See also* Support groups; Workaholics Anonymous

Work anorexics, 72

Work binges, as symptom of workaholism, 65

Work bulimia, 72, 79

Workers' Compensation costs of workaholism, 228–229

Work ethic: promoting loyalty to company, 216–217; role of denial in workaholism, 40, 47, 117, 190; as shield for workaholics, 190–192. *See also* Puritan work ethic

Work hangovers, 5

Work highs, 5, 50; as substance abuse, 3–6, 48–50

Working (Terkel), 174

Working hard vs. workaholism, 16–19

Working optimally vs. workaholically, 233–235

Work moderation, 52–53, 81–82; in Workaholics Anonymous, 103

Work patterns, varying, of workaholics, 68–77

Workplace: home as, 38; as cause of workaholism, 45; workaholism in, 209–235

Work smarter, not longer, 136

Work trances, as symptom of workholism, 66

Work week: average length of, 2–3; among the Japanese, 36; during the 1980s, 35

World Business, 217

World Service Organization for Workaholics Anonymous, origins of, 242–243

Wright, Leslie, 219

About the Author

Bryan E. Robinson, Ph.D., is Professor Emeritus of Special Education and Child Development at the University of North Carolina at Charlotte and a psychotherapist in private practice in Asheville, NC. He is the author of over twenty-five self-help and academic books and has published his research in over one hundred scholarly journals. He was recipient of the American Counseling Association's Research Award and the University of North Carolina at Charlotte's First Citizen Scholars Medal for his pioneer research on the negative consequences of workaholism. He hosted the PBS documentary *Overdoing It: When Work Becomes Your Life* and he has been featured on numerous television programs including ABC's *20/20, Good Morning America, World News Tonight, NBC Nightly News,* and *The CBS Early Show.*